ETHICS IN ACTION

CASE STUDIES IN ARCHAEOLOGICAL DILEMMAS

Chip Colwell-Chanthaphonh,
Julie Hollowell, and Dru McGill

SOCIETY FOR AMERICAN ARCHAEOLOGY

The SAA Press

Contents

Acknowledgments

Through the years we have been the recipients of remarkable gifts of generosity offered, perhaps not entirely unexpectedly, from those dedicated to thinking and talking about the ethics of archaeological practice. Help has come in many ways, in many forms. Every year since 2003, we have recruited student teams who are the core of the Ethics Bowl's success, an event upon which this book is based. We have also depended on the time and energy of a host of professionals who have served as moderators, judges, and sponsors. The SAA Board of Directors and the SAA Committee on Ethics have been extremely supportive, helping the Ethics Bowl along from a slightly quirky exhibition to an annual and regularly well-attended event. Lynne Sebastian (President of the SAA when we first launched the event), Alex Barker (Chair of the SAA Committee on Ethics during our tenure on the committee), and Joe Watkins (final round moderator extraordinaire for four years running) deserve special thanks. We are also very fortunate to have had the Association for Practical and Professional Ethics—notably Robert Ladenson who created the Intercollegiate Ethics Bowl, and Brian Schrag who now organizes it—allow us to borrow the Ethics Bowl format and make it into our own. Alas, the list of colleagues we should thank is now too numerous to fully enumerate here; with so many to acknowledge, leaving someone out seems to be a greater risk than a blanket acknowledgment! We are truly, deeply, and genuinely grateful for all those who have helped the SAA Ethics Bowl through these initial years.

The list of people to whom it is somewhat easier to offer our thanks catalogues those who have contributed to case studies used in the Ethics Bowl. These kind folks have given their ideas, words, and editing skills to the case studies, helping to make each scenario more insightful and provocative. Although our names appear on the front of this book, writing almost all of these case studies truly has been a team effort so here we appreciatively acknowledge our colleagues who contributed to the case studies used in this volume: Jeffrey Altschul, Catherine Carlson, Brandi Carrier Jones, Cheryl Claassen, Julia Costello, Krista Farris, Jeffery Hanson, Paula Lazrus, Randall McGuire, Martin McAllister, Madonna Moss, Earl Neller, Sven Ouzman, Heather Pringle, K. Anne Pyburn, Karen Olsen-Bruhns, Kimberly L. Redman, and Robin Stevens. This volume's Case 16 is based on Case 24 in Cassell and Jacobs (1987). Further support, inspiration, and assistance was generously given to us through the years in editing many of the scenarios in this book as well as writing the larger set of case studies used in the four years of Ethics Bowl competitions: Alex Barker, Meg Cannon, T. J. Ferguson, Mark Hackbarth, Jason Jackson, Janet E. Levy, Karen D. Vitelli, and Alison Wylie. Additionally, a number of former Ethics Bowl participants also munificently wrote "tips" for this volume (see Chapter 4). We are thankful for their contributions.

The peer reviews of this volume, provided by Jeffrey H. Altschul and Larry J. Zimmerman, were exceptional and we are grateful for the time and consideration the reviewers gave to our work. Patty Gerstenblith and Alison Wylie were also kind enough to help us with lingering questions in the manuscript. Alison's feedback especially added clarity to chapters 1 and 2. David G. Anderson, editor of the The SAA Press, has been remarkably enthusiastic about this book since its inception. We are tremendously thankful for his encouragement and the efforts he and the staff at The SAA Press, as well as The SAA Press Editorial Committee, have put into this volume.

Finally, we especially want to acknowledge the students who have participated in the Ethics Bowl. To be in the Ethics Bowl—to prepare for weeks, to sit under the spotlight in front of your peers, to debate on the spot without notes, and to answer pointed questions from esteemed scholars—takes more than a little mettle. And so we applaud and thank those who have taken up the challenge and helped us make the Ethics Bowl a success.

To Karen D. Vitelli,
our mentor, colleague, and friend,
for co-founding
Indiana University's Archaeology and Social Context Program

1

Ethics in Archaeology

Ancient artifacts pilfered in Mexico for pesos sold at auction in New York City for a small fortune. . . . African Americans protesting the excavation of a slave burial ground. . . . subdivisions and cell phone towers erected on sacred sites. . . . millions of tourists pouring into the fragile and ancient cliff dwellings of Mesa Verde year after year. . . . a small burial container thought to be evidence of Jesus' existence until proven a fake. . . . the annihilation of millennia-old Buddhist statues by Islamic fundamentalists. Given such controversies in recent years—and these are just a few—it is little wonder that professional ethics have become a growing part of contemporary discourse, training, and practice in archaeology. Almost daily, newspapers report some new crisis, but the reasons for paying attention to ethical issues in archaeology go much deeper than what we see in the news, especially for aspiring and practicing archaeologists.

Why Ethics In Archaeology Matter

As archaeologists, we are confronted all the time by situations that ask us to make delicate, complicated, and influential decisions, whether in the field collaborating with others, in the lab or office deciding how to treat data, in our interactions with colleagues, our publications, or in the classroom. Ethics are an inherent and essential part of everything we do and how we do it, whether we are aware of the principles we are acting from or not (Winter 1984). Archaeological ethics are specific to the roles, responsibilities, and obligations of those who do archaeology. As these roles and responsibilities have changed over time, so have the ethics that give them meaning. The field of cultural heritage management, for example, has its own built-in conflicts of interest and ethical contradictions among responsibilities to scholarship, the archaeological record and its creators, and seemingly

I

inevitable forces of development. It is no wonder that heightened attention to ethics in archaeology comes at a time when archaeologists have begun to recognize the implications of their practice for living peoples and to wrestle with the many new roles that archaeology is asked to play in a global and multicultural world.

Philosopher Alison Wylie (2003) defines an "ethic" as a set of principles or values that guide our actions or sanction conduct, often encoded in the standards of a profession. An ethic expresses what you should or ought to do. In archaeology, a set of ethics establishes parameters or norms for what would be considered a "good" archaeologist. An explicitly archaeological ethic, then, is an ideal that can guide what an archaeologist should do when faced with a difficult situation. Wylie distinguishes between a "moral code," which has broader applications in society, and a "code of ethics," which outlines responsibilities specific to a particular profession. Likewise, an "ethos" describes a shared worldview often associated with a particular set of goals or practices that might well inform or orient one's sense of obligation or ways of acting, but which are more broadly construed than an "ethic." Specific codes of ethics differ substantively in their approaches and content. Some are based on broad moral principles that set out ideals (ceilings) for how to behave while others are framed to specify minimally acceptable standards (floors) for practice, often accompanied by rules for enforcement.

On the other hand, "ethics" as a field of inquiry is different from a code or a set of standards. It is the philosophical study of these standards and principles, a way to evaluate how these principles affect our research, other people, and the decisions and choices we make. Ethics or morals—terms many people use interchangeably—involve a continual examination of how our principles for right behavior are put to work in the world and their potential for both harm and good (Hamilakis 2005:100; Meskell and Pels 2005).

There are many ways to approach ethics in archaeology, but they all involve thinking about how to conduct ourselves in various situations. Having a code of ethical principles won't solve the inevitable conflicts that arise in the course of everyday practice. Indeed, there are no hard and fast rules for ethical professional behavior (and we should be worried if there were). Open and critical discussion among colleagues, however, gives us some tools for applying lofty principles to actual situations and some experience with how to think through these ethical dilemmas critically. Most professional organizations actively seek to engage their members in discussions about ethical practices and professional development. The SAA has long taken a lead in shaping these debates, from the development of its Principles of Ethics to forums held at annual meetings, debates in *American Antiquity* and *The SAA Archaeological Record*, and, more recently, in its sponsorship of the Ethics Bowl.

This book is designed to introduce the Ethics Bowl as a way to explore the challenges and complexities of ethical issues that arise in archaeological practice.

As a pedagogical tool, the Ethics Bowl offers those anticipating a career in archaeology much more than a set of case studies to contemplate; it allows you to move from being detached observers to active and engaged problem solvers. Working through case studies based on concrete situations helps you become a more sophisticated thinker, better prepared to address ethical problems when you face them—as you inevitably will—in your professional lives. For those who are already professional archaeologists, grappling with case studies can help you think clearly and carefully through ethical predicaments similar to those you might actually face. The ultimate goal of the Ethics Bowl, and of ethics education more broadly, is to help the discipline become ever more ethically aware and engaged.

What Are Professional Ethics?

What happens when allegations about malpractice or the misconduct of a self-interested researcher compromise the quality of the work or, worse yet, cause harm to others? Most colleges and universities have policies that curtail and punish behaviors they deem unethical, such as plagiarism, fabrication of data, forms of harassment or discrimination, and more. These policies generally hold people to a higher standard than the law affords, but many forms of ethical conduct are governed only by professional organizations. A brief look at the origins of professional ethics lends some explanation as to why this is so.

A profession is an occupation that requires specialized training and study to master a specific body of knowledge and skills. A profession usually has its own association, code of ethics, and some form of certification. In ancient Greek and Roman times (which, for better or worse, provided the foundation for much of our current "Western" educational and legal systems), only a few professions were recognized—at first, only medicine, law, ministry, and the military. Members of these professions were typically required to take an oath that "professed" their duty to adhere to a specific code of ethics. Over time, as occupations became more and more specialized, other professions were recognized, typically governed or regulated by guilds and "colleges" and certified by the state. To this day a "master's degree" signifies mastery of a certain "discipline," and a Doctor of Philosophy means that an individual has grappled with a discipline's philosophical foundations. Today we recognize many different professions: teaching, business, policing, librarianship, civil engineering, and nursing, to name a few. Each is associated with a special set of knowledge and skills and a heightened sense of accountability for how these are practiced.

Professional ethics can promote exclusivity by drawing a line between those who have certain forms of training or who practice according to certain standards and those who do not. This division has its own inherent dangers, but the original purpose of professional ethics was to hold individual members to higher standards of accountability in their work and actions. Just what these standards should be and even the question of "accountable to whom?" change over time.

What Are Archaeological Ethics?

Ethics in archaeology—as in all disciplines—are historically contingent and based on moral arguments, world views, and goals founded in certain ways of relating to the past that may or may not have a sound foundation or be shared by everyone. Many of the same goals inform and orient archaeology today as a century ago (see Hall 2005), though their meanings may have shifted, since what counts as "science," "preservation," or "accountability" changes over time. Changes in professional ethics also reflect new duties faced by a profession and shifts in broad moral attitudes that occur when rights or social responsibilities that previously may have gone unrecognized are acknowledged (Patton 2006). It seems incredible to us today, but not that long ago many Aboriginal peoples and their ancestors' remains were not even considered fully human by some research standards (Hill 1988:12). While we can trace broad historical trends, it is important to recognize that archaeological ethics are not universally held. There are many crosscurrents of thought and even oppositely held notions of good behavior in a single generation of archaeologists. Still, to understand the nature of archaeological ethics, we must try to understand the shifts in worldviews, orienting goals, and modes of practice in the discipline's past that contribute to what we consider professional ethics today.[1]

Ruins and Relics

A history of ethics in archaeology might begin with an *ethos of antiquarianism* that became fashionable among European intellectuals by the seventeenth century and incited scholarly explorations of antiquity. One expression of these sentiments was a zeal for collecting that focused on curiosities of natural and cultural history from distant and exotic peoples, times, and places (Helms 1993; Trigger 1995). Ruins and relics held a special fascination as remnants of previously powerful civilizations; the "antique lands" became a popular destination for scholar-adventurers (Leask 2002). By the early 1800s, an *ethos of science* pervaded much of Europe, and it went hand-in-hand with a goal of discovery, marked by the quest to map and to claim the last unknown regions of the planet (Figure 1). "Specimens" of material culture and human remains collected for newly established national museums filled missing links in the "scientific" study of human progress, synonymous at that time with linear notions of human evolution and world civilization (Ames 1992). These ideas in turn helped provide a rationale for colonialism; for example, Martin Hall (2005) identifies a persistent (if unrecognized) strategy of using archaeology as a justification for colonialism throughout the history of African archaeology.

Figure 1. The "discovery" of ancient Maya sites in the 1800s was a source of great curiosity and excitement—here Tulum near Cancún, Mexico is being cleared of the jungle canopy for study and documentation. (From *Views of Ancient Monuments in Central America, Chiapas and Yucatan,* Frederick Catherwood 1844:Plate 24)

In the first decades of the twentieth century, a gradual transition took place in studies of the ancient past. Expeditions to sites of ancient civilization led by wealthy scholar-explorers gave way to more systematic archaeological investigations and excavation as a mode of practice. Often the goal was tracing the origins of Western civilization to earlier "high" cultures and reconstructing "lost" civilizations and the reasons for their collapse. Huge multiyear excavations in the Near East, North Africa, Central America, and South America engaged scores of local workers to recover tons of objects that headed for European and American expositions and museums (Fagan 1975, 1977; Meyer 1973). The excavation methods of many archaeologists during this time were often similar to those of relic collectors, although there were notable exceptions such as the work of Flinders Petrie (Drower 1995). The appropriation of ancient materials for display in world centers was justified by appeals to salvage, preservation, and art appreciation—values that continue to validate and inform museum practices, private collecting, and attitudes toward the global antiquities market today—as well as by hardly less overt allusions to imperialism (Trigger 1984; Vrdoljak 2006). In recent years, many nations have requested the return of antiquities taken during these times as objects of cultural patrimony (Bush and Barkan 2002; FitzGibbon 2005; Greenfield 1989).

In the United States, growing antiquarian interest in ancient civilizations of the Americas stimulated an extensive market in relics for collectors, tourists, museums, and expositions (Bassett 1986; Hutt et al. 1992). In the late nineteenth century, more "scientific" methods of excavation and documentation developed after people realized the kinds of information that could be gained with systematic and detailed *in situ* analysis (Lynott 2003). Increasingly, researchers engaged not just in digging and collecting, but also reporting their work in written journals, and archaeology and anthropology became embedded in universities. Thus, an *ethos of scholarship* was promulgated, which held that researchers should be allowed to pursue scientific goals free of constraints placed on their subjects, methodologies, and interpretations.

The passage of the Antiquities Act in 1906 called attention to the unauthorized and unscientific removal of archaeological materials from sites of national significance (Harmon et al. 2006). The Act established the means to designate national monuments and instituted a commitment by the state to protect and manage historically important sites, which were set aside as public lands, with federal agencies as their stewards. It also required permits for collecting artifacts or excavating on federal lands, making a clear delineation between those authorized to do archaeology and others. Although many positive things have flowed from the Antiquities Act, it was in many ways another means by which the nation appropriated the heritage of Native peoples and their connections to these lands (Colwell-Chanthaphonh 2005; McLaughlin 1998).

Science and Salvage

The reclamation and development projects of the 1930s ushered in a new era of commitment to archaeological salvage on the part of the U.S. government. The majority of human remains in Smithsonian collections originated from WPA projects conducted during this time for construction of flood control dams and highways—and simple relief work (Johnson 1990:16). The depression-era archaeology programs represented the first time that major archaeological research projects were publicly funded (Figure 2). However, these endeavors were not undertaken to advance archaeological science, but to provide relief for unemployed laborers. While the programs successfully created new jobs and expanded research opportunities, often little money was set aside for analysis and reporting. In subsequent decades, an obligation of reporting developed as scholars recognized that field research should go hand in hand with publication.

When the Society for American Archaeology (SAA) was founded in 1934, its members were a mix of trained and untrained archaeologists whose common ethic was the need for careful documentation in excavation and reporting. The Society's original bylaws contained a clause that allowed the expulsion of mem-

Figure 2. WPA workers excavating the Stockdale Site in Benton County, Tennessee in the 1930s for the Tennessee Valley Authority prior to dam construction. (Courtesy Frank H. McClung Museum, The University of Tennessee, Knoxville)

bers for using archaeological objects or sites for personal gain or satisfaction or for other unspecified misconduct. This clause was partly a reaction to the zealous excavation of sites such as Spiro Mounds by commercial diggers. One of the SAA's first actions was to work jointly with the American Council of Learned Societies to establish the Committee for the Recovery of Archeological Remains (CRAR) and, through CRAR, to begin to define the role of archaeology in federal development projects. By 1945, federal agencies largely agreed that government funds should be used for archaeological salvage work and for monitoring the impacts of projects on significant sites. By the mid-1950s, some agencies required survey and salvage of archaeological resources on public lands under construction. With this change came a call to define minimum standards for who was an archaeologist and thus worthy of employment, and for the first time formal training became important in the United States—an expression of a budding ethic of professional practice (Kehoe and Emmerichs 1999; Lynott 2003:19–20; McGimsey 1995).

The destruction wrought by World War II prompted UNESCO in 1954 to adopt a major international treaty aimed at safeguarding tangible cultural heritage, the Convention and Protocol for the Protection of Cultural Property in the Event of Armed Conflict. Known as the 1954 Hague Convention, this agreement called for special protections for sites of cultural significance in times of war or occupation, as well as in times of peace (Climent 1994; Colwell-Chanthaphonh and Piper 2001; Meyer 1993). One hundred and sixteen nations have ratified or accessioned (meaning, brought into law) the Convention so far; the United States is not yet among them. Although the Hague Convention highlights the effects of civil unrest and human tragedy on archaeological sites and monuments, it has not prevented major destruction from occurring in the aftermath of war and occupation (Cultural Policy Center 2006).

In 1960, the SAA appointed a Committee on Ethics and Standards to examine the need for professional standards and a code of ethics, and the following year, the Committee issued "Four Statements on Archaeology" (Champe et al. 1961; see Appendix 2). The document contained a mixture of principles to aspire to and "bottom line" directives for how an archaeologist "must" behave, in some cases at the risk of expulsion. The statement devoted to ethics focused heavily on promoting an *ethic of professional accountability* toward other members of the profession, to scientific methods, and to sharing data with other scholars. The "[d]isregard of proper archaeological methods" could be grounds for expulsion, as was the "willful destruction, distortion, or concealment" of archaeological data. The latter was partly a reaction to data hoarding, long a quasi-acceptable practice in archaeology. The fourth statement concerned the need for specialized training. There is no mention at all of accountability to the public, except for an obligation to secure permission from property owners before excavating!

Resource Management

Legislation in the United States and other countries enacted and implemented during the 1960s and 1970s authorized archaeologists to manage and protect archaeological resources for the state in a climate where historic preservation often conflicted with development. The SAA and CRAR worked with politicians to develop archaeological resource protection statutes. With the loss of major archaeological sites along the Missouri River to flood control, the proliferation of urban and suburban development projects, and drainage projects that opened vast tracts of land to agriculture, the view emerged that a successful project was one that kept archaeological sites intact (Dunnell 1984; LeBlanc 1979:361-362; McGimsey 1972). This shift in values from salvage and excavation to *in situ* preservation and protection of what was coming to be seen as a diminishing resource was termed the *conservation ethic*, an orientation that embraced new goals, guidelines, and modes of practice (King and Lyneis 1978; Lipe 1974).

The National Historic Preservation Act (NHPA) of 1966, along with the National Environmental Policy Act (NEPA) of 1969—as supplemented by Executive Order 11593, which required all Federal lands to be archaeologically inventoried, and the Archeological and Historic Preservation Act of 1974 or Moss-Bennett Act, which created a mechanism for salvaging archaeological resources endangered by Federally supported projects that alter the land—required federal agencies to fund archaeological impact and mitigation studies, opening thousands of jobs to archaeologists in public agencies and private firms and promoting a particular set of archaeological resource management practices. By the mid-1980s, more than half of all professional archaeologists worked outside of academia in cultural resource management (CRM) fields (Elia 1993). Many professional archaeologists were now publishing in a burgeoning "grey literature" and dealing with legal contracts. A growing *ethic of public accountability* that included clients with very different interests and situations created new dilemmas in professional standards, methods, and the handling of data (Raab et al. 1980).

The Society of Professional Archaeologists (SOPA) and the American Society of Conservation Archeologists (ASCA) both came into being in response to the rapidly changing face of archaeology. In 1973, a resolution passed by the SAA urged the development of minimal standards and a system of certification for archaeological work. Meetings in 1974 resulted in the Airlie House Report, which recommended the establishment of a professional registry, an idea that passed the SAA in the following year after heated debate, with the stipulation that the organization be both voluntary in membership and legally separate from the SAA (McGimsey 1995; McGimsey and Davis 1977). SOPA was born in 1976, and a committee met to draw up a code for minimal standards of conduct.[2] A grievance process allowed members to be adjudicated and censured or expelled for violating the standards (Davis 1984). The SOPA code built upon the Four Statements of 1961, but it embraced accountability to the public and covered new obligations arising within a CRM context characterized by clients, employers, contracts, and other business obligations. The establishment of a set of standards also served the purpose of assuring contractors and agencies that they were paying for quality research. In other words, a visible code of ethics was good for business.

High Stakes

By the 1970s the market for antiquities had expanded to an illicit trade that depended on global networks of looters, couriers, art dealers, and private collectors (Coe 1993; Meyer 1973) and fueled undocumented digging of sites the world over (Brodie et al. 2001; Renfrew 2000; Tubb 1995). Archaeologists developed a strong stance against commercialization and turned to legal instruments, education, and ethical codes to try to stem the antiquities trade (Coggins 1969; Messenger 1999). In 1970, UNESCO passed the Convention on the Means of Prohibiting and Preventing the Illicit Import, Export and Transfer of Ownership of Cultural Property—often referred to as the 1970 UNESCO Convention—which the United States accepted and signed into law with the 1983 Cultural Property Implementation Act (CPIA). Since then, the United States has developed bilateral agreements with several "archaeologically rich" countries to regulate the import of certain objects entering the United States. Only recently have the United Kingdom and Switzerland, historically two of the largest importers of antiquities, signed the Convention.

A growing number of museums now have a code of ethics forbidding them to acquire or sometimes even exhibit antiquities imported after 1970 or 1981 (Gerstenblith 1998), but many still are reluctant to stop acquiring ancient treasures without proof of illicit provenance (Brodie and Renfrew 2005). The conviction of antiquities dealer Frederick Schultz in 2004 was an important step in upholding previous United States federal circuit court decisions that recognized the cultural property laws of foreign countries (Baker 2003; Gerstenblith 2002). Since then, Italy, Egypt, and Greece have taken active stands in seeking the return of certain antiquities that left their borders illegally, and other countries will likely follow suit. A handful of international charters, many of them promulgated by the International Council on Monuments and Sites (ICOMOS), deal with protecting and preserving world archaeological heritage. While all of these measures have raised awareness about the illicit antiquities trade and its repercussions, archaeologists are becoming more cognizant of their own role in influencing the appreciation that sells antiquities and wrestling with the fact that war, social instability, and economic inequalities often underpin the undocumented destruction of archaeological sites.

In the 1980s, one of the loudest calls in archaeology concerned the need for public outreach as a necessary component of professional practice. Public education was perceived as the solution to many of the dilemmas facing archaeology, especially looting, site protection, and support for historic preservation efforts (SAA 1990). It had become apparent that the same archaeological site or object could easily represent something very different to special interest groups, and the ways these various values were prioritized could create unavoidable conflicts in deciding how cultural resources should be managed (see Lipe 1984). Archaeologists had to acknowledge that they were but one group among multiple "publics" who had a stake in the past, and not necessarily the group with the greatest influence (McManamon 1991; Prott and O'Keefe 1984:28). Consultation became a mandatory aspect of professional practice in heritage management, and the field of public archaeology blossomed.

Respect and Reckoning

The World Archaeological Congress (WAC) formed in 1986, in the midst of controversy surrounding the boycott of South African archaeologists to its first Congress. WAC envisioned itself as a broad-based global organization, representing the values and experiences of those affected by archaeology, not limited to professional archaeologists (Ucko 1987). From its inception, WAC promoted an *ethos of social justice* and a conception of archaeology as having a social responsibility to work to address global inequities, including access to funding, technology, and information (Stone 2005). A glance at the program of any WAC Congress or Inter-Congress immediately conveys the organization's emphasis on the social and political contexts of archaeology. As debates and discussions about repatriation unfolded in the 1980s, and dozens of U.S. states passed repatriation laws, WAC addressed the volatile issue of human remains with an international conference in 1989 that resulted in the Vermillion Accord (see Appendix 2). In 1990, WAC adopted its First Code of Ethics: Members' Obligations to Indigenous Peoples (Zimmerman and Bruguier 1994), which included eight "principles to abide by" and seven "rules to adhere to" that recognize obligations to Indigenous peoples that come with the privilege of archaeological research, and on a commitment to respect as one of the core values underlying ethical professional practice. The Code of Ethics of the Australian Archaeological Association, adopted in 1992, was modeled directly on the WAC Code and also reflects the political context after the Mabo decision, which recognized Aboriginal rights to lands and cultural heritage (Lilley 2000; Smith and Burke 2003:188).

By this time, many tribal governments had developed archaeology programs suited to their own needs and objectives, with archaeologists working with and for them (Dongoske et al. 2000; Ferguson 2003; Klesert and Downer 1990; Swidler et al. 1997). At the same time, the "post-processual turn" in archaeology questioned the primacy and subjectivity of Western science and encouraged other readings of the past (Hodder 1986; Preucel 1991). This opened the door to the development of alternative archaeologies incorporating new perspectives, methodologies, and approaches from feminist, Marxist, and Indigenous orientations as well as a stance of critical reflexivity toward archaeological practice (Conkey 2005; Conkey and Gero 1997; Hodder 1997; McGuire 1993; Nicholas 2007; Smith and Wobst 2005; Spector 1993; Watkins 2000). Post-processualism recognized the validity of alternative histories and the inherently political nature of archaeology (Schmidt and Patterson 1995). Not everyone has welcomed these perspectives, which perhaps is an indication of just how significant a shift they represent. David Clark is even quoted as saying, "I like to keep my archaeology dead" (in David and Kramer 2001:31).

In 1990, passage of the Native American Graves Protection and Repatriation Act (NAGPRA) marked—even mandated—an ethical sea change for archaeology in the United States and reflected similar moral and legal claims by Indigenous peoples in other parts of the world such as Canada, Australia, and New Zealand. For the first time, the interests of American Indians, Alaska Natives, and Native Hawaiians (at least those recognized by the federal government) were legally declared to outweigh those of archaeologists or museums when it came to human remains, grave goods, sacred objects, and objects of cultural patrimony. The spirit of this new law was furthered in 1992 with amendments to the NHPA, which compelled greater participation of tribes in decisions affecting important traditional cultural properties (Ferguson 2000; Parker and King 1998).

The passage of NAGPRA raised a host of new concerns about cultural affiliation, the study of skeletal materials, and the professional practices of archaeologists and others (Anderson 1996; Meighan 2006; Mihesuah 2000; Rose et al. 1996; Zimmerman 2006). Some archaeologists decried NAGPRA as a breach of archaeological ethics (Goldstein and Kintigh 1990:587). Others felt that academic freedom should not automatically trump respect for the wishes of indigenous peoples. Geoffrey Clark, one of the more outspoken critics, has called NAGPRA "anti-science" and biased toward the beliefs of a "demon-haunted world" (Clark 1999). On the other hand, Anthony Klesert and Shirley Powell (1993:348) asserted that archaeologists needed a professional ethic that "values the rights of those studied and their cultural descendents and places academic pursuits in the proper context." A decade later, many archaeologists at first wary of NAGPRA had changed their positions after experiencing the benefits resulting from the spirit of collaboration that has pervaded many NAGPRA negotiations (Watkins and Ferguson 2005; Zimmerman 1998). Appreciation of the diverse values at stake in heritage management decisions has continued to grow (Carman 2005; Carver 1997; Darvill 1993), as well as recognition of the role archaeologists often play in a system of governmentality (Smith 2004). Still, interest in collaboration is neither universal nor uniform (Bonnichsen et al. 2005).

The SAA Principles

In 1991, the SAA established an Ethics in Archaeology Committee to look into issues of growing concern that might warrant a new ethics policy. The Society was particularly concerned with the effects of the global antiquities market on site looting, the use of looted materials in scholarly publications, and the cooperation of archaeologists with commercial shipwreck salvors, as well as with the mounting concerns of Native Americans over treatment of sites, objects, and human remains. Alison Wylie, a philosopher of archaeology, was asked to prepare a discussion paper on how the SAA might best address these and other problematic issues. Wylie urged the SAA to begin a process of self-inquiry to evaluate and clarify its own ethical positions. She emphasized that the SAA needed to acknowledge the existence and possible validity of other non-archaeological interests and gather empirical evidence from actual practice to address questions such as: "What counts as looted data? What research value does it have? And what are the implications, trade-offs and consequences of its use?" (Wylie 1995). She suggested the SAA initiate a process of widespread discussion among interested parties as a way to understand the range of standpoints, explore the potential for common principles, and gather evidence to assess the best courses of action.

In November 1993, the committee met in Reno, Nevada with an open-ended mandate from the SAA Board. Interestingly, funding for the meeting came from the National Park Service and the Ethics and Values in Science Division of the National Science Foundation (NSF), after NSF's Archaeology Program declined support "on the grounds that its funds should not be diverted from primary research to secondary concerns such as disciplinary ethics" (Wylie 2005:52). The committee discussed expanding the existing bylaws, which since the late 1970s had endorsed a conservation ethic and censured commercialism, but instead decided to articulate a series of ethical principles that described conduct archaeologists should aspire to—ceilings for behavior rather than minimum standards (Lynott and Wylie 1995a; Wylie 1995, 2003, 2005). The committee drafted six principles and introduced them to the membership at a forum held at the annual meeting the following spring. After a period of widespread dissemination and comment, eight Principles of Archaeological Ethics were passed by the Board of Directors in 1996. At the same time the Board created a standing Committee on Ethics, charged with promoting discussion and education on ethics in archaeology and making revisions to the Principles. Though they are admittedly intertwined, the SAA Principles appear in rank order, with an *ethic of stewardship* as the primary tenet of professional practice. In their deliberations, the committee did broach the question of whether the SAA should develop an enforceable code of conduct and grievance procedure, but left this for future consideration. SOPA partially filled this role when it became an inter-society association, the Register of Professional Archaeologists (RPA), in 1998, and the major archaeological associations in the United States all strongly encouraged their members to register.[3]

Hindsight

Looking back, we see that what comprises ethical practice in archaeology has undergone significant transformations in the past generation, not to mention over the past century. It is no longer enough to be accountable to the profession itself. While many of the orienting goals of archaeology have persisted, their interpretations and expressions have changed with changing roles and responsibilities and as the profession has become more cognizant of the social context and repercussions of its practices in the wider world.

As late as 1961, the context for doing archaeology was limited to data collection, analysis, and working with other archaeologists. Most archaeologists assumed science always took priority over other interests. In contrast, today many archaeologists would recognize situations where a commitment to protect archaeological resources might outweigh the desire to glean as much scientific information as possible from them (Wylie 2003:9-10). We can all look back on situations that in hindsight seem racist, ethnocentric, or lacking in the kind of sensitivity or respect that would be obligatory today, but what will archaeologists eschew fifty years from now that we find acceptable today? Indeed, we will likely come to see the work archaeology does in the world in a new light, recognizing aspects that previously appeared invisible (Moody-Adams 1997).

Recent Critiques of Archaeological Ethics

In many ways, the vitality and relevance of the profession depends on critiques of its ethics both from within and outside of the various associations and societies. The SAA Principles have certainly had their critics, some arguing the principles went too far and others not far enough. In 1993, the strongest objections came from SAA members who felt that an ethic of science should continue to be the primary tenet of the profession, not a messy and potentially contentious concept like stewardship (Wylie 1997:17). Many had—and some continue to have—the attitude that politics do not belong in archaeology. But archaeology has always been implicated with politics, from excavations funded by imperialist and nationalist desires to the Nazi regime's expeditions in search of Aryan origins (Arnold 1990; Pringle 2006), and more recently the destruction of the Bamiyan Buddhas in Afghanistan and the looting of Iraq that has emerged in the wake of the second Iraq war (Colwell-Chanthaphonh 2003; Garen 2006) (Figure 3). The question is, what ethical responsibilities do archaeologists have to respond to such situations, and what are the best ways to do so? In any case, good ethics today includes questioning what agendas our work supports and who is empowered or disenfranchised as a result (Smith and Burke 2003:191).

The SAA Principles of stewardship and accountability have also been the subject of particularly cogent critiques from those who feel some do not adequately recognize the ethical responsibilities of the profession or its privileged position (Groarke and Warrick 2006; Welch et al. 2006; Wylie 1999, 2005; Zimmerman 1995). Had the insularity of the discipline actually deluded archaeologists into thinking that they were the only ones who cared about the archaeological record? Or was it that only recently other voices had become strong enough to be heard, compelling archaeologists to listen and recognize their impact on the lives of others (Zimmerman 1995:64)? How could archaeologists claim to be stewards "for the archaeological record for the benefit of *all* people" when there are so many interests, each with their own ideas of how to treat "the past" (Groarke and Warrick 2006)? On whose behalf, then, do archaeologists act as stewards: for living people, whose interests are invariably not homogenous or even compatible, or for the archaeological record, which, some argue, is an amorphous concept created by and for archaeologists (Hamilakis 2003; Smith and Burke 2003)? Who are the real beneficiaries of archaeology? Shouldn't archaeologists recognize all people as stewards of the past (Hodder 2002; Zimmerman 1995:66)? Those who drafted the "stewardship clause" were well aware of such ambiguities and had hopes that the principle would be interpreted as advocacy for collaborative models of stewardship rather than in ways that would re-entrench disciplinary priorities.[4]

Others have questioned the contradictions inherent in a professional commitment to preservation, again asking what interests this serves (Hamilakis 1999; Layton et al. 2001; VanderVeen 2004; Vitelli and Pyburn 1997; Zimmerman 1995:66). How do we justify archaeologists excavating sites that are not threat-

Figure 3. The 53-meter-tall Buddha statue in the Bamiyan Valley, before its final destruction by the Taliban in 2001. (Photograph by John C. Huntington, courtesy of the Huntington Archive)

ened? How do we avoid contributing to the commercial value of objects when their values go up every time we publish a related article? Critics of the principle of public outreach point out that education needs to be a two-way street and the idea that looters, with the proper education, would understand the value of archaeological preservation is myopic, or at best naïve (Hollowell 2006; Matsuda 1998; Pendergast 1994). Even WAC has been criticized for not living up to its own principles in the face of imperialist acts and the atrocities of war, and accused of being more concerned with the fate of sites, museums, and objects than with human lives and needs (Hamilakis 2005). The fact is that only by a continual sincere and critical examination of our ethics will archaeology transform itself to meet the challenges and obligations that the future holds.

Are there any signs telling us where to go from here? One small but significant ethical leap facing the SAA in coming years is whether to acknowledge the special responsibilities that archaeologists have to Indigenous peoples, based on their distinctive relationship to the archaeological record, something that the archaeological associations of Canada, Australia, and New Zealand have already done (Rosenswig 1997; Wylie 1997). The SAA's Committee on Native American Relations has drafted several proposed amendments to the Principles of Ethics on this topic for consideration by the SAA Committee on Ethics.

Ethics on the Horizon

What ethical orientations can we see emerging in archaeology today? We seem to be at the edge of a new era of accountability, one in which archaeology is presented with the challenge of coming to terms with the effects its work can have in the world (Pyburn 2003; Wood and Powell 1993). This commitment to accountability is an engagement not only with the past, but also with the present. It is an engagement that requires sensitivity to the particular contexts and contours of each and every situation at the same time that it recognizes archaeology's unavoidable entanglements with broad political and economic movements. As Lynn Meskell (2005:129) has noted, archaeologists and heritage managers are increasingly answerable to institutions and individuals at local, national, and global levels all at once, and our current ethics are not adequate to guide us as we work in these multiple sociopolitical landscapes and transnational contexts. The real substance will be in how professional commitments to "engagement," "accountability," and "social responsibility" work out in everyday practice.

What is this change in accountability likely to mean in the context of archaeological research? We are seeing projects that bring local or descendant communities and archaeologists together to create collaborative research designs, with questions and objectives that address different agendas and have different, not always shared, outcomes (Figure 4). The research process is likely to include community review and new forms of access and ownership of the processes and products of research (Brugge and Missaghian 2006). This change in professional practice also expands on an ethic of collaboration (Colwell-Chanthaphonh and Ferguson 2004, 2007; Kerber 2006; McDavid 2002), building new relationships based on shared commitments to reciprocity and dialogue that will change not only the face of archaeology, but transform the research process (Conkey 2005; Ferguson and Colwell-Chanthaphonh 2008; Nicholas and Andrews 1997; Wilcox 2000).

How will opening up the processes of archaeology to these new forms of collaboration and accountability affect what we do? In his work at Çatalhöyük, Ian Hodder (1998, 2002) has asked whether archaeologists have a social and ethical obligation to take account of the questions and objectives of other interested groups rather than solely designing research around their own academic questions. Politicians, funders, Goddess societies, and local villagers are all attracted

Figure 4. Zuni cultural advisors Octavius Seowtewa and John Bowannie point out a sacred shrine to archaeologist Sarah Herr at a site in northern Arizona during a collaborative research project. (Photograph by Chip Colwell-Chanthaphonh, August 14, 2006)

to Çatalhöyük for different reasons. They each have their own interpretations of the site, its meanings in the past and the present, and of the work being done. Hodder (2002:176) believes it is an archaeologist's ethical duty to engage with all those who "use the distant past to make claims about origins and identities" and, in particular, to offer other interpretations and alternative perspectives, both as part of an ethic of engagement and as way to counterbalance essentialist views of the past.

Hodder is hardly the only one to tackle these questions. A growing number of "archaeological ethnographies" (Meskell 2005) describe archaeologists and communities engaged in forms of research that are as diverse as the people participating in them (Colwell-Chanthaphonh 2006; Dowdall and Parrish 2003; Edgeworth 2006; Green et al. 2003). These ethnographies give examples of how innovative forms of practice work in the world. They have a role to play, not only in helping archaeologists understand local situations and the potential consequences of our ethics and actions (or non-action), but also in developing research designs and questions that incorporate local objectives. Indeed, Lisa Breglia (2006:174) defined ethnography of archaeology as an "eminently ethical engagement between archaeologists, ethnographers, and local communities."

This commitment to accountability reformulates and refocuses the obligations archaeologists have toward living peoples—a radical shift from the ethic of antiquarianism that is at the root of archaeology's development (Table 1.1). It includes working for social justice, with the recognition that preservation of the past carries responsibilities to work with living peoples to sustain a viable future, with all of the personal and professional obligations this entails (Hodder 2002; Pyburn and Wilk 1995). The underlying motivation for such an orientation becomes apparent when we look at the difference between how we treat the archaeological record and how we treat living people.

Ethics Education

Recent media coverage of cases involving ethical misconduct, particularly in the natural sciences, has called attention to the role of higher education in teaching ethics, since this is the place where young women and men are first exposed to the ethics of a profession. As students, you learn about professional ethics from your instructors, your mentors, and from events and meetings you attend, implicitly or through osmosis if nothing else. In 1980, a report from the Hastings Center on *Ethics Teaching in Higher Education* laid out five worthwhile goals in the teaching of ethics: (1) stimulating the moral imagination, (2) recognizing ethical issues, (3) developing analytical skills, (4) eliciting a sense of moral obligation and personal responsibility, and (5) tolerating—and resisting—disagreement and ambiguity (Callahan and Bok 1980). Still, few colleges, universities, or even professions require an ethics course as part of their curriculum or training,

Table 1.1. *The Shifting Ethos (A Shared Worldview) and Ethics (A Set of Principles and Values) of Archaeology.*

Ethos and Ethics	Date of Manifestation
Ethos of Antiquarianism	1600s
Collecting	
Ethos of Science and Discovery	Early 1800s
Justification for colonialism	
Ethos of Scholarship	Early 1900s
Salvage	
Preservation	
Art appreciation	
Ethic of Scientific Method	1930s
Excavation	
Documentation	
Ethic of Professional Accountability	1950s
Publication	
Formal training	
Conservation Ethic	1960s
Cultural Resource Management	
Ethic of Public Accountability	1970–1980s
Public outreach	
Anti-commercialization	
Consultation	
Ethic of Stewardship	1990s
Collaboration	
Respect	
Ethos of Social Justice	2000s
Reciprocity	
Dialogue	
Benefit-sharing	

although this is changing rapidly in the medical fields, where bioethics issues loom larger and larger.

In 2006, the Council of Graduate Schools received a grant from the NSF to expand its programs in ethics education to eight more United States universities, adding to the ten piloted in 2004. These efforts have almost exclusively focused on biomedical, behavioral, and natural science fields, with the exception of a recent workshop organized by the Association for Practical and Professional Ethics (APPE) with NSF funding specifically for discussing ethics in social science research, in which archaeology played a prominent role (Schrag 2006). The

Council now recommends that graduate students working in any research field be encouraged to take an interdisciplinary course in research ethics and have the option of attending additional courses and workshops on ethics within their own departments, with the idea that universities should work toward making these experiences mandatory (Brainard 2006).

Teaching ethics through case studies is thought to be one of the most effective approaches because it places abstract ethical principles in the context of realistic situations. To be effective, however, as one ethics educator put it, "This evaluation needs to go beyond a simple justification by appeal to general ethical principles to consider the complexities of the context of the situation" (Muskavitch 2005:433). This means stepping out of the more comfortable role of judging the actors and into the role of agent, attempting to see yourself in their shoes, with their conflicting obligations and responsibilities, and thinking through what actions you would take while also considering potential consequences. Only through such a contextualized evaluative approach to case studies do we learn to apply critical thinking skills that lead to better informed and more equitable and just decisions.

Another vital aspect of ethics education is interacting with others, both from within and outside of your profession, especially those who may have very different perspectives. Thus one of the leading recommendations for best practices from the Council of Graduate Schools (2006) is making ethics a visible and regularly discussed topic though public forums and events such as the Ethics Bowl. The very fact that people are discussing a common problem openly generates a sense of collegiality, peership, and shared decision-making.

In one study that suggests what a well-balanced ethics education should entail, it was found that senior researchers used a combination of formal principles or guidelines (such as codes) and "practical wisdom" to tackle ethical dilemmas arising in everyday practice (Deming et al. 2007). Three practices reportedly contributed to developing practical wisdom: self-reflection, sincere skepticism, and open dialogue with colleagues. This is one of many reasons why the online tutorials being packaged and sold by some companies as the answer to the need for ethics education are not nearly enough (Muskavitch 2005).

William Perry (1970) has defined stages in intellectual and moral development that are particularly vigorous during the college years. In brief, students generally progress from thinking that all problems are solvable (wanting to know the right answer); to acknowledging multiple equally valid answers (ethical relativism, see Chapter 2); to using reasoning to evaluate different solutions; to finally integrating knowledge, experience, and reflection to make a commitment and understanding the consequences of that commitment. Ethics education provides every student with opportunities to wrestle with all of these stages. The Ethics Bowl, for example, asks you to acknowledge multiple answers, develop reasoning methodologies, integrate learned knowledge and personal reflection, and make commitments to solutions while thinking about their consequences and responsibilities.

Will participating in an Ethics Bowl instill certain core values about archaeological practice? There has been some disagreement over whether the goal of ethics education is—or should be—to change a person's core values and beliefs—which could amount to a subtle form of propagandizing—or to increase an individual's reasoning and critical thinking skills. The ability to think critically is clearly important in all aspects of education and in life in general. Critical thinking has been described as "the art of thinking about your thinking while you are thinking in order to make your thinking better: more clear, more accurate, or more defensible" (Paul et al. 1995:361). A critical thinker is someone with a sense of curiosity, who listens carefully to others, seeks evidence to support assumptions or beliefs, and is generally a good problem solver (Ferrett 2002). Critical thinking skills can and do improve with focus, practice, self-confidence, and experience. In general, studies done in introductory interdisciplinary ethics classes have shown that training in ethics didn't significantly change personal values or opinions, but did increase students' abilities to identify and analyze problems, generate alternatives, think through the consequences of various decisions, and appreciate opposing viewpoints (Klugman and Stump 2006). The situation could be a bit different, however, when ethics education occurs within the bounds of one profession, which advocates a particular set of professional values or, moreover, in the Ethics Bowl, where students are "judged" by their professional mentors.

There is even some debate over whether ethics can really be "taught" at all (Marino 2004), based on studies indicating that training in ethics does not necessarily change an individual's behavior when faced with the personal and professional pressures of real life, particularly in high-pressure science careers with competitive funding environments and the high costs of keeping labs running (Brainard 2006). In any case, it's ultimately true that how ethics play out in real life will involve a myriad of unforeseeable circumstances and compromises. In the end, it's not that more knowledge or more experience analyzing case studies stands to make anyone a more ethical person, but having to reflect closely on and defend your position in front of others might cause you to think more carefully about the facts involved, the implications of your actions, and the responsibilities archaeologists have in the world today.

Origin of the Ethics Bowl

The Ethics Bowl is the brainchild of Robert Ladenson, a philosophy professor at the Illinois Institute of Technology (IIT). In 1993, Ladenson invented the rules and procedures for an Ethics Bowl, held at IIT, which subsequently began to attract teams from nearby universities. The Intercollegiate Ethics Bowl went national in 1997 at the annual meeting of the Association for Practical and Professional Ethics (APPE), and has since been held every year at the annual meeting. By 2004, the APPE was turning teams away after filling the 40 slots reserved for the annual competition.

The event is a distinctive mode of ethics education that compels students to engage directly with the complexities of working through moral dilemmas. As Chapter 3 describes, it consists of teams presenting arguments about how they would resolve ethical dilemmas raised in hypothetical case studies. Although centered on hypothetical dilemmas, the Ethics Bowl is anything but abstract; participants must investigate how professional codes of ethics, legal mandates, historical examples and considerations, and different moral philosophies all inform problem solving in a range of situations. A panel of judges scores each team based on criteria of intelligibility, depth, focus, and judgment. The APPE Intercollegiate Ethics Bowl uses interdisciplinary case studies from a variety of disciplines and professions and recruits judges from a similar diversity of backgrounds.

In 2004, an interviewer from *The Chronicle of Higher Education* asked Ladenson why he thought the event had sparked so much interest among students. He attributed it to filling a void created by a general lack of consensus on ethical issues in society today. "The Ethics Bowl appeals because it's an activity that allows for tremendous ranges of disagreement and interpretation," he said, "but in a framework that highlights the aspects of ethical thinking that are common," in contrast to the "really awful kind of intellectual bullying" that we see all over the media these days (Borrega 2004). Rather than turn teams away, in 2006-2007, preliminary rounds were held for the first time at college campuses across the country, months before the final event, which brought together 32 teams, all of them already winners, at the annual APPE meeting.

An Ethics Bowl for the SAA

Each year the annual business meetings of most SAA committees take place simultaneously in one large room with dozens of tables buzzing with agendas. In 2003, K.D. Vitelli, past chair of the Committee on Ethics, and Chip, her doctoral student at that time, introduced the idea of holding an Ethics Bowl at the SAA annual meeting to the Committee on Ethics. Chip had witnessed the Ethics Bowl in action earlier that year at the APPE meeting and found himself duly impressed by the well-prepared teams who performed to a rapt and overflowing audience at the end of a long conference day. He and K.D. felt that an event that could stimulate so much collective enthusiasm about ethics could only benefit the SAA. The Committee saw it as an excellent way of getting students involved in discussions about the many complex dilemmas that confront the profession, exactly suited to its mission of "promoting discussion and education about ethical issues in archaeology." Chip and Julie, then both members of the Committee on Ethics, took on the appointed task of organizing an Ethics Bowl for the 2004 meetings in Montreal.[5]

The Committee's chair, Alex W. Barker, had no trouble getting the enthusiastic support and endorsement of the SAA Board and its President, Lynne Sebastian, for the Ethics Bowl. Lynne helped us promote the Ethics Bowl in numerous ways, including her quip: "More exciting than the Rose Bowl; warmer than college hockey's 'Frozen Four'; more cerebral than the NCAA 'Sweet Sixteen.' Don't miss the SAA Ethics Bowl in Montreal—the premier intercollegiate competition in archaeology!" The SAA's Executive Director Tobi Brimsek let us know diplomatically that all of the venues and rooms for the annual meetings were booked five to seven years in advance, and it would be no small challenge to find a way to fit the Ethics Bowl into an already jam-packed meeting schedule. So far, Tobi has magically managed to find more than adequate space, although we look forward to the day when the preliminaries outgrow hotel meeting rooms and take over 20 hotel rooms, as they do at the APPE.

It was all we could do to muster two teams the following year in Montreal. We saw that first year as an exhibition event of sorts that would show people how an Ethics Bowl worked, how much fun it could be, and inspire participation for following years. Due to a last-minute change in plans, one team ended up composed of three students, all from different universities. They did a superb job, in spite of obvious disadvantages of distance and time, but after that we decided that a team should represent no more than two universities (both of whom would have their names engraved on the silver trophy). Our distinguished judges that first year were Rosemary Joyce, Brian Fagan, and Janet E. Levy. Janet fortunately had prior experience as one of the many judges for the APPE Ethics Bowl. She was enormously helpful and later wrote an essay on how to prepare for the competition (Levy 2006). Each year members of the Committee on Ethics, and many SAA members, have pitched in as moderators or helping to find sponsors for the event (Table 1.2). One of the cleverest aspects of the Ethics Bowl is the trophy itself—a hefty silver bowl engraved with the names of each year's winners. After engraving, the bowl is shipped to the home of the winning team and comes back to the annual meeting the following year.

Even those of us who are not fond of competitions or trophies have become steadfast fans of the Ethics Bowl. Participating teams and their mentors have committed untold hours preparing for the event by the time they arrive at the annual meeting. Many have put together notebooks of ethics resources and strategies for evaluating each case study. Teams show up with an entourage that often includes faculty mentors and fellow students, some of whom have prepared alongside their cohorts but are not sitting for the competition. The atmosphere is at once festive and serious, and the spirit and determination of each team is palpable. Everyone is well prepared, yet ready for the unexpected—nervous, yet ready to go.

The competence and team spirit of all of the participants is indescribable to witness, whether they advance to the next round or not. Many teams return the

Table 1.2. *Teams, Moderators, Judges, and Sponsors for the SAA Ethics Bowl, 2004–2007.*

Year	Teams	Moderators and Judges	Sponsors
2004	Cambridge University, **Indiana University/ University of Nevada-Reno**	Brian Fagan, Rosemary Joyce, Janet E. Levy, Joe Watkins	Archaeogear, Center for Desert Archaeology, Cultural Resource Technologies Inc., *Journal of Social Archaeology* (Sage Publications), Marshalltown Company, Rite in the Rain
2005	Indiana University, Longwood University, San Diego State University, **University of Arizona**	Jeffrey Altschul, Sonya Atalay, Alex Barker, Alexander Bauer, Jane Eva Baxter, Hester Davis, Lynne Goldstein, Ian Hodder, Paula Lazrus, Shereen Lerner, Janet E. Levy, Madonna L. Moss, Gordon F. M. Rakita, John R. Welch, Joe Watkins, Larry Zimmerman	Archaeological Institute of America, Art Loss Register, *International Journal of Cultural Property* (Cambridge University Press), Center for Desert Archaeology, Register of Professional Archaeologists, Rite in the Rain, Saving Antiquities for Everyone (SAFE)
2006	Boston University, College of William and Mary, **San Diego State University**, University of New Mexico, Utah State University	Mitch Allen, Alex Barker, Catherine Carlson, Chip Colwell-Chanthaphonh, Meg Conkey, Pat Garrow, Eric Kansa, Paula Lazrus, Heather McKillop, Eduardo Neves, George Nicholas, Lynne Sebastian, Dean Snow, Sarah Tarlow, Joe Watkins, Melinda Zeder	American Institute of Archaeology, Center for Desert Archaeology, Rite in the Rain, Register of Professional Archaeologists, Saving Antiquities for Everyone (SAFE)
2007	**Brown University**, Indiana University, Michigan State University, Northwestern State University, University of California-Berkeley, University of Massachusetts-Amherst, University of New Mexico	Alex Barker, Alexander Bauer, Mary Jane Berman, Tamara Bray, Jeffery J. Clark, Linda Cordell, Sam Duwe, Paul Fish, Lisa Frink, George Gumerman IV, Paula Lazrus, Karlene Leeper, Janet E. Levy, Diana Loren, Carol McDavid, Lena Mortensen, Gordon F. M. Rakita, Vincas Steponaitis, Nina Swidler, Joe Watkins, David Whitley	Archaeological Institute of America, Center for Desert Archaeology, *International Journal of Cultural Property* (Cambridge University Press), *Journal of Social Archaeology* (Sage Publications), Left Coast Press, Marshalltown Company, Register of Professional Archaeologists, Rite in the Rain

Note: Winning team is in bold.

next year. We hope to see participation in the Ethics Bowl develop into a legacy that is passed down among students in a department. The effects of working together as a team cannot be underestimated. Team members typically collaborate in deciding how to respond to the case studies, and their deliberations make them aware that their colleagues may well have different opinions on the same issues and solid arguments to back them up. Such interactions make us all reflect upon our own ethical positions and the moral arguments that support them, which is always a positive thing to do.

Admittedly, one reason for strong support for the Ethics Bowl on the part of the SAA Board and administration is that it is a positive way to attract students to the annual meeting and get them involved in the organization. As its organizers, we see the Ethics Bowl as having less to do with inculcating a specific set of professional values than with critically exploring how these tend to work out in practice and what else might need considering, based on the evidence. Although it is always impressive when a participant cites a section from one of any number of codes as if it were a law, this is not really the spirit that the Ethics Bowl is trying to convey.

Some Frustrations

Organizing the Ethics Bowl has not been without its frustrations. One of the biggest frustrations for us as volunteer organizers is the time and energy it takes to recruit teams each year. We can only hope that some of this is due to the newness of the event, now entering its fifth year. Every year a major effort is made to contact graduate archaeology programs across North America and archaeology listservs with a call for participation. Each year five or six very committed teams come forward, but there are always unforeseen last-minute changes. We'd like the event to grow, and hope this book helps with this goal.

Coming up with ways to get the word out has been another time-consuming but creative job, which should improve with experience. In 2007, Sam Duwe, a University of Arizona graduate student and veteran of an Ethics Bowl himself, worked with fellow members of the SAA Student Committee to send notices to major university anthropology and archaeology departments surrounding Austin, Texas, the site of the annual meeting. (The idea being that students nearby could more easily participate as expenses would be minimal for them.) Even so, recruiting teams remains a challenge. It has also been a constant struggle to ensure visibility for the Ethics Bowl in the programming for the annual meeting, and here our efforts have not been so successful. On the other hand, the SAA Webmaster has always been very responsive to our periodic requests for updates and new pages of ethics resources for SAAweb, the society's website.

Perhaps even more frustrating is our inability to support participating students for their travel or other expenses. Our plan is, in time, to offer *all* participants a discounted registration fee or a one-year membership in the SAA. As a first step toward this goal, in 2007, the RPA donated registration fees for the winning team, and we set up the necessary protocols for distributing this generous prize. We've had more success acquiring prizes such as books, journal subscriptions, memberships to other organizations, and archaeological gear. We have thought seriously about writing a NSF grant to support the Ethics Bowl, but this requires an inordinate amount of time and energy for a grant that might expire in two or three years while our goal is to create a long-term sustainable financial program. The APPE Ethics Bowl has used major corporate sponsors, something we have yet to try. We have successfully encouraged and assisted teams and individual students in applying for travel funds for professional development through their universities or departments, arguing that participating in an Ethics Bowl is at least as important a professional activity as giving a twenty-minute paper.

Surprising Outcomes

The Ethics Bowl has generated many positive outcomes, some of them quite unexpected. There is a surprising sense of satisfaction watching the next generation of archaeologists wrestle with complex ethical issues—almost a sense of relief that they represent the future of the profession. A good percentage of participants have already gone on to become leaders in professional activities and associations.

Another unexpected surprise has been the overwhelmingly positive reactions from those who have served as judges, or who play such an important role as mentors and sounding boards. Recruiting judges is a great deal of fun because people are so eager to participate. For the final round, we choose individuals who hold distinguished positions in the profession—past and future Presidents of the SAA, influential thinkers, and important figures. Judges for the preliminary rounds come from all subdisciplines and backgrounds. They seem to value the experience tremendously, and often ask to be invited back. So far, we have tried to spread this experience around, since it is a good way to get the word out about the Ethics Bowl.

We can say that there will never be a dearth of case studies for the Ethics Bowl. Each year, it actually seems easier to come up with a dozen or so strong cases, thanks in part to suggestions from the SAA membership and to the proliferation of pertinent issues in the mainstream news. We are aware that some of the case studies come quite close to the real life situations from which they are drawn, but so far no one has flinched (not much, anyway).

One very interesting development is that individuals have started to come to us with case studies based on real life dilemmas and personal experiences. Sometimes these represent situations that occurred to that person or to a colleague many years ago, but which were never fully resolved. Other times they are events that a person has recently struggled with in his or her own practice. Remarkably, the act of writing up these cases and turning them in seems to create a space for resolution, whether by allowing people to think through things and move ahead, or possibly as a sort of catharsis that lends some sense of closure. We encourage this and see it as one of the unexpected benefits of the Ethics Bowl.

Last but not least, another positive outcome of the Ethics Bowl is that each year a new set of case studies becomes available as a resource for ethics education in archaeology. We love to hear that individuals, groups, or classes are using these case studies or developing their own! Part of our intention in writing this book is to let more people know about these resources and to spread the word about this practical and invigorating framework for using them. We hope those of you who undertake to write up case studies (a learning process in itself) will share your scenarios with the Ethics Bowl organizers so they can be used in the annual event and made widely available on the SAA website, or in future editions of this book.

The Book Itself

The primary audiences for this volume are graduate and advanced undergraduate students and their instructors who will find the case studies and the Ethics Bowl useful and edifying in classes on archaeological ethics, as part of a theory or methods course, or as an extracurricular activity. Hopefully many of them will do so as preparation for the annual SAA Ethics Bowl! The resources and methods here would also be valuable and appropriate for many introductory archaeology courses as an end of the year project or for extra credit.

Another important audience is professional archaeologists more generally, who will benefit from reading the case studies and discussing them with colleagues. Each year since the inauguration of the Ethics Bowl, the RPA has sponsored a forum at the annual meeting using several of that year's case studies to spark discussion, demonstrating their relevance and usefulness to active professionals as well as students.

The materials here will also be a useful resource for those in other disciplines, particularly fields related to archaeology. Liz Kryder-Reid and Larry J. Zimmerman of the Museum Studies program at Indiana University-Purdue University Indianapolis, for example, recently adapted the SAA materials with their students to stage a successful Ethics Bowl.[6] With the growing presence of archaeological ethics in the media and other public spheres, discussions of case studies could easily provide the basis for a public forum, university roundtable, or simply enliven a faculty meeting. The interested non-professional will also find plenty of food for thought here about ethical predicaments that archaeologists face at every turn, sometimes just as interesting and intriguing as the dilemmas of Indiana Jones.

The chapter that follows, "Thinking About Ethics," introduces some essential rules, intellectual devices, and reliable strategies that you can use to work through ethical dilemmas. Chapter 3, "Learning from Ethical Dilemmas," introduces the format and strategies of the Ethics Bowl so that the reader can more effectively create, oversee, and participate in ethical debates. This chapter also features a collection of "Tips," solicited from past student participants, judges, moderators, and faculty mentors. The fourth part, "Case Studies," includes 36 case studies selected from previous SAA Ethics Bowl competitions, covering a broad but representative range of provocative ethical dilemmas that arise in archaeological practice. The cases themselves are hypothetical insofar as they consist of fabricated scenarios, but most were inspired by actual problems archaeologists have faced in recent years. Although there are no neat divisions in themes or obligations—indeed, partly what makes a case study work is when multiple duties clash—for the purpose of selecting the case studies, we followed three general themes. In the appendices, you will find the current competition guidelines and scoring sheet for the SAA Ethics Bowl, a listing of professional codes and principles of ethics, and a bibliography of suggested readings covering eight different topics.

In conclusion, for new and seasoned professionals, professors and students alike, this book will engage the reader with a range of topics, including looting, fakes, access to data, public accountability, collaboration, intellectual property, illicit collections, sexual harassment, manipulated data, conflicts of interest, and more. We hope the volume is one way for archaeologists to come to grips with the discipline's past, contend with its present predicaments, and imagine its future possibilities.

Notes

1. Since most readers of this volume will be based in the United States, we focus our introductory history around archaeology's development there. However, an in depth study of archaeological ethics should indeed take a more global perspective.

2. At its height, SOPA had between 500 and 750 members, then about 20% of the SAA membership (Jeffrey H. Altschul, pers. comm., 2007).

3. Today, there are about 2,000 registered RPAs, or about 29% of the SAA membership (Jeffrey H. Altschul, pers. comm., 2007).

4. Alison Wylie, pers. comm., 2007.

5. We were both still students at that time, in the last stages of our Ph.D.s, in the Archaeology and Social Context Program at Indiana University. As the new kids on the block, we saw this as a way of contributing to the Committee, and of encouraging the SAA membership to engage with ongoing ethical dilemmas. Dru McGill, a recent graduate student in the program at Indiana University, joined the Committee in 2006 and helped to coordinate the Fourth Annual Ethics Bowl; Dru now takes the organizational lead of the event.

6. For their class materials, check out: www.iupui.edu/~mstd/a403503/ethicsbowl1.html. The rules and procedures of the SAA Ethics Bowl, as well as tips for preparing, case studies from former years, and many other ethics resources can be found on the drop-down menu of the Ethics Bowl page on the SAA website at http://www.saa.org/aboutSAA/committees/ethics/ebowl.html.

2

Thinking Through Ethics

What would you do ... if you discovered a colleague hiding data that challenges his or her theories? ... if your professor made a pass at one of your fellow graduate students? ... if the museum you worked for planned to exhibit looted artifacts? ... if your Native American collaborators wanted some books removed from the library shelf because of language offensive to them?

When people hear the word "ethics" they often think about abstract theories, armchair philosophers, or even preachers at their pulpits, but as the questions above reveal, ethics aren't something outside of what archaeologists do, they are potentially in everything they do. From collecting, reporting, and storing data, to their relationships with mentors and colleagues, to their responsibilities in presenting the past to the public, to productively working with diverse stakeholders—ethics are inescapable!

Archaeological ethics, at their core, are about the real world problems archaeologists face and how to go about solving them in a way that is reasonable, responsible, and right. Ethics aren't just about coming up with abstract principles. They're about enacting principles. Putting ethics into action concerns not merely what you *can* do, but also what you *ought* to do in any given situation. Applying ethics is about uniting practice and theory: acting in the right way and being able to explain why convincingly.

Disagreements about ethics are so intriguing and interesting because the right thing to do is rarely obvious. The great debates in contemporary public life—abortion, the death penalty, animal welfare, global warming, affirmative action—all have credible points on both sides and endless arguments in between. These debates are so heated because they are so important, yet none of them have unequivocal solutions. They are tremendously complex because, as a whole, the right behavior for individual citizens and society is murky and uncertain.

However, just because ethical problems don't have clear-cut answers—or for that matter because we can't be absolutely positive which solution will be the right one—does not imply that all answers are equally good. Skepticism about right answers and humility about our own limitations are constructive feelings to have, but we should not let them paralyze us when generating potential solutions to ethical dilemmas. The realization that we need to decide about courses of action, even if our knowledge is imperfect, leads to the question of *how* we can determine which answers are the best ones. How can we solve ethical problems?

In this chapter, you will be given some tools to begin untangling the knots of ethical dilemmas. Although there is no single approach—to be sure, exactly how to tackle ethics has been argued about for thousands of years from Plato to Confucius to Nietzsche—there are some basic rules, intellectual devices, and sound strategies that you can use to conceptualize and solve ethical problems archaeologists face. We will begin with a discussion of some basic ground rules and areas of moral agreement, and then move on to different factors that should be considered in your deliberations. We will conclude by working through a hypothetical case study, using a step-by-step procedure for ethical decision-making. This chapter aims to help you to begin thinking through different ways of approaching ethics, as well as thinking through problems you may face with an ethical lens.

Beginning Points

Ethical dilemmas typically emerge when there is disagreement about what to do in a given situation. In this way, ethics are usually about variance and dissent. While people of course can say, do, and believe what they choose, we need to agree about some basic ways of thinking and talking about ethics in order to have productive conversations.

Some Ground Rules

Know the facts. When deliberating on ethical predicaments, such as the case studies in this volume, we should be sure to know the facts. This is important because the facts of the case shape our understanding of what issues are at stake. From the information given, we must critically examine those things we know for sure, those things that are plausible, and those things that are unlikely. So, for example, a rumor about a looter could be plausible or unlikely (depending on the source and claims), while the need for an assistant professor at a major university to have publications to get tenure is a fact. An intervention of UFOs or reading someone's mind using ESP may be entertaining to ponder, but, because they are highly unlikely, would not provide realistic solutions to real-world problems. Getting the facts straight is important because we need to justify our claims based on the reality of the world as we know it.

Use your ethical imagination. At the same time, we should be careful not to let the facts of a case constrain our thinking. In thinking through dilemmas, you should use your "ethical imagination." In any given case study, only so much information can be provided. Rather than dwelling on what is unknown, the unknowns should encourage you to think about the possibilities of a case. Think to yourself: If X, Y, or Z were to happen, then what would be the result? Examining alternative possibilities will also encourage you to think about the *unintended consequences* of certain choices. In other words, any potential solution to an ethical predicament is likely to create new ethical predicaments, and these should be considered, so far as it is possible, in your deliberations.

Be logical and consistent. When discussing ethical cases, your arguments should be based in reason. They should be logical and consistent. If, to solve one dilemma, you say that it is okay for an archaeologist to lie to someone, then in the next case, you shouldn't say that archaeologists must always, in every case, tell the truth. Applied ethics is about being able to persuade the people around you that a given course of action is the right thing to do. If you argue based only on your feelings or unfounded beliefs, or if your point of view seems haphazard, you will convince few people.

Consider other viewpoints. Ethical dilemmas often involve different people with different values and interests. Although you will likely have your own interests in a case, it is important for you to try to be impartial. This is important because people often unfairly let their own welfare take precedence over others. For example, suppose an archaeologist wants to excavate Site X, but the local town and nearby Native American community do not want the site disturbed. It would be entirely unjust for the archaeologist to dismiss the interests of these other communities *only* because archaeologists will benefit by excavation. The archaeologist instead should consider the viewpoints of all the people involved, and strive to come up with a solution that equitably considers the interests of all. Whenever possible you should use your imagination to understand where other people are coming from, and use your good listening skills to hear what other people have to say.

Respect, Beneficence, and Justice

In 1932, a medical experiment to study the effects of a contagious organism called *Treponema pallidum* on the human body was launched (see Jones 1992). The disease that results from *Treponema pallidum* is commonly known as syphilis. The Tuskegee Syphilis Study, as the experiment came to be called, wasn't about treatment, but rather about observing the course of the grisly disease that can lead to paralysis, insanity, and death. Even as, over time, treatments for syphilis became widely available, the medical doctors participating in the study did not make them available to the participants. Forty years later, more than 600 men had participated in the experiment, all of them African Americans, and most of them living in dire poverty. The men, in place of treatment, or even information about its possibility, were given free meals, physicals, and medical help for minor ailments when they visited the researchers. They were also given a burial stipend.

If anything could be said to be a positive outcome from this appalling breach of medical ethics, it was a national dialogue about the moral duties that should bind researchers. Not since the trials of Nazi medical experimenters at Nuremburg had Americans in one voice proclaimed that a license to conduct research is not license to do as one pleases. A direct outcome of the controversy over the Tuskegee Syphilis Study was new federal legislation to regulate the actions of researchers who conduct research on human beings. On July 12, 1974, the National Research Act was signed into law, creating the National Commission for the Protection of Human Subjects of Biomedical and Behavioral Research. In the spring of 1979, the Commission released *The Belmont Report: Ethical Principles and Guidelines for the Protection of Human Subjects of Research*. This important report gives us three basic ethical principles—respect for persons, beneficence, and justice—that should guide researchers when their work involves people.

Respect for persons involves two important points. First, people should be treated as autonomous agents; that is, researchers must recognize that people are independent and responsible for themselves. Second, people who have diminished autonomy, such as infants or invalids, warrant special protection and consideration. In practice, this principle compels researchers to ensure that people take part in research voluntarily and with sufficient information.

Beneficence is the doing of good, an active pursuit of goodness, kindness, and charity. With this second principle, the report emphasizes that researchers should not only protect research participants from harm, but should make a concerted effort to secure their well-being. Here, beneficence is seen as an obligation that is expressed in two complementary ways: (1) do no harm, and (2) maximize possible benefits and minimize possible harms. These expressions mean honestly providing participants with information about risks and benefits and then allowing them to make decisions "according to their best judgment." Risks and benefits should be thought of in terms of both individuals and society at large.

Justice, the report's third principle, relates to questions about "fairness in distribution" or "what is deserved." As the report states, "An injustice occurs when some benefit to which a person is entitled is denied without good reason or when some burden is imposed unduly. Another way of conceiving the principle of justice is that equals ought to be treated equally." However, equality is not a simple concept. The report emphasizes that distinctions among individuals—for example, based on age or deprivation—should be made in research endeavors. Formulations can therefore be made about the distribution of benefits and burdens. The principle of justice seeks to ensure that the people who are the subject of research reap at least some benefit from participating in a project.

How do the principles of respect for persons, beneficence, and justice apply to archaeology? Don't archaeologists deal in dead things and not living people? Although archaeologists by definition study material culture, the pursuit of archaeology is a social practice. You cannot divorce the social context in which archaeology takes place, because all archaeology involves relationships— relationships with fellow researchers, students, community members, government officials, tourists, land owners, avocationalists, future generations, descendant populations, and still others. Additionally, it is important to understand that some of the materials archaeologists work with, such as human remains and sacred objects, are considered living spirits by some stakeholders (e.g., Ferguson 1990; Turner 1994). Recently, some have persuasively argued that archaeologists should be subject to the restraints of the National Research Act "where there are identifiable living persons with a stake in the disposition of the artifacts and information being studied" (Bendremer and Richman 2006:114). The principles of *The Belmont Report* are a crucial beginning point—whether or not archaeological researchers are subject to the National Research Act—to begin deliberating how archaeological ethics shape professional responsibilities in the social present, as well as obligations to the material past.

Approaching Ethics

Thinking through ethics requires thinking broadly. The complexity and number of issues raised in ethical dilemmas means that you must be open minded and creative, as well as ready to draw from many areas of knowledge. In this section, you will learn about five key aspects of moral thinking that will help in the explication of ethical quandaries.

Thinking from Moral Philosophy

Contemporary moral philosophers generally discuss three key approaches to ethics: consequentialism, deontology, and virtue theory. There are, of course, many variations and many threads of theory intertwined. Here we present a brief introduction to the three approaches, not to emphasize one over the others, but to ensure that when approaching ethical dilemmas, you are aware of the different theoretical orientations you may draw from.

Consequentialist-based Ethics. Consequentialism is the theory that ethical decisions should be made on the basis of the expected outcome (or consequences) of a given action. The most well-known kind of consequentialist-based thinking is Utilitarianism, which as a formal theory was born in Western Europe in the 1700s. Its most famous proponents were Jeremy Bentham and John Stuart Mill. Utilitarian theory is focused on the consequences of our actions, the end result of our moral decisions. It is a kind of cost/benefit analysis because its method involves weighing the costs of a certain course of action against the good that will result. In classical Utilitarian theory, the good is happiness. As Mill (1987[1863]:16) wrote, "The creed which accepts as the foundation of morals utility or the greatest happiness principle, holds that actions are right in proportion as they tend to promote happiness, wrong as they tend to produce the reverse of happiness. By 'happiness' is intended pleasure, and the absence of pain."

The calculation that results from this principle is largely indifferent to how happiness is achieved or who receives the happiness. Here is a somewhat oversimplified example: If 100 people are living in dire poverty, suffering terribly, to serve 10 wealthy people living in blissful happiness, then the calculation of Utilitarianism says that such a situation is immoral. One of the more serious problems with classical Utilitarianism is that it is a "cold" system that largely disregards our human relationships. We value our friends and family not just as human beings (as we value strangers), but as intimates who provide us with companionship and love. Another problem is that when thinking about ethics, consequences are not all that matters. Rachels (2003:107) provides a provocative case to illustrate the problem:

> Suppose a Peeping Tom spied on Ms. York by peering through her bedroom window, and secretly took pictures of her undressing. Further suppose that he did this without ever being detected and that he used the photographs entirely for his own amusement, without showing them to anyone. Now under these circumstances, it seems clear that the only consequence of his action is an increase in his own happiness. No one else, including Ms. York, is caused any unhappiness at all. How, then, could Utilitarianism deny that the Peeping Tom's actions are right? But it is evident to moral common sense that they are not right. Thus, utilitarianism appears to be unacceptable.

Despite these and other problems, Utilitarianism can be a powerful way of thinking about ethical dilemmas. For one, it emphasizes that consequences *are* relevant to ethical decisions—that we should care deeply about what will be the result of our actions. For another, it emphasizes that we should be concerned about the happiness and well-being of *all* those who have the potential of suffering. While we care about our friends and colleagues, it is unfair to excessively weigh—without reason—our own interests and the interests of those we are personally close to. Later versions of Utilitarianism, which are "rule-based," can be especially compelling, as they formulate rules derived from consequences of the rule rather than specific acts.

Deontological Ethics. The second approach is called deontological ethics—from Greek, "for that which is binding"—and holds that "the rightness of an act is derived from its logical consistency and universalizability" (Pence 2000:14).

Unlike Utilitarianism, which focuses on consequences, deontological approaches, on the contrary, emphasize duty—that we must do the right thing irrespective of the consequences. A duty-based ethics was most brilliantly put forth by the eighteenth-century philosopher Immanuel Kant. He argued that actions are intrinsically wrong or right—that we should search for ethical rules that can be followed absolutely.

Imagine that you are sitting at home one night, and there is a knock at the door. You answer it to discover a man, frantic and out of breath. He asks you to hide him in your house because he is being chased by a man who wants to kill him. You naturally agree, for he seems innocent enough, and bring him into your home. Just as you are hiding the man under your bed, there is another knock at the door. It is a large man carrying a large ax and he is very angry. He then asks you if you are hiding a man.

If you were in such a situation would you lie or tell the truth? Kant argued that it is extremely difficult to predict the outcomes of events. Yet we can know whether or not a specific action is right or wrong. In an essay originally published in 1797, Kant (1994) reasoned that lying was wrong because you could not anticipate what will result from the lie. Perhaps, if you lie, the murderer will turn away in frustration and he will meet a moment later the man who has climbed out of your bedroom window when you were at the door. Your lie would then in part result in the man's death, for if you had told the truth, the murderer would have entered your home while the would-be victim escaped out of the window. If you lie, then you are responsible for the lie's consequences; whereas if you tell the truth, then you have done nothing more than what morality demands of you. Therefore, Kant says that you should tell the potential murderer the truth. From such reasoning, Kant (1963[1785]:88) derived what he called the categorical imperative, which states, "Act only on that maxim through which you can at the same time will that it should become universal law." In sum, this means that, for example, you should tell the truth in particular situations because telling the truth is an act that you can universalize, that is, an act you can and should always do.

Rachels (2003:122–127) points out two problems with Kant's approach. The first is that it is overly pessimistic about anticipating consequences. Of course, there is no absolute guarantee that the large man carrying the ax will kill the man you are hiding if you tell the truth, but surely you could suppose a high probability. Thus, in this scenario, intuitively, lying seems okay because you can reasonably guess that telling the truth would lead to murder. The second problem is that certain rules cannot be easily reconciled. While "It is wrong to lie" can be a universalized rule, so can the rule "It is wrong to facilitate the murder of innocent people." What rule could you establish to settle a conflict between rules? One of the great strengths of Kant's writings, however, is that he is fundamentally committed to coming up with rational and consistent theories. In thinking about ethical dilemmas, we are often tempted to make exceptions in order to get a particularly desirable result—often exceptions that will benefit ourselves or that fit our preconceptions. But Kant insisted that we come up with rules that we can reliably apply. The point is that we must use caution when we want to make exceptions and we should strive to be as rational and consistent as possible in our thinking about right behavior. In a connected argument, Kant also powerfully argued that we must never treat other human beings merely as a means to an end. That is, we should not use people only to satisfy our own desires. Such arguments require that everyone be treated as autonomous moral agents.

Virtue Ethics. The third and final approach to engaging ethical dilemmas begins not with questions of consequences or rules, but questions of character. Virtue Ethics addresses the qualities people should cultivate in order to behave in the right ways at the right time. Because this approach examines what traits of character make a person good, it has been associated with many kinds of philosophy, from ancient Chinese sages to modern European existentialists. Among the most reflective philosophers to promote an ethical theory based on virtue was Aristotle (1985:17), who posited more than 2,300 years ago that "the human good turns out to be the soul's activity that expresses virtue" (Figure 5).

Virtues are the "excellences of character that include (as the cardinal virtues) courage, wisdom, self-control, and justice, as well as other admirable traits such as loyalty and compassion" (Pence 2000:55). Rachels (2003:176) lists a number of virtues that humans cultivate in order to flourish:

Benevolence	Fairness	Patience
Civility	Friendliness	Prudence
Compassion	Generosity	Reasonableness
Conscientiousness	Honesty	Self-discipline
Cooperativeness	Industriousness	Self-reliance
Courage	Justice	Tactfulness
Courteousness	Loyalty	Thoughtfulness
Dependability	Moderation	Tolerance

The cultivation of specific virtues involves finding the right balance—"the golden mean"—between excess and deficiency. For example, in truthfulness about oneself, the extreme is boastfulness while the deficiency is self-deprecation (Aristotle 1985:110). Instead, we must try to honestly present ourselves as we are, between arrogance and meekness.

For Aristotle, good character is not something a person is born with, but something each person must strive to cultivate. As he wrote, virtues "we acquire, just as we acquire other crafts, by having previously activated them. For we learn a craft by producing the same product that we must produce when we have learned it, becoming builders, [for example], by building and harpists by playing

Figure 5. A marble portrait of Aristotle. (Photograph by Eric Gaba, July 2005, Creative Commons Attribution ShareAlike 2.5 License)

the harp; so also, then, we become just by doing just actions, temperate by doing temperate actions, brave by doing brave actions" (Aristotle 1985:34). Aristotle, among other philosophers, emphasizes that ethics should be about human flourishing, the ability to excel in one's life and ensure excellence in society. So choices we make should avoid actions that will limit our capacity to flourish or restrict our moral sensibilities. Hence, moral thinking is moral work. We should seek to nurture our moral sensitivity, engage in sincere and candid moral deliberation, and open ourselves to potentially transformative criticism.

A major limitation—among others—of Virtue Ethics is that it provides no quick fixes. In the real world, in real crises, to explain to someone that she or he, like a builder needing to build more, should just practice being more virtuous would be strangely unhelpful. On the flip side, this notion of ethics is positive because it recognizes that no human is perfect, that being ethical is hard work but unquestionably attainable.

Thinking About Codes and Principles

When archaeology emerged as a professional pursuit in the early 1900s, it was a field made up of a handful of men (and they were mostly men) with relatively similar backgrounds and similar ideas of what archaeology could and should be (McGimsey 1995:11). By the 1960s, as archaeology became more popular and more universities launched anthropology departments, the field gradually began to change from a small group of like-minded individuals to a large and diverse community. Into the 1970s, change was further propelled by the emergence of business-oriented cultural resource management (CRM) companies, Native

Americans' increasingly vocal objections to disrespectful archaeological practices, and rising commercial interests in ancient objects (Lynott 1997:590). Archaeology was becoming increasingly fragmented.

A written set of professional standards has several important functions. They help professionals define for themselves the nature of their work, announce to the world a shared set of values, and distinguish professionals from nonprofessionals (Lynott 1997:591). The last point is especially important in archaeology because defining oneself as a professional allows a person to secure public funding, permits to work on public lands, and access to many kinds of resources (such as museum collections). The need to define what made a professional underpinned one of the first declarations of archaeological ethics (Champe et al. 1961; see Appendix 2). Approved by the SAA board in 1961, the "Four Statements for Archaeology" defined an ethical archaeologist as one who endeavors to do good fieldwork, preserves records, refrains from buying and selling artifacts, obtains permission as needed for research, and honestly reports and retains archaeological data.

In the spring of 1996, the SAA board adopted a new set of professional standards. Rather than delineating specific rules for behavior, the SAA's leadership and membership instead elected to offer principles that are "edifying," meaning they offer guidance on how the most ethical archaeologist would behave (Lynott and Wylie 1995b:8). As one key author of the new principles wrote: "The principles have been defined as ideals ... ideals that should serve as the goals for professional behavior, rather than to define standards of minimally acceptable conduct among archaeologists" (Lynott 1997:597). These principles address eight areas of archaeological ethics: stewardship, accountability, commercialization, public education and outreach, intellectual property, public reporting and publication, records and preservation, and training and resources.

The ideals of practice set forth by the SAA contrast with codes of ethics and conduct promulgated by other organizations. The RPA, for example, has a law-like code that approves and disapproves of specific behaviors. Notably, however, the RPA is an organization that can de-register archaeologists for misbehavior and so its codes serve a different purpose. The American Institute of Archaeology (AIA) has also been a leader in promoting a dialogue about archaeological ethics; its one code is short and focused on the antiquities trade, while its other code applies only to "professional members" and has a well-developed grievance procedure. WAC has a strong set of statements about ethics, which is closer to the American Anthropological Association's (AAA) code in its focus on the rights and needs of living people. Codes and principles have become an essential part of archaeological organizations. Nearly every major national and international organization now has a code (see Appendix 2), and careful study of the similarities and differences between these codes should be a part of everyone's effort to untangle the knots of archaeological ethics.

These codes and principles have their pluses and their minuses. Taken as a whole, a general sense of ethical behavior emerges: archaeologists should be good stewards of archaeological resources while addressing concerns that living communities have about the material past. However, when specific guidance is compared, contradictions become apparent. For example, is the anthropological archaeologist's first responsibility to the archaeological record (SAA) or the people she or he studies (WAC)? Given such glaring incongruities, how should you go about deciding which principle is the better one? The answer is that you must think about the underlying arguments for these principles rather than thinking of these principles as immutable laws. You should think about each code's form and function and try to understand each statement's potential and its problems (O'Keefe 1998).

More pluses and minuses. Plus: Statements of ethics put forward by archaeological organizations are clear statements about shared values. Minus: Not everyone necessarily shares those values. Codes and principles tend to be centrist, in large part because getting thousands of people to agree to a statement about ethical behavior requires diplomacy and compromise. But the result is that the "extremes" on the spectrum of ethical arguments—which in fact may hold the better arguments—are rarely codified by professional organizations.

Plus: Statements of ethics capture the spirit of professionals at a given historical moment. Minus: These statements once written can be seen as set in stone. Indeed, the original drafters of codes and principles often recognize that principles do and must evolve over time. "These principles are not intended to be the final word on archaeological ethics," Mark Lynott (1997:597) wrote, "change is inevitable." But as time goes on, as more people read and come to rely on codes, they can come to be depended on as unchangeable, like edicts from a power above. Changing written codes is no easy task. When we think that the SAA code took three years of wrangling (plus thousands of dollars), revising the principles will take a large commitment of energy and resources. Thus, the SAA code perhaps better captures the spirit of archaeological ethics in 1996 than it does now, more than a decade later.

Plus: Statements of ethics shape and guide our conversations about right actions. Minus: Sometimes people use codes and principles to end conversations rather than start them. It has been observed that, "Ironically, the very codification of behavioral standards can provide a means for escaping ethical requirements as well as enforcing them" (Smith and Burke 2003:191). Indeed, every ethical predicament is unique, set within its own social and political circumstances. Because of this, it is extremely difficult to solve an ethical problem simply by citing a code or principle. For example, the SAA principle of stewardship states that, "It is the responsibility of all archaeologists to work for the long-term conservation and protection of the archaeological record by practicing and promoting stewardship of the archaeological record." But if the museum you are working for has in its collection a sacred mask that a local Native American community says should be allowed to decay naturally, what would you do? Does "long-term" mean forever, or just a long period of time? Does "conservation" mean preserving the *physical* remains of the past, or does it mean the *social meanings* embodied in artifacts? In this case, does being a good "steward" mean ignoring or heeding the concerns of the Native American community? Thus, a simple citation of "SAA Principle No. 1, Line 2" cannot by itself solve such dilemmas. Codes and principles must not be the end of our conversations about ethics, but instead should prompt, guide, and inform them. As Lynott (1997:593) persuasively argued, statements of ethics are fundamentally "directional beacons" for us in our deliberations about archaeological ethics.

Thinking about Laws

The relationship between law and ethics is often complex and rarely straightforward. As the philosopher Kent Greenawalt (1998) has outlined, some laws make no reference to morality—and some arguments of morality make no reference to law. For example, a treaty between two countries may be about trade or peace but have no reference to why the countries should act in such a way. Oppositely, if you tell a friend "don't lie to me," this statement says nothing about law. At the same time, ethics and law are often intertwined, for the moral values of a society are often mirrored in its laws (Greenawalt 1998:8). Laws about abortion, murder, perjury, divorce, and so forth concern not simply rules that govern, but claims about what is right and what is wrong for individuals and society as a whole. Greenawalt (1998:9) further points out that while we are, by definition, legally obliged to follow laws, we are not always or necessarily morally obliged. He writes that while we should obey morally neutral laws and moral laws, we are not required to follow immoral laws. Thus, some laws are unethical, and some ethical actions may be illegal. Laws do not always equal ethics.

Yet, with cultural property laws, the ideals of archaeological practice often work in concert with legal obligations. For example, the SAA principle of stewardship is in line with most of the state and federal laws regarding cultural heritage in the United States. But conflicts do emerge. Joe Watkins (1999:341) has pointed out that some archaeologists working for the federal government may be put in a double bind: they may be compelled to comply with a law that gives preferential treatment to some publics, which in some way may impair archaeology as a profession, while the SAA principles emphasize that archaeologists should be concerned about the discipline's well-being.

Despite some tension between laws, codes of ethics, and moral obligation, there are many cultural property laws that seek to protect archaeological resources and promote the pursuit of archaeology. In the United States, as early as 1906, the Congress passed the Antiquities Act, which established the foundation of cultural and natural resource preservation in the United States; it codified the "ethic of protection" that had been developing in America (see Chapter 1). This legislation, only several pages long, diminished indiscriminate excavations on federal land; recognized looting as a crime; quelled the overt commercialization of ancient objects; authorized the creation of national monuments; and established the principle that government should serve as steward of a nation's cultural, historical, and natural heritage (Harmon et al. 2006).

The National Historic Preservation Act (NHPA) of 1966 is an important law that established a national policy for historic preservation. One of the key parts of the NHPA says that the federal government must consider how its actions will affect the country's historic resources. This law encouraged the growth of the CRM industry by compelling government agencies to "mitigate" the negative effects of federally sponsored projects (such as dams, roads, and utility lines) through archaeological research. The Archaeological and Historic Preservation Act of 1974—also known as the Moss-Bennett Act—stands out because it was the only law of this era designed exclusively by archaeologists and perhaps best represents the archaeological ethos of this time. Another important law is the Archaeological Resources Protection Act (ARPA) of 1979, which controls who can conduct archaeological research on federal lands and stipulates penalties for those caught looting on public land. The Native American Graves Protection and Repatriation Act (NAGPRA) of 1990 has been instrumental in reshaping dialogues about archaeology and its relationship with Native peoples. This law says many things, but mainly provides for the repatriation of funerary remains and other important objects to federally recognized tribes from institutions that have received federal funding; it also guides the disposition of funerary remains discovered on federal lands after 1990. Although these are some of the most important pieces of legislation in the United States, many other local, state, and national laws should be considered in ethical deliberations (see Craib 2000; Cunningham 2006; Gerstenblith 1995; Richman and Forsyth 2004).

International laws can also inform local dilemmas. One of the primary international laws relating to cultural property is the 1970 UNESCO Convention, which "establishes a framework for international cooperation to reduce the incentive for pillage by restricting the illicit movement of archaeological and ethnographic material" (Kouroupas 1995:83). The Convention aims to resolve a problem of national law: that is, typically nations are not legally bound to uphold the laws of other nations. So, for example, it may be illegal in Peru to loot archaeological sites, but if those looted objects come to the United States, the United States—even if it knows the objects were looted—is not legally compelled to prosecute those holding the stolen objects. (That said, the United States can choose to prosecute those who import "stolen" property into the country.) The 1970 UNESCO Convention helps fix this problem by creating a framework that allows nations to uphold the cultural property laws of other nations. (In fact, the United States does now have a bilateral agreement with Peru, so in many cases it is illegal in the United States to possess artifacts illicitly taken from Peru.)[1] A second major international law is the 1954 Hague Convention, which attempts to curb the destruction of cultural property during war. Although this law has had some limited successes over the last half century, the United States has not yet ratified (meaning, brought into domestic law) the Convention (Colwell-Chanthaphonh and Piper 2001). There are many more international laws and treaties that can be examined to understand the how archaeology and heritage often operate beyond national borders (see Appendix 3).

In sum, laws are important to consider in our deliberations on ethics. Where laws are moral, it is right to follow the law, because then our actions will be both legal and moral. However, where laws are immoral—and indeed, if we consciously subvert laws in order to do the moral thing—then we need to be aware of what laws are wrong and in what ways, and perhaps even work to change them. We also need to be aware of the legal consequences of our actions. In many ways, laws are akin to codes and principles in that they should guide our approaches to ethics, but they should not necessarily restrict them. Discussions of laws should not replace our discussions of ethics.

Thinking Historically

It was a cold November morning in 1864 when a regiment of Colorado Volunteers attacked a peaceful encampment of Cheyenne along Sand Creek. The unsuspecting Cheyenne fled in terror, but hundreds, mostly women and children, were cut down by a hail of bullets. Even the wounded and dead were not safe from brutalization—bodies became the trophies of slaughter. "As the wounded moaned unattended, drunken soldiers moved from body to body, scalping, mutilating, and collecting sordid souvenirs," David Hurst Thomas (2000:53) has recounted. "Fleeing children became moving targets for marksmen, and several still living Cheyennes were scalped. One woman's heart was ripped out and impaled on a stick. Several soldiers galloped around the battleground, sporting bloody vaginas as hatbands." Some of the Cheyenne bodies were further mutilated, though in the name of science instead of war. Some bodies were decapitated, defleshed, and sent eastward to the Army Medical Museum in Washington D.C. These remains, and those of thousands more, were eventually transferred to the Smithsonian Institution.

Archaeology, we know, does not operate in a social vacuum, but neither does it exist in a historical vacuum. The practice of archaeology, and the moral predicaments that result from it, are historically contingent. In the same way the Belmont Report discussed at the beginning of this chapter is the outcome of the Tuskegee experiment, so too NAGPRA is the outcome of horrendous practices such as battlefield pillaging of the kind witnessed at Sand Creek (Figure 6). Many nineteenth-century anthropologists were far from scrupulous. The anthropologist Robert W. Shufeldt, in 1891, advised his colleagues "to make sure they

Figure 6. A drawing made shortly after the Sand Creek Massacre, illustrating the Third Colorado Regiment entering the Cheyenne camp. (Denver Public Library, Western History Collection, X-33806)

'secured' unusual remains after dark when everyone was asleep" (Parezo 2006:102); and even the father of American anthropology, Franz Boas, opined, "It is most unpleasant work to steal bones from a grave, but what is the use, someone has to do it" (Thomas 2000:59). On the crest of the repatriation movement, the Smithsonian Institution alone had more than 18,500 human bodies in storage (Marshall 1989:1184). Given such a past, a turbulent future for the discipline should have been anticipated. Our modern moral predicaments are often the result of historical injustices.

History can and should inform our thinking about ethics by providing us with "historical considerations" and "moral motivations." The historical considerations include identifying contemporary stakeholders and interest groups: given a project's history, or the discipline's history as the case may be, it is important to ask who has been affected and who will likely be affected by a course of action. History also is an important source of empathy and knowledge about different worldviews. Imagine hearing that the Cheyenne were requesting from the Smithsonian Institution the return of some ancestors from a place called Sand Creek, but you knew nothing about the Cheyenne's historical experiences. Then, imagine hearing the request in the context of stories about the 1864 slaughter at

Sand Creek. Understanding history, then, contextualizes our understanding of different people's collective and individual experiences.

History also provides us with the moral motivations to pursue justice and to overcome past prejudices. Grasping stories such as the Sand Creek Massacre should spur us on to ensure that at least some measure of justice has been gained, and that such acts are never repeated again. Past events and institutional processes lead to power differentials in the discipline—whether based on gender, race, or class—and we must come to grips with these historical processes in our negotiations with colleagues and the public alike.

Thinking Locally, Thinking Globally

When Moses brought down the Ten Commandments from Mount Sinai, there inscribed upon the stone tablets were moral imperatives quite literally written in stone. Adopted through the generations by a myriad of Jewish, Christian, and Muslim believers, these principles have long been thought to be universal and immutable. And yet, we know that there are many societies around the world in which the principles of the Ten Commandments are unknown—and in many cases opposite beliefs are held. What of the society that has more than one god? What of the society that does not keep holy the Sabbath? What of the society that allows adultery?

One of the great questions theologians and philosophers have debated is the conundrum of whether there are universal principles to which every human must or should subscribe. Some argue that undeniably there are clear rules that all humans ought to follow; some argue that there are a few basic values that every society must agree to in order to perpetuate itself (a society that freely murders its children, for example, will not last very long); while others argue that universals are difficult to discern, but that we have good reasons to continue the search for moral ideals all people can share and cultivate (Ladd 2002; Momeyer 1995; Moody-Adams 1997; Rachels 2003:20).

Archaeologists likely will not be able to fully resolve the difficult question of whether a universal morality exists. As a beginning point, though, we should be clear to make a distinction between "cultural relativism" and "ethical relativism." Philosopher Merrilee H. Salmon explains that in the tradition of Franz Boas, cultural relativism involves "trying to understand and evaluate the practices of other cultures in their own historical context"; it is a powerful means to ensure that we do not always judge people simply by our own standards (Salmon 1997:49). However, ethical relativism is the much stronger claim that "denies the existence of universal moral truths and proposes that right and wrong must be defined variously, based on differences in cultural norms and mores" (Pence 2000:19). While cultural relativism is sure to give us a helpful perspective on differences between societies and sheds light on our own behaviors, ethical relativism is a forceful moral and philosophical stance that denies the possibility of any universal moral principles.

And indeed, there are reasons to be skeptical of extreme forms of ethical relativism. If ethical relativism were correct, then its implications would be dire (Rachels 2003:21–22). We would have no grounds to disapprove of apartheid in South Africa or the extermination policies of Nazi Germany. Ethical relativism is highly problematic because it reduces ethics to a "majority rules" mentality whereby if people are doing it, then it is difficult to say it is bad. To figure out the right thing, all we would have to do is consult societies to see what they are already doing. But equally, there are reasons to be cautious about claims of universal moralities. Often, claims of universal morals are regularly suffused with ethnocentric beliefs—that simply *our* way of doing things is better than *their* way. Universal claims are often draped in hubris and intolerance.

Archaeologists may be best served by taking a "practice-oriented" approach, which recognizes that just because there are clear moral differences between communities does not mean that those same communities can never find common ground.[2] On the contrary, even communities with very different beliefs can and often do come to mutual understandings. We may never find universal morals (or if we do, convince others of them), but we can work on a case-by-case basis toward discovering discrete moral commitments that are shared between communities and will be the foundation for local negotiations.

The phrase "thinking locally, thinking globally" is useful to illustrate two other points. First, solving ethical dilemmas often involves opposing impulses. One impulse is to focus on constraints, that is, all the issues that restrict future possibilities: the grumpy professor, the locked gate at a site you want to visit, the need for a paycheck to pay the bills. These include all kinds of real world factors that limit our choices. The other impulse, however, is to escape from these restrictions and imagine a world without limits: a ten million dollar grant, a professor who never complains, winning over a local looter—many archaeologists have had these dreams. Both of these impulses are good ones in moderation, and indeed, both play an important role in thinking through ethical dilemmas. The key is to strike a balance between recognizing constraints that limit our choices and dreaming of possibilities that allow us to move beyond constraints and imagine alternative solutions.

Second, thinking locally and globally also means recognizing ways in which immediate and local problems are frequently linked with much larger ones. For example, the looting of sites in "Third World" settings is not only about the lack of alternative local economic opportunities, but also about a global system of trade and aesthetics that transforms antiquities into commodities worth thousands of dollars (Hollowell 2003, 2006; Matsuda 1998). Real solutions to real world problems will recognize how local problems relate to global ones, as well as balance creative solutions and practical limitations. Furthermore, archaeologists around the world are dealing with ethical dilemmas. Although Americans might be more familiar with the ethical dilemmas that have emerged in the United

States, archaeologists oftentimes are debating similar issues in Japan, Sweden, Peru, Australia, and still many other places (Fawcett 1986; Karlsson 2004; Ritter 2006; see Appendix 3). These issues are important for all archaeologists to know about and reflect on in today's global world.

Applying Archaeological Ethics

Assistant Professor Travis Hitchcock is about two years away from tenure review at Southwestern University. The department chair, Professor Beeman, one day invites Hitchcock to discuss his progress toward tenure. Beeman emphasizes to Hitchcock that his case will be significantly strengthened by one more major publication in a leading journal. Hitchcock replies that for the past three years he has been gathering data on Archaic projectile point variability in the Santa Rialto River drainage and that he plans to submit his results to American Antiquity.

*   What Hitchcock doesn't tell Beeman is that he is uneasy about the data on which the study is based. Several years ago a local "avocational archaeologist" named Derek Judge loaned Hitchcock an unparalleled collection of lithic points. Judge also turned over hand-drawn maps and notebooks with contextual information, which indicated that all of the points came from several of the large, private ranches in the region. Hitchcock felt that Mr. Judge was honest in their dealings, and Judge had even served a term as President of the Santa Rialto Archaeological Society, a group of dedicated nonprofessionals interested in archaeology. However, when Hitchcock visited Judge at his home, the young professor couldn't help but notice the extensive collection of ancient and historic artifacts littering the house—and more recently he had heard a rumor that Judge had a valuable collection of nineteenth-century bottles dug up from a railroad camp on public land, a violation of the Archaeological Resources Protection Act.*

*   Professor Hitchcock desperately wants tenure, and he feels Judge's collection of points will be vitally important in understanding the history of the Santa Rialto River. But at the same time he is registered with the RPA and is concerned that his association with Judge might imperil his good standing.*

What Would You Do?

This case study, which we wrote with our colleague Jeffery Hanson, is based on a situation not too distant from real life. The case raises several issues archaeologists have dealt with in various situations. Each person faced with such situations has to resolve the problems on her or his own terms. But how would you go about solving it? If you were Travis Hitchcock, what would you do?

In the last section, you were introduced to different aspects of ethical thinking; in this section, we will put together these aspects to try to solve Hitchcock's predicament. Here, we apply a framework for moral reasoning, put forth by Judith P. Swazey and Stephanie J. Bird. Swazey and Bird (1997:12) recommend a

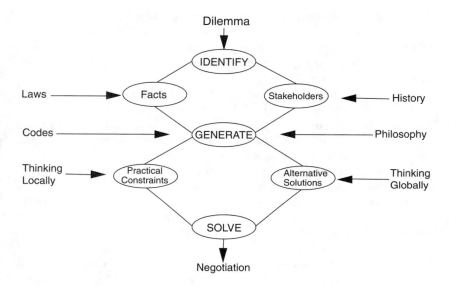

Figure 7. A framework for ethical problem solving. (Based on Swazey and Bird 1997:13)

structured procedure with seven steps that is particularly effective for probing case studies, a "framework that focuses on learning how to use ethical principles and moral reasoning skills to identify, analyze, and decide how best to respond to ethical issues." Our model includes a total of eight steps (Figure 7). Although we think the model above is a good one, especially in the context of the Ethics Bowl, we offer it as just one of many possible ones that may be used (e.g., de Bono 1990, 1993; see also Chapter 3). We thus use this approach to show just one way of working through an ethical dilemma.

When a dilemma emerges, the first step is to identify precisely the nature of the predicament. What kind of problem is it? Is it truly an ethical dilemma, or is it perhaps only a legal problem? In some cases, there may be more than one dilemma. The second step is to properly identify all the facts of the particular case. What do we know for sure about the case? What can only be guessed at? What is opinion or superfluous information? What laws, if any, apply to this situation? The third step is to identify the stakeholders, a process that should be guided by historical considerations. Who are the people involved, and what is their stake in the predicament? The fourth step is to generate possible solutions, which can be informed by codes and principles as well as theories of moral philosophy. The fifth step is to think about any of the practical constraints that might constrict possible solutions. What personalities are involved? What resources (monetary or otherwise) are realistically available in the given situation?

What would be the consequences of the possible solutions? Then, given these constraints, the sixth step is to think about ways around them. What alternative solutions are possible? The seventh step is to arrive at a solution, or several possible solutions. The last step is then to consider how you would negotiate your solution with the potential stakeholders.

Now, to apply these steps to Professor Hitchcock's dilemma:[3]

1. Identify the dilemma. The primary ethical predicament here is whether Hitchcock's publication of the projectile points would in some way aid or abet looting. In this case, the objects have already been gathered, so publication would not directly result in an increase in looting, but it would provide legitimacy to a collection that might very well be illegitimate according to some. However, publication could indeed increase looting due to people seeking similar objects now that they have become "known" or famous from publication. Publication could also give clues to people about where to look. A secondary issue is the relationship between professional and avocational archaeologists. Hitchcock should be concerned about how his decision (and how he deals with it) will affect his relationship with Judge, an individual who clearly has a great interest in archaeology. If the projectile points were only taken from private land, and he has done a faithful job recording their location, then Judge has perhaps done a good service by providing for archaeological study a group of objects that would otherwise be unavailable. A tertiary issue is Hitchcock's standing as a good professional. His pursuit of tenure and his standing in the RPA are not irrelevant, but these concerns must be balanced with how his actions will affect—negatively or positively—the archaeological record and his relationship with a key stakeholder.

2. Identify the facts. Here is what we know for sure: (1) Hitchcock needs tenure; (2) Hitchcock is registered with the RPA; (3) if Hitchcock publishes looted data, then he imperils his good standing in the RPA and possibly undermines his tenure bid; (4) Judge has maps and notebooks with purported contextual information; and (5) if Judge looted the artifacts from public lands without a permit, then he has violated ARPA. As the law states in Section 6(a): "No person may excavate, remove, damage, or otherwise alter or deface any archaeological resource located on public lands or Indian lands unless such activity is pursuant to a permit issued under section 4, a permit referred to in section 4(h)(2), or the exemption contained in section 4(g)(1)." Here are some questions from the purported facts: (1) Is Judge honest? Hitchcock in his dealings with Judge feels him to be honest; (2) Does Judge own looted artifacts? Hitchcock has reason to be skeptical of Judge, given his extensive personal collection and the rumors circulating about Judge; and (3) Even if Judge owns looted artifacts, does this necessarily mean he's lying about the projectile points he claims to have collected from private ranches? Not necessarily.

3. Identify the stakeholders. There are four main stakeholders in this dilemma. The first is the archaeological community, which has dedicated itself to ensuring that the discipline does not encourage or participate in the looting of archaeological resources while at the same time ensuring that accurate scientific knowledge circulates. The second is the community of avocationalists, an important community for archaeologists, as they provide much material and political support for the discipline. The third is the general public, which has at least some stake in preserving our shared cultural resources, as indicated by public law. If Judge has taken artifacts from public lands without a permit, then he has violated ARPA and is liable to prosecution. Depending on the value of the artifacts and damage done to the site, Judge could be liable for up to $20,000 and sentenced to two years in prison (ARPA, Sec. 6(d)). The fourth is Hitchcock and his family, as both will be greatly affected by the course of events.

4. Generate possible solutions. Solution 1—Hitchcock proceeds with his research and tries to publish it in *American Antiquity*. He doesn't tell anyone about his concerns. This solution would fit with the RPA Standards of Research Performance, section VI, which states, "The archaeologist has responsibility for appropriate dissemination of the results of her/his research to the appropriate constituencies with reasonable dispatch." However, Hitchcock would have to admit that this solution sits less comfortably with the SAA Principle of Public Reporting and Publication, which in part states, "An interest in preserving and protecting *in situ* archaeological sites must be taken in to account when publishing and distributing information about their nature and location." To justify this approach, Hitchcock might use an utilitarian-like calculus that emphasizes the "greater good" of publication: although these particular objects may have come from looted contexts, the greater benefit would be that science would have a permanent record of them.

Solution 2—Hitchcock proceeds with his research and tries to publish it— but he engages in a dialogue about his decision. This would entail speaking with his colleagues (including his department chair) as well as Judge and other avocationalists. A serious conversation with Judge is important too, to try to determine whether the rumors about the avocational archaeologist are in fact true. When Hitchcock writes his article, he could include a discussion of the ethical quandary and his arguments for why the benefits of publication outweigh the possible harm to the archaeological record. This approach has more of an emphasis on stewardship as well as the virtues of honesty and relationship building. By openly engaging in a dialogue, Hitchcock would try to not only publish this important collection but also improve the relationship between archaeologists and avocationalists.

Solution 3—Hitchcock stops his research and does not try to publish his work. This approach would be the most literal interpretation of the SAA Principle on Public Reporting and Publication. It would also be in line with scholars who argue that archaeologists not be the first to publish on materials known to be, or suspected to be looted (e.g., Kleiner 1990). This is a rather deontological approach, in that it recognizes a rule that can and should be generalized.

5. *Generate practical constraints.* Solution 1—If Hitchcock is successful in publishing his article in *American Antiquity*, and it comes to be known that the materials were looted, then trouble would surely follow. Colleagues would ask why Hitchcock did not ask the appropriate ethical questions and why he proceeded with research and publication given the uncertain nature of the collection. If it turns out the artifacts were looted—although keep in mind it was only rumored that Judge's bottle collection came from public lands, not the point collection—and this fact comes to light, then Hitchcock would be seen as abetting an illegal and unethical act. The RPA Code of Ethics says in no uncertain terms that archaeologists shall not "Engage in any illegal or unethical conduct involving archaeological matters or knowingly permit the use of his/her name in support of any illegal or unethical activity involving archaeological matters" (Sec. 1.2.a). Nor shall archaeologists "Engage in conduct involving dishonesty, fraud, deceit or misrepresentation about archaeological matters" (Sec. 1.2.c). Another possibility to consider: Suppose the artifacts were looted, but no one ever finds out. By publishing the collection, Judge may believe he acted correctly and continue his illicit behavior: in other words, Hitchcock could be implicitly encouraging Judge by continuing with his research and not asking him the hard questions. Furthermore, we might ask if it is right for Hitchcock to not question the laws that state that it is okay to excavate on private land, but not on public land. Even if the collections were legally collected, from the perspective of stewardship and a conservation ethic, we might expect Hitchcock to ask why so much collecting (and presumably some excavation) occurred on land that was not threatened, on resources that were already preserved on these large ranches.

Solution 2—If Hitchcock admits in his article that the artifacts were possibly looted, the editor of *American Antiquity* might refuse to publish it. Also, even admitting that he is working with a collection that was possibly looted might bring censure from some colleagues. Such a move would surely bring not only Hitchcock under public scrutiny, but also Judge. If Hitchcock voices his concerns, it might even lead to an ARPA investigation of Judge.

Solution 3—If Hitchcock doesn't pursue his research on the points, he may very well be missing out on a scientifically important—and indeed archaeologically rare—collection of artifacts. If it turns out that the artifacts were all taken from the surface of sites on private land (and all the documentation is correct), then Hitchcock's decision could be a bad one. By not pursuing his research, a great harm may be inflicted on the archaeological record, especially as a stigma might emerge around the rejected collection. If Hitchcock won't touch it, who will? Furthermore, he potentially cuts off a positive relationship with Judge.

6. *Generate alternative solutions.* Alternative Solution 1—Proceeding as if nothing is wrong carries some big risks for Hitchcock (and Judge too). Secrets

always carry with them the danger of being revealed. Even if only a few people come to learn of the potential problems with the collection—say a few close colleagues who were also approached by Judge—Hitchcock's actions could set a troubling precedent. Some might ask themselves: if Hitchcock did it, why can't I? Perhaps Hitchcock could try to speak with these few individuals and explain his reasoning, but this would mean Hitchcock's actions would be only slightly less than a secret.

Alternative Solution 2—If Hitchcock seeks to publish his work while raising its moral questions then this won't be an easy path. With a real concern for Judge's welfare, Hitchcock could begin with an informal though honest conversation with the collector. If Judge promises that the artifacts were not illicitly acquired, then Judge should not have a problem with Hitchcock raising the issue of the artifacts' provenience in his work. Indeed, the fact that Hitchcock raises the issue will show that neither he nor Judge have anything to hide or fear. Plus, Judge, as an avocational archaeologist should himself have some greater concern for the archaeological record. If the editor of *American Antiquity* refuses to publish the article this is not the worst thing that could happen to a person. Publication elsewhere, even in a regional peer-reviewed article, will carry some weight in Hitchcock's tenure review.

Alternative Solution 3—Even if Hitchcock doesn't publish his study in a peer-reviewed journal, he could still try to publish it in the "grey literature." This would have the effect of making the collection at least known and available for study by some, while at the same time (because of limited distribution) not bringing much attention to Hitchcock or Judge. However, because Hitchcock needs tenure, this alternative solution would detract—in time and energy—from that effort.

7. *Solve the dilemma.* The revised second solution—seeking publication with open discussion—is the best solution. It shows Hitchcock's concern for stewardship and accountability, as well as publication of an important collection. At the same time, it emphasizes honesty and the importance of Hitchcock's relationship with his colleagues and avocational archaeologists. If it turns out that the collection was looted, then it is clear that Hitchcock was hiding nothing.

8. *Prepare for negotiation.* The first step for Hitchcock is to speak with Judge. Assuming Judge maintains that the collection is legal, he should proceed with discussions with Beeman and his colleagues as well as other stakeholders, such as other avocationalists. In the spirit of dialogue, Hitchcock should be ready to listen. But he should also be ready to defend his choices, knowing that he carefully considered all the issues and arrived at the best possible solution.

Right Answers

If nothing else, working through this case study shows how complex moral predicaments are for those stuck in them. In a way, Hitchcock does not have the luxury of a perfect solution: he just has the best solution in a pool of several not-so-good ones. In the end, Hitchcock's choice may be a good or bad one. Perhaps more evidence can be located showing that the collection is on the up and up. Or, perhaps, a District Attorney reads the article in *American Antiquity* and decides to pursue an ARPA case. Who knows what could happen? Given that we cannot fully anticipate the outcomes of our decisions, it may be tempting to decide nothing at all. But unfortunately, while readers of hypothetical case studies can afford such indulgences, the real life Hitchcocks in the world must pursue some course of action.

What will *you* do when you are faced with a moral predicament? In truth, you probably can't answer this question until you find yourself confronting one. But, by thinking through the possible dilemmas you will likely face—and by honing the skills you'll need to clearly think through them—you'll be in a good place to begin finding the right answers.

Notes

1. Notably, due to ongoing ethical and legal conflicts between archaeologists in the United States and Peru, the Peruvian government has recently taken the extraordinary step of restricting U.S. archaeologists from working in the country by changing the permitting process. Subsequently, the Colegio Profesional de Arqueologos del Peru (COARPE) and the RPA have taken the unprecedented step of creating an arrangement to provide archaeological opportunities to professional archaeologists in both countries (Jeffrey H. Altschul, pers. comm., 2007).

2. Based on arguments put forth by Alison Wylie, pers. comm., 2007.

3. The solution we offer here is only one possible one, and perhaps you will not agree. Indeed, you probably will not. But, this is a good thing; it is the basis of the Ethics Bowl. If you disagree, how would you go about solving the dilemma? What would be your rebuttals to the arguments?

3

Learning from Ethical Dilemmas

[Those educated persons who] have never thrown themselves into a mental position of those who think differently from them ... do not, in any proper sense of the word, know the doctrine which they themselves profess ... So essential is this discipline to a real understanding of moral and human subjects that, if opponents of all-important truths do not exist, it is indispensable to imagine them and supply them with the strongest arguments which the most skillful devil's advocate can conjure up.

—John Stuart Mill (not an Ethics Bowl participant)

As you approach the stage with your team you look out into the audience, out to your peers, your colleagues, and your faculty mentor, not to mention three judges waiting to critique whatever argument you make. You finally take your seat. After months of preparation, the final event is here. The moderator reads the case. It is one of the cases assigned to you—the case that has kept you up at night for the last two weeks:

You are an underwater archaeologist who has been approached by a wealthy collector who has offered to finance a three-year excavation of a rare, previously inaccessible shipwreck. All he asks in return is ownership of the "best" pieces—the rest he will donate to your institute for study. As an archaeologist, you know you should not participate in the commercialization of the record, but you also know that if no researcher accepts the collector's offer, then a commercial salvage company will gladly do the job with no concern for context, publication, or preservation. Is it better to not participate, or to "salvage" as much data as possible from this potentially important site? Why are archaeologists still collecting everything when there is a curation crisis at hand anyway? By limiting public access to artifacts, are archaeologists only furthering the divide between science

Figure 8. The winner of the Second Annual Ethics Bowl, the University of Arizona team with the silver trophy. (Photograph by Joe Watkins, March 31, 2005)

and the public, creating more of a demand for already unavailable artifacts? In the next 24 hours, you have a decision to make that could perhaps be the defining mark of your career. What do you do? The moderator finishes reading the case. Your five-minute response begins ... *now*.

This stressful though exhilarating situation is a scene from the SAA Ethics Bowl (Figure 8). Each year, teams of three to five students are provided with a set of hypothetical case studies written to present ethical challenges in modern archaeological practice. Teams prepare for the Ethics Bowl by constructing responses to each case, as well as rebuttal statements and answers to potential questions from judges. Teams are questioned by a panel of distinguished archaeologists acting as judges, who score the students on four criteria: intelligibility, depth, focus, and judgment (see Appendix 1). Although a certain level of excitement builds around the scoring and winners, the real excitement is in seeing how students and judges respond to and think about the myriad situations that encompass archaeological ethics.

In recent years, archaeologists have increasingly come to realize that the discipline of archaeology is fraught with ethical dilemmas (see Chapter 1). Our ethically turbulent present is the result of a history of practice that often ignored—or mistreated—stakeholders, participated in colonial enterprises, and assumed con-

Social Ethics

John R. Welch, Simon Fraser University

Ethics, archaeology, and, most especially, ethical archaeology, are intrinsically social pursuits. We derive maximal benefits from our thoughtful work not while holed up in our labs and offices, but while sharing experiences, information, and perspectives with diverse groups of individuals who care about the same places and issues without necessarily adhering to the same goals, interests, and rationalities.

My advice for those seeking the right ethical path: look within, to be sure, but never at the expense of the bonanza of perspectives within an arm's reach. The best Ethics Bowl teams forge common ground on the basis of divergent views, thereby becoming greater than a sum of individuals and evincing inspiration from ethical perspectives that have expanded and complemented their personal trainings and inclinations. The best outcomes reflect individual commitments to a fusion of archaeology with high ethical standards and to a team process that integrates diverse approaches and ideas.

trol and ownership of cultural properties. In the previous chapter, we outlined strategies for thinking through ethics and offered one possible framework for unraveling and resolving modern ethical dilemmas of archaeology. This chapter will focus on the ways in which case studies can be used in ethics education and what students who are preparing for an Ethics Bowl should know. We first explore how to integrate the case studies into an archaeology curriculum and other professional settings and then offer a series of suggestions (including "tips" from previous Ethics Bowl participants) about how to prepare for ethical debates.

As the chapter's opening scene indicates, learning from ethical dilemmas is not necessarily an easy and straightforward experience. How would you go about preparing a response to the ethical dilemma described above? What factors guarantee a good performance in an ethical debate? How would you facilitate ethical discussions about this case in a classroom? By the end of this chapter, you will be able to more effectively create, oversee, and participate in ethical debates, whether in the form of an Ethics Bowl, in informal settings, or even in the midst of your everyday life as a professional archaeologist.

For the Teacher: Ethics in the Archaeology Classroom

In a sense, when we debate ethics, it is a reciprocal endeavor. Everyone is a teacher and everyone is a student. We learn from other people's perspectives by introducing ourselves to alternative ethical standpoints. The archaeology class-room is a unique and mostly safe context in which to learn about theoretical and practical ethics and the profession of archaeology.

Public education methods have been discussed by a variety of scholars (Jameson 1997; Little 2002; Smardz and Smith 2000). Indeed, "public archaeology" has been an important part of archaeology since the 1970s (Derry and Malloy 2003; King 1983; McGimsey 1972; Merriman 2004). In our definitions of "public," however, academic archaeologists have rarely discussed in print the public with whom they have the most direct contact: college students. Yet, college students are, potentially, training to become the next generation of archaeologists. Many more students take an archaeology class out of interest, while majoring in another subject; these students become a part of the "general public" that archaeologists in part serve. Why then has so little been written about archaeological pedagogy (Hamilakis 2004)?

In recent years, some effort has been made to discuss what college students are learning in terms of professional training in archaeology classrooms (Bender and Smith 2000; Colley 2004). Efforts have also been made to diversify undergraduate curriculum to address the changing nature of archaeological research and practice (e.g., M.A.T.R.I.X. Project 2003). Other scholars have explored the teaching of archaeology as a revolutionary act (see *Archaeologies* 1[2] 2005) and given advice for active learning in university classrooms (Burke and Smith 2007). However, the collegiate classroom continues to be an underutilized tool for discussing the contemporary contexts of archaeological research. We feel the best way to learn about and eventually confront these contexts in the classroom is to engage archaeological ethics through case studies, discussion, and even debate.

Skepticism and Goals for Ethics in the Classroom

Some of you, undoubtedly, already utilize ethical dilemmas to teach archaeology—thus, we may be "preaching to the choir." Others, however, may have skepticism toward ethics-based education. Common skepticisms toward ethics education include thoughts like: ethical problems only happen to unethical people; ethics is just being a good person; and every situation is unique so guidelines and case studies are useless and cannot solve real problems (Lo 1993:151–153). These are unfair criticisms for a number of reasons. First, in life we are confronted by difficult choices all the time, often because of the situations we find ourselves in—not through some fault of our own. Ethical dilemmas arise for everyone, and practical ethics is more about choosing the best course among alternative actions. Second, ethics is much more than just being a good person. Every "good person" lives in a society made up of people with multiple, often differing perspectives—that is, moral pluralism. What happens when your well-intentioned action conflicts with another "good" person's actions? Applied ethics involves reasoned accounts for your actions that help you solve actual predicaments. Third, skepticism about specifics is a form of relativism, which, as explored in the last chapter, has its limits. Simply stated: yes, each context of archaeological research is different, but archaeologists pride themselves on learning from the past. Therefore, we should be able to learn from discussions of previous contexts and consequences of archaeological research. Learning from the past helps frame and guide our present dilemmas.

There is no more important context to address the above skepticisms of the relevance of archaeological ethics than the classroom. Students are renowned skeptics! As educators, however, archaeologists hope to prepare students for a future in anthropology or archaeology. To succeed in archaeology in the twenty-first century, students will need training not only in cultural resource management, lithics analysis, methods and theory, but also in ethics (Anderson 2000:142; Lynott and Steponaitis 2000). The goals of teaching professional ethics should be to challenge assumptions about archaeology and to promote critical thinking. As Swazey and Bird (1997:5) advise, the goal of teaching research ethics "is to teach people who want to do good science about the ethical standards and issues in their work, and how to deal with ethical problems that they encounter as scientists."

It is vitally important that young scholars be trained to address the ethical dilemmas they will inevitably face as archaeologists. This training should include pedagogical instruction for graduate and advanced undergraduate students. Graduate students, specifically, are in a unique position of learning how to teach and to develop their own methodologies for practicing archaeology. Archaeologists should follow the recommendations of educators in multicultural education and anthropology that call for students to engage global issues and identity politics in the classroom through participation, dialogue, deliberation, and debate (Banks 2004; Castles 2004; Parker 2004). These authors argue that students who are introduced to ethical dilemmas and global issues become more tolerant, concerned, and active democratic citizens and critical thinkers. Archaeology instructors should learn to teach ethics, and students should demand ethics education as part of their learning experience.

Organizing an Ethics Bowl in the Classroom

Now, to jump into some ethical dilemmas! We guarantee that one effective, interactive, and fun way of doing this is by organizing an Ethics Bowl of your own. Here are eight simple steps for putting ethics into action in your classroom by creating a mini Ethics Bowl.

Step 1: Divide the class into teams. There is no practical limit on the number of teams, though each team should consist of at least three students. The Intercollegiate Ethics Bowl held every year at the Association for Practical and Professional Ethics annual meeting has 32 teams that qualify to participate from regional matches. You can easily organize a round-robin style tournament for eight or more teams.

Step 2: Find a panel of three judges. Associate instructors, graduate students, or other faculty all make excellent judges. Students could also rotate being judges for other student teams. In fact, some professors who have used the Ethics Bowl in their classes report that their students say they learned the most while in the judge role, so you might want to restrict nonstudent judges to the final, "championship" round. Ensure that the judges know about and are familiar with the criteria for evaluating student responses (see Appendix 1). You will also need a moderator for each round.

Step 3: Distribute case studies to the teams and judges. If teams are preparing for an end of the semester competition, they will need at least a month to adequately prepare. You could create cases related to specific topics you wish to discuss in class. Draw from the 36 topically organized cases in the next chapter and create a set of 10–12 cases. It can also be a great exercise to have the students write their own case studies, derived from their readings or experienced dilemmas, to add to the mix. Judges should also review the cases so they understand the ethical issues involved and can think about potential complications and solutions.

Step 4: Walk teams through a case study. Choose a single case study to work through as a whole class. Identify the relevant facts and stakeholders. As a class, generate potential solutions by utilizing codes, standards of professional behavior, moral philosophy, or other means. Critique your potential solutions by looking for practical constraints, inconsistent arguments, and alternative solutions. Finally, come to a conclusion and formulate a presentation as a class.

Step 5: Encourage preparation. Getting ready to be in an Ethics Bowl takes time. So be sure that the participants have the time they need to prepare. You can make time during class, or encourage the students to have brown bag round tables once a week. Answering cases in written form—writing an abstract for a case by listing the relevant facts, describing the moral and ethical issues involved (including conflicts), discussing possible courses of action, or arguing for a particular solution—can also be made into class assignments. The more time and guidance available for preparation, the better students will be able to understand and engage the complex issues in each case study.

Step 6: Arrange Logistics. For room layout, you will need at least three tables with chairs at the front of the room (one for each team and one for the judges), a podium for a moderator, and seats for an audience (Figure 9). Be sure to invite other students, faculty members, and even deans and university administrators to watch. Judges will need multiple copies of the judging sheets (available in Appendix 1), student teams should have name-placards, and the moderator needs a stopwatch or a watch that counts seconds. Also, the organizer is responsible for deciding in advance which cases will be used for which rounds. For example, in the typical SAA Ethics Bowl, 10 cases are disseminated for the students to study, but if there are only three rounds, then only six cases will actually be debated in the event—two per round. Additionally, the organizer is responsible for coming

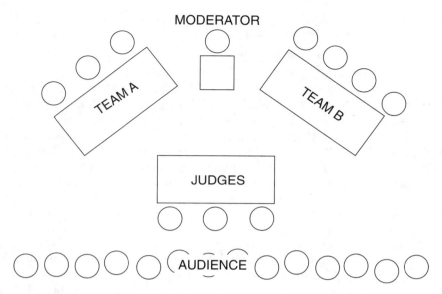

Figure 9. The recommended Ethics Bowl room layout.

up with the first question for each case that the moderator will ask. The question is usually broad, such as, "If you were person X in this scenario, what would you do?" These questions should be written in advance and given to the moderator at the beginning of each round.

Step 7: Debate! Follow the rules and guidelines as set out in Appendix 1. These rules and guidelines allow for an initial response by Team 1 to a case read aloud by the moderator, a rebuttal by the opposing team (Team 2), and a response by Team 1 to Team 2's rebuttal. This interchange of responses is followed by a period of questions from the judges for Team 1. Then, Team 2 has a final rebuttal. After the questions, the roles are reversed and a new case is read. Each round (between two teams) will take at least one hour if you follow the rules for the SAA Ethics Bowl. You could, of course, shorten the matches by shortening the responses if you are limited by time. (Also: you shouldn't be afraid to modify the rules, unless the students are preparing for the SAA Ethics Bowl. The ideas from the Ethics Bowl still come across well in abbreviated formats!)

Step 8: Plan for follow up. Celebrate the time, energy, and critical thinking skills the students have put into the event. One way to do this is by hosting a reception for participants after the final round. Have a follow up activity to ensure that participants carry with them the lessons they learned into the future. For example, have a writing assignment where each student must choose her or

Case Studies in the Classroom

Joe Watkins, University of New Mexico

Using scenarios developed from the Ethics Bowl allows archaeology instructors to guide discussions about ethical issues in the practice of archaeology. Archaeologists actively working in the field contribute scenarios to the Ethics Bowl based on real (or nearly real) situations. Students often have limited experience relating to archaeological issues, and classroom scenarios can serve to make them aware of some of the issues archaeologists face. The scenarios also help the students examine their own ideas and help them work toward better understanding of other perspectives on these issues as well.

Divide your class into groups of 3–5, and have each group prepare a response to one of the scenarios from the previous Ethics Bowls. Provide the scenarios to the entire class as a packet, and then ask each group to present their thoughts on the issues. After each presentation, lead the discussion toward other issues and perspectives. Ask leading, open-ended questions that require conversation and cannot be answered with simple "yes" or "no" answers. You'll be surprised at the number of perspectives that are discussed as well as the ideas the students will offer (and carry away with them). Written papers based on the scenarios complete the educational package.

Gordon F.M. Rakita, University of North Florida

One of the aspects of critical thinking that is an important part of any comprehensive education is the ability to cogently and convincingly develop a position on an issue and logically defend that position. The use of the ethics scenarios in this book provide you with a way to develop those skills in your students while also developing their sense of ethical issues confronting modern archaeology. I recommend that after presenting a given scenario to your students, you have them identify their point of view or position on the issues raised. You should then be able to divide the class into two or more groups of students, recognizing that there may be more than two sides in any given situation. At this point, I assign the groups to defend a position different from the one the students in that group believe or accept and then initiate debate on the scenario's issues. By forcing students to defend a position where they may not agree with, you encourage them to polish their skills at developing logically coherent and persuasive argumentation. I find that the contrast between what they believe and what they can effectively defend heightens their recognition that defending a position depends upon more than simply what they believe.

his favorite case study and explain how it should be solved. Then, look forward to your next Ethics Bowl!

Additional Uses for Case Studies

Holding an Ethics Bowl is perhaps the most compelling use of ethical case studies in the classroom, but it also takes a lot of time, planning, and preparation. The case studies in this volume can be used in many other ways to cultivate innovation and critical thinking about complex ethical dilemmas. Below are a few additional ideas, which we offer to remind you that case studies can be used in a variety of formal and informal pedagogical contexts.

1. Case studies as homework. In a course section on ethics, assign a case study from Chapter 4 to your students. Have each student work individually, although you should encourage the students to discuss the case outside of the classroom. One approach would be to have students each write an analytical response to a case, outlining the core ethical predicament, the relevant sections of codes, principles, and laws, and some possible responses. Have the students turn in their written responses, and use them to spark informal discussion about solutions with the class as a whole. As a follow up assignment, have the students write out their "best case" solutions to predicaments raised in one or more of the case studies.

2. A semester long project. The case studies in this volume can form the core of a semester-long project for your students. Have each group of two to three students choose four case studies at the beginning of the semester. Then, once a month, ask each group to share its thinking processes and solutions to one case study. At the end of the semester, have each group summarize its approach to archaeological ethics. The aim with a long-term project such as this is that students learn ways to systematically approach ethical dilemmas. This project also encourages the students to explore and even create their own methodologies of moral thinking.

3. Informal opportunities. The case studies do not only have to be used in formal settings. Hold a brown bag series, in which students and faculty are invited, and each week introduce a new case study and debate it on the spot. If you're teaching a theory or method class, hold onto this book for a day when all the students seem sleepy or not especially engaged—then, offer a case study and debate it then and there. Other possibilities include briefly debating the cases at faculty meetings, staff meetings (if you're in a CRM firm or museum setting), or anthropology club meetings.

4. Role-Playing. The "Six Thinking Hats" technique (de Bono 1990) asks you to adopt a perspective other than your own as your group works through a case study or ethical dilemma. Each person dons a differently colored hat, with each hat signifying a particular style of thinking (factual, emotional, logical positive, logical negative, creative, and process-oriented). Individually, each hat contributes insights into possible solutions and their consequences; together, the six hats represent a well-balanced perspective. (In another twist, each hat can represent a different stakeholder.) This compelling technique not only promotes risk-free communication and nonhabitual modes of thinking, it highlights the interplay of individual positions and group dynamics in solving complex problems.

5. *Constructing visual models.* Constructing visual models of a dilemma is another extremely productive technique for generating deeper understandings of a situation, the actors involved, logical steps toward decisions, and potential consequences. Edward de Bono (1993), who also developed the Six Thinking Hats, encourages the use of a "flowscape" to visually simplify the features that make up a complex issue and the relationships among them. He calls his approach "water logic" because it asks you to consider "What does this lead to?" and focuses on what constitutes a dilemma as a rational flow of ideas and actions, rather than as separate building blocks of "rock logic" ("what is"). Another approach to visual modeling that is easily and fruitfully adaptable to ethical issues and case studies comes from the field of ecological anthropology, where anthropologists are using a series of symbols that represent stakeholders, sources and flows of energy and information, and hindrances to these flows to "map" complex dilemmas (Pavao-Zuckerman 2000:56). Through creating the model, many aspects of a dilemma become visible that otherwise were not apparent, thus opening up new possibilities for moving toward a well-thought out solution

These and other models, such as the decision-making framework in Chapter 2, serve as conceptual tools that help you think critically and holistically about any ethical dilemma and deepen your understanding of its complexity. As with most visual models, the real insights occur in the act of constructing the model and the new perspectives generated in the process. Using these tools in the classroom or in preparation for an Ethics Bowl is not only a great deal of fun, but it will also hone students' critical thinking skills and enrich their approach to the case studies and how they work together as a team.

For the Student: An Insider's Guide to the Ethics Bowl

This chapter began with a nail-biting scenario from the SAA Ethics Bowl. Faced with the same experience, how would you proceed? What steps would you take to prepare? What are the important considerations in judging ethics? Preparing to debate archaeological ethics on a national stage or in the classroom may seem arduous and frightening, but there are simple tips for preparation and performance that will help ease your trepidation. The rest of this chapter is devoted to providing an insider's guide to ethical debates in the Ethics Bowl (Figure 10). Our own recommendations on preparing for, performing in, and judging ethical debates will be augmented by "tips" from previous participants in the SAA Ethics Bowl.

Figure 10. The final round of the Fourth Annual Ethics Bowl in action. (Photograph by Chip Colwell-Chanthaphonh, April 26, 2007)

Preparation

We've already talked about many ways to prepare for your discussion of a case study in the Ethics Bowl, but here we offer some specific tips from former Ethics Bowl participants that recommend several things to take into account for a successful Ethics Bowl experience. These "tips" include how to allocate responsibilities within a team, the importance of conducting a literature review and contemplating various codes, making sure to consider alternative perspectives, and sticking to the facts.

Organization

When analyzing case studies for an Ethics Bowl, most teams choose to assign certain cases to certain individuals. This approach divides the workload and ensures every case has a ready-to-go speaker for the competition. However, although one person may be responsible for a case, that person benefits greatly from the input of their team. Sharing responsibility for cases will not only introduce diverse perspectives and help analyze potential alternative arguments, but it will also bring your team closer together (Figure 11).

Preparation for Ethical Debates

Brandy Rinck, Boston University 2006 Team

Preparing for both sides of a case (answer or rebuttal) is the best idea for groundwork [since you don't know in advance if your team will make the first arguments, or go second and have to respond] … Prepare all three types of responses to questions and comments: a five-minute discourse, a response to the most ethical point of view, and a question for the other team that challenges the position you think they will take in case the other team gets first shot at an issue. This way you will have all your bases covered even before the debate begins. Remember, you can't bring your notes inside, so each person should memorize both sides of the argument of their specific studies. Also, bring notes for your teammates to the SAAs with you in case someone in your group cannot attend. That way you will be prepared to study up quickly on the issue at hand.

Joe Watkins, University of New Mexico

Advance preparation is the key. In every scenario, there are numerous things that can be discussed—Is artifact collecting legal yet unethical? Are artifacts objects of art or items of scientific importance? Ethics are moral guidelines, not legal instruments, and they will always have shades of gray. It is not necessary that you identify every possible ethical dilemma, but what you believe to be the primary issue. Teams should focus on issues driving the question in preparing their response. Be certain to prepare for both sides of the argument as you would for any debate, and then use key words to organize your presentation and to help you recall the points you want to emphasize.

Many teams prepare for the SAA Ethics Bowl months in advance (unlike when a scenario is used in an informal classroom setting). Some teams learn the hard way that it is important to budget time and set deadlines. Steps taken during preparation (literature review, case analysis, generating solutions, etc.) can take a deceivingly long time. When setting your deadlines, be sure to include enough time to practice your response with even a small audience and incorporate the critiques you receive into your performance before the final competition.

Literature Review

As every student eventually comes to realize, most "new" ideas are never actually "new." Important discussions of archaeological ethics have been occurring now

Divide scenarios among team members and focus individual energy. Meet often before the Ethics Bowl to hone your presentations. Be certain that each individual has strong arguments on both sides of the issue. Prepare outlines and pass them among team members so that, at the Ethics Bowl competition, each team member can jot down notes on scenarios and can pass the notes to the presenter. The presenter should be the individual who prepared for the scenario, but other team members should prepare for all eventualities.

Robby Robinette, Boston University 2006 Team

The best way to handle the case studies is to have each participant handle two or three cases. That person is responsible for that question and is considered the "expert." The person should conduct background research on the issue and think of salient points, counterpoints, examples, and how to effectively convey all possible points of view. Each "expert" should write one or two pages about all the information collected.

Then, all the participants should get together to test out how each person might respond to possible questions, including rebuttal questions. Each person should be given a critique of their response and suggestions for what to change in the future.

Finally, each participant should make copies of their outlines and responses to distribute to the other participants. Doing this ensures that everyone will have a basic understanding of each case so that all the participants can respond to questions from the judges.

for more than 100 years. In Chapter 1, we summarized the history of ethics in archaeology. The history of archaeology is, unfortunately, replete with examples of ethical dilemmas and professional crises (e.g., the Elgin Marbles, Nazi archaeology, archaeologist spies, Kennewick Man). This history is a valuable source of information for those considering modern archaeological contexts.

In preparing for an Ethics Bowl, consult the plethora of literature available related to archaeological ethics (see Appendix 3). Beyond referring to the classic "red" and "white" books (Vitelli 1996; Vitelli and Colwell-Chanthaphonh 2006; Zimmerman et al. 2003), seek out articles from international journals by international archaeologists. Ethics exist both locally and globally. Challenge mainstream perspectives by expanding your horizons. Also, remember that archaeol-

Figure 11. The San Diego State University team works together during the final round of the Second Annual Ethics Bowl to answer a judge's question. (Photograph by Joe Watkins, March 31, 2005)

ogy is, at least in the United States, a subdiscipline of anthropology. Anthropologists have been engaging ethical dilemmas for years (e.g., Project Camelot, the "Darkness in El Dorado," Franz Boas' comments on anthropologists as spies). Be sure to take advantage of the salient resources that exist on anthropological ethics (e.g., Caplan 2003; Fluehr-Lobban 2003; Turner 2005), and professional ethics in general (Cooper 2004; Martin 2000).

Finally, when preparing a literature review, don't forget to consult recent news stories. A quick Web search for "archaeology" can lead to hundreds of important news articles and give you an idea of how the public sees the discipline. Whether reading modern news articles or peer reviewed journal articles, you should look for facts and opinions, but also seek to understand the ethical dilemmas at the heart of a given set of events and circumstances.

Codes, Principles, and Standards of Professional Practice

As suggested in Chapter 2, thinking through ethical codes helps us create moral and intellectual stepping stones to generating solutions to ethical dilemmas. A basic knowledge of archaeological codes and standards for professional behavior

Ethical Principles and Codes

Paula Lazrus, St. John's University

The Ethics Bowl scenarios push us all to consider difficult ethical and moral situations. While it is easy at times to simply fall back on the "laws" and codes to establish right and wrong in a situation, ethical arguments should push participants (and listeners, judges, etc.) to consider the deeper implications of the actions delineated in a scenario both in the long and short term. This means thinking not only about the big issue, but about all the ways different stakeholders might view the same rules, or infringement of them. Ethical thinking asks us to consider actions from multiple perspectives and to try and understand how competing conclusions (and thus actions) might be drawn from a set of circumstances/facts. At the same time, one must then decide what course of action must be taken to address the ethical dilemma proposed.

Gordon F.M. Rakita, University of North Florida

Archaeologists derive their ethics, in part, from the professional associations and societies to which we belong. However, not all societies' ethical standards are the same. When competing in the SAA Ethics Bowl it is very important for teams to consider the full range or types of ethical statements of the various professional archaeological organizations. For example, the SAA establishes ethical goals or ideals to strive toward. These include, among others: stewardship of the record, accountability to all stakeholders, and public education and outreach. The RPA and the AIA, on the other hand, provide minimum standards for ethical behavior. These standards often take the form of "shall ..." and "shall not ..." statements. Included in these codes are, for example, giving credit to work done by others, not refusing a reasonable request to share research data, and recording and maintaining appropriate provenience data for specimens. Both of these types of ethical creeds are important and should be adhered to as much as possible. While framing their answers, Ethics Bowl teams would do well to consider the implications of both.

is necessary if we are to understand archaeological ethics and debate the future of our discipline (see Appendix 2). The principles constructed by organizations such as the SAA are important standards for professional behavior in archaeology.

But, do not rely on codes and moral philosophy too much. Remember, there may be universal human values, and perhaps even universal "truths"—don't tell

---

Stakeholders

Janet E. Levy, University of North Carolina at Charlotte

Always consider the broad issue of stakeholders. There are likely to be multiple, often competing, stakeholders in each scenario. You may wish to give preference to the interests of certain stakeholders over others; that's fine, but be prepared to explain and justify that choice. Remember: life is full of hard choices, and archaeologists have to make some. It is acceptable to acknowledge competing interests, even when you ultimately privilege one set over another. In fact, your argument will be more realistic and compelling if you explicitly acknowledge the multiple stakeholders than if you suggest that there is one simple answer.

Remember, ethical dilemmas are just that: dilemmas. If they were easy to answer, we wouldn't need codes and debates and Ethics Bowls. You can expect that an appropriate solution to some scenarios will be unsatisfactory to some parties and/or will be imperfect. Acknowledge that honestly in your response, but clarify your decisions and choices. Ethics, after all, is about the reasons we have to guide the choices we make.

Dr. Jones—but ethical codes and moral philosophies are not written in stone.[1] These frameworks for the discussion of ethical situations are meant to be malleable, mutable, and sometimes, controversial or even contradictory. Challenging ethical codes can be an effective tool in learning from ethical dilemmas. Remember, archaeological research requires practical solutions that are contextually specific, effective, and relevant.

Considering Alternative Perspectives

Once you have structured each case in an ethical framework and discovered the relevant facts, you can begin generating potential solutions. When working through these solutions, as John Stuart Mill (1956[1859]:45) suggested in the quote that began this chapter, it is critically important to consider alternative perspectives. The practice of archaeology is surrounded by "those who think differently." Archaeology does not exist in a political, economic, or social vacuum. Our work affects the lives of others in numerous ways. The many diverse stakeholders in the archaeological record should not be ignored in archaeological practice or in your framing of a response to a case study.

There is a vast array of material on stakeholders and contemporary contexts of archaeological research related to topics such as: cultural property, indigenous rights and repatriation, ethnicity, nationalism and internationalism, intellectual property, popular culture, and tourism (see Appendix 3). It is also a good idea to

> ## "Due Process"
>
> *Larry J. Zimmerman, Indiana University-Purdue University Indianapolis*
>
> A few Ethics Bowl case studies and many ethical dilemmas in real life involve accusations of colleagues against others. Don't forget that accusations are not the same as proven ethical violations. Many legal systems work according to the long-held maxim: "innocent until proven guilty." As well, the 5th Amendment of the U.S. Constitution and other legal systems demand "due process of law," which guarantees that one has a right to hear any charges against them, a hearing by an impartial jury, and a right to face one's accusers, among other things. Ethics Bowl teams sometimes fall into the trap of presuming guilt before it has been proven. As you prepare for the case studies, carefully avoid solutions that may violate someone's rights. In fact, you may gain points by raising the problem while presenting your case or during questions.

read ethnographic examples of how actual projects have faced difficult situations (e.g., Gero 2000; Meskell 2005). The One World Archaeology series often openly deals with the issues raised by multiple stakeholders (e.g., Layton 1989, 1994), and there are also volumes now out on community archaeology and applied archaeology (e.g., Derry and Malloy 2003; Shackel and Chambers 2004).

Stick to the Facts

Finally, when generating potential solutions, it is also important to base your decisions on the facts of the case in front of you. For instance, in a case where an archaeologist is accused of smuggling antiquities out of a war-torn country in violation of their law, you could debate the extent to which stewardship should guide the archaeologist's actions, present possible solutions for the repatriation of the artifacts, and discuss how the archaeologist should be punished. However, you would have made a fundamental error if you had assumed the archaeologist was guilty *merely* because he had been accused of unethical behavior.

Performance

Ethics Bowls are just as much about performance as they are about preparation. In the SAA Ethics Bowl, the goal is for teams to present clear and focused responses based on an understanding of the facts and an appreciation of alternative perspectives. The key words here are *clear* and *focused*. A wonderfully intelligent argument will not go far without public speaking skills. Remember, you're not just trying to make a sound argument; you're trying to convince the panel of

Performance

Sam Duwe, University of Arizona 2005 Team

By the time of the actual Ethics Bowl you've already read everything relevant to your case studies, but being able to recite NAGPRA front-to-back doesn't guarantee eloquent speech during the competition. The key to performing well during the debates is to practice speaking your arguments. The first part comes from not only knowing your cases back-to-front, but also being able to present your initial arguments and to answer tough questions from the judges. Our 2005 University of Arizona team found the best way to prepare is to have your advisors and other teammates quiz each other on their cases. Practice your statement, and rebuttal, under fire. Identifying difficult questions during practice will guarantee fewer surprises during the competition itself.

Another tip: pack the audience with friends. The more students and professors are there to cheer you on, the better. Have confidence! Everyone wants to see you do well.

Joe Watkins, University of New Mexico

The Ethics Bowl is as much a performance as a competition. You have to convince the judges that you have given reasoned consideration of the issues and that you are presenting the best possible solution, and your performance will reinforce that perception.

Take a watch or timer and have a teammate act as timekeeper. Most Ethics Bowl teams rarely make adequate use of the time allotted. Present your perspectives at an even pace, words distinctly enunciated, and with points presented clearly. Breathe normally. Don't be too animated, but don't be robotic either.

Use notes to count down remaining time and save the last minute to summarize your points. Open the last minute with "In summary ..." so

judges that your solutions and the reasons behind them are the best possible ones. The best way to perform a clear and focused response is to practice. Practice, after all, makes perfect, right? Don't believe us? Then be sure to read the tips from previous Ethics Bowl participants.

Judging Ethics

For many people, when they think of ethics, they think of esoteric debates over complex issues that rarely have a right or wrong answer. Indeed, many people that the judges know you are summarizing. Explain why you chose the perspectives you have presented, but also recognize other relevant perspectives. Ultimately, however, YOUR opinion is the most important and you must defend it.

As with all things, practice and advance preparation will make you a better performer and presenter, and will increase your success.

Janet E. Levy, University of North Carolina at Charlotte

You should also practice oral presentation. Develop some strategies for focused, snappy presentations: like a verbal version of bulleted lists on a PowerPoint presentation. Work on the capability to use the allotted time effectively. You don't want to hear the buzzer when you are in the middle of a sentence; on the other hand, you don't want to finish with two full minutes remaining that you could use to state your case. So, you need to practice enough to get a feel for what two minutes are and what five minutes are.

Develop good posture; you will be seated at a table, so sit up straight. Project your voice outward; look at the audience as much as you can even if you have to consult notes. There will be a microphone, so practice using one. (However, also be prepared to speak effectively with or without a microphone; this will serve you well in the future!) Practice extemporaneous, but substantive, speaking so that you can pause without using fillers like "um" or "I guess." Breathe instead. Don't be afraid to pause and take a quiet breath.

Finally, remember that the Ethics Bowl is intended to be enjoyable and educational. No one is out to "get you." In fact, everyone involved—the organizers, moderators, and judges—will want to see you succeed! And simply by preparing, showing up, and earnestly sharing your thoughts, you'll find a measure of success. So relax—and have fun too (Figure 12).

may only know moral philosophy as a type of "spaceship ethics," conceived as theory "far removed from the realities of practice" (Benjamin 2001:29). Practical, applied ethics differ from this in that they expressly aim to make abstract philosophies relevant and useful to real problems. Although our ethical decision-making may be guided by Kantian, Utilitarian, or Virtue ethics, the profession of archaeology exists in a world of moral pluralism where practical decision making is necessary. As stated by Martin Benjamin (2001:30), "Ethics without the capacity to ameliorate, if not fully resolve, concrete practical issues is empty."

Practical, applied ethics does have the capacity to help archaeologists resolve ethical dilemmas. Although it may be true that some archaeological dilemmas will not have a "right" answer, there are such things as better and worse answers. For instance, when posed with a case involving gender inequality and discrimination in a CRM firm, arguing that the principal investigator should remove all the women working in the firm in order to resolve the problem would not be considered the "best" answer. Hence, with better and worse solutions potentially at hand, judging ethics becomes a realistic part of debating ethics.

As described in Appendix 1, responses from teams in the SAA Ethics Bowl are evaluated on the basis of four criteria:

1. *Intelligibility*—Has the team stated and defended its position in a way that is logically consistent? Has the team expressed its responses with enough clarity and precision that the judges can understand them?

2. *Depth*—To what extent does the team's statement and defense of its position indicate an awareness and understanding of the issues that the judge views as ethically central to the case?

3. *Focus*—To what extent does the team's statement and defense of its position avoid issues that are ethically irrelevant to the case?

4. *Judgment*—To what extent, in the judge's view, has the team made a careful and reasonable comparative assessment of considerations it identifies as ethically relevant to the case?

These criteria incorporate all the elements of preparation, performance, and judgment described above. In order for an argument to be logically consistent, it should be steadily situated in a framework, all conclusions should follow from sound premises, and answers to questions from judges should not contradict earlier opinions offered. "Intelligibility" is also judged based on the consistency, clarity, and precision of an argument. These skills are developed through practice and performance. For "depth," the best way to become aware of the issues ethically central to any case study is to have done an adequate literature review and to make sure you have addressed the standpoints of other stakeholders. "Focus" requires avoiding ethically irrelevant issues by sticking to the facts and taking a minute to organize your response before beginning an argument. Finally, a comparative assessment of ethically relevant considerations will necessitate the fair and full criticism (or "judgment") of multiple, sometimes contradictory, viewpoints to come up with a plan for action that is as fair and equitable as possible.

Afterwards

The above sections have aimed to prepare you for participating in debates about archaeological ethics through case studies and the Ethics Bowl. We hope that this volume is just the beginning of your explorations in archaeological ethics—or a means to continue the ongoing work of understanding how our professional

Carrying Ethics Forward

Emma Bate, Indiana University 2004 Team

Once the Ethics Bowl is over, you may wonder what to do with all of your preparation and experience. Our team mentored a group of undergraduates in an archaeological ethics class who were doing a project based on the SAA Ethics Bowl cases. We met with the students once or twice a week for a month, discussing the cases, suggesting readings, and helping them to construct arguments for each case. By the time they wrote their final papers, we were confident that they could have competed in the Ethics Bowl and done well. More importantly, it was clear that they had a more complete understanding of the ethical issues crucial to the practice of archaeology. The graduate students also realized that mentoring the undergraduates helped us understand archaeological ethics more clearly and argue more effectively. Our mentoring experience not only better prepared us for the Ethics Bowl the following year, but also ultimately made us all better archaeologists. Perhaps this is the best use of our Ethics Bowl experience: to carry our understanding of the issues and the habit of discussing them forward into our professional lives.

behavior affects the archaeological record, our colleagues, and the many publics who have a stake in our work. In the spirit of open dialogue, we hope this book inspires you to pursue still other forms of interchange and public forums. Why not:

- Initiate a roundtable discussion with faculty and students to discuss research ethics.
- Invite the Director of your local Institutional Review Board (IRB) to give a presentation on Human Subjects compliance in social science research.
- Participate in multidisciplinary workshops or conferences on ethics, organized by groups such as the Association for Practical and Professional Ethics (APPE).
- Involve yourself in public archaeology education activities.
- Create a public forum on ethical issues and concerns in archaeology for your state's Archaeology Week or Archaeology Month activities.
- Utilize your experience and the experience of your colleagues to draft case studies for future SAA or Intercollegiate Ethics Bowls.
- Organize a team for the APPE Intercollegiate Ethics Bowl or the Annual SAA Ethics Bowl.

The real test of ethical thinking—and, indeed, ethical behavior—will not come in a lecture, workshop, term paper, or Ethics Bowl competition. It will

Figure 12. The teams from the Fourth Annual Ethics Bowl final round (Brown University and University of New Mexico) with the final judges, moderator, and organizers—all smiling. (Photograph by Kaitlin Deslatte, April 26, 2007)

come when, perhaps, you hear of a colleague hiding data, a landowner who writes an angry letter in the local paper about your fieldwork, or a fellow student whose work was purloined by her professor. The Ethics Bowl and these case studies will not solve such problems for you. But, we believe if you have trained yourself in identifying ethical dilemmas and the issues at stake, analyzing codes and laws, and coming to moral predicaments with seriousness and earnest, then you will be well on your way to making the right decision.

Note

1. At the beginning of *Indiana Jones and the Last Crusade*, Dr. Jones opined, "Archaeology is the search for fact ... not truth. If it's truth you're looking for, Dr. Tyree's philosophy class is right down the hall."

4

Case Studies in Archaeological Ethics

Reading hypothetical scenarios is a way to work through the kinds of real crises and dilemmas that archaeologists face. These case studies are fundamentally stories in which you are encouraged to insert yourself squarely in the narrative—as both the protagonist and antagonist. This leap of imagination is key because it allows you to understand that in every ethical dilemma there is much at stake, and as importantly, that there are almost always multiple stakes.

Some of these cases are set in rather farfetched circumstances that few researchers will likely ever face, while other cases bring out predicaments that most professionals will experience at some point in their careers. All of the scenarios, however fanciful their settings and actors, raise difficult questions about the fundamental values and practices that underscore archaeology. In this way, the case studies are really not a game of solving particular problems, but rather a vehicle for you to explore the nature of stewardship, accountability, respect, trust, and much more. These scenarios ask you to seek potential solutions to the knotty but vital questions of who cares about archaeology, who owns the past, and who makes history.

The themes given for each case study are intended to help guide you in starting your inquiries. They are not meant to limit you in your research, thinking, or arguments. Indeed, where can archaeologists draw the line between principles such as stewardship and accountability? Each standard necessitates the other, so the division into sections and themes offered below is somewhat artificial, but hopefully will provide you with some guidance about the major issues inherent in each scenario.

Keep in mind: Although many of these case studies were inspired by actual events, the scenarios are intended to be educational and hypothetical. If you're using these scenarios in an Ethics Bowl, participants should only consider the provided information. Finally, we again acknowledge and thank all those who have contributed to these cases through the years.

Who Cares About Archaeology?
Stakeholder Interests and the Community of Archaeology

1. Are Avocational Archaeologists Allies or Adversaries?

Belinda Smith is the President of the Colorado State Archaeological Society, a nonprofit organization of volunteers dedicated to bringing together those interested in archaeology. A recent controversy has erupted over whether to publish the results of an excavation conducted on an archaeological site in the society's Special Report Series. The archaeological work submitted for publication was not the result of an illegal dig, but rather a dig on private land, on a site that has never been reported to the state. The state of Colorado has no laws that require a private landowner to record archaeological sites on their private property and does not claim ownership of artifacts found on private land. The excavation was done with landowner permission using appropriate archaeological field techniques by experienced amateur archaeologists. The landowner, deeply skeptical of the state government, chose not to record the site with state authorities and asked to retain ownership of everything that was excavated.

The Colorado State Archaeological Society is composed of both amateurs and professionals, including many private landowners. One of the organization's missions is to work with landowners and amateur archaeologists to enhance sharing of information and advance the study of archaeology. Because of the organization's efforts in recent years, a growing number of private landowners and amateurs have made the decision to record archaeological sites with the state, donate collections to the state museum, monitor sites for looting, and stop activities that otherwise might have led to further loss of the archaeological record.

One vocal group of society members has argued to Mrs. Smith that publishing the results of the excavation is a positive example of solid archaeological research conducted on private land, which will encourage more private landowners to sponsor archaeological research. However, a second group, including several of the society's powerful board members, has insisted that publishing this report is a step backward, an implicit encouragement of private landowners to do with archaeological sites and artifacts as they please. Both groups are demanding that Mrs. Smith make a presentation of her decision to the divided board very soon.

Themes: public reporting and publication, public education and outreach, looting

2. Bad Press

Tad Sullivan is the field director of a CRM project—a colonial-era Native American village in the path of a highway realignment—south of Buffalo, New York. One day while working on the site, Rosie Hanson, a reporter for the *Buffalo News*, approaches Mr. Sullivan and starts to ask questions, making apparent her intention to write a story for the paper.

At that moment, nearly a dozen graves are in the midst of being excavated, and, without asking for permission, the reporter takes out her camera and starts taking pictures. Mr. Sullivan explains that the local Native American groups have asked that no pictures of graves be taken, let alone be published. He kindly asks her to stop and not publish any information about the graves. Ms. Hanson becomes belligerent and argues that since this project is being funded with public money and conducted on public land, the public has a right to know about the excavations. Moreover, she demands, don't archaeologists have a responsibility to inform all the different parties about their work?

Ms. Hanson storms off the site saying that she is going to publish the photos of the graves and whatever else she pleases.

Themes: burials, respect, public reporting

3. Touring Troubles

The famous Go Cave is commonly regarded as the premier heritage site of a small country in Africa. It was the focus of many archaeological expeditions during the colonial era, and not long ago was listed as a UNESCO World Heritage Site. The cave currently draws around 10,000 visitors a year, but the national government has long sought to increase tourism to the site. The country's Ministry of Tourism recently revealed plans (with USAID money) to conduct additional archaeological research and to construct a Fantasia Light Show that will illuminate the inside of the cave with colored lights set to the music of Beethoven.

Although the Ministry of Tourism has promised that no physical damage to the cave will occur and the cave's heritage integrity will be preserved, controversy has emerged. Some people in the nearby town are concerned about the effects of an increase in tourism; others make clear their desire for more tourist dollars. Additionally, several towns over is the Xu religious cult, a group of several hundred people who somewhat illicitly use the cave during rituals. However, during these rituals, site guards are present and no physical damage to the cave is done. The cult leaders now insist that silence is vital to preserving the sacred spiritual power of the site, and they already dislike the current levels of tourism in the cave. The Ministry of Tourism has been quick to point out that these activities are illegal and claims that the Xu rituals sometimes entail defacing the ancient sculptures in the cave. Despite these somewhat local conflicts, Go Cave is considered a national symbol, and much of the country's population supports the government plans.

Dr. Samantha Sacks has long done research in the country, but has never had the chance to do any work in the cave, which has been closed to researchers for nearly 30 years. She is convinced new research will shed light on the cave's ancient uses and users, and in turn potentially inform the cultural history of the entire country. Dr. Sacks has been invited by the Ministry of Tourism to start research in the cave immediately, as $800,000 has already been secured from USAID for archaeological research and the development of public exhibits and outreach programs.

Themes: development, public outreach, sacred place, tourism, preservation

4. What is Protection? What is Stewardship?

In western Australia several major mining companies have ore extraction projects, which inevitably cause massive disturbance to the land. At the same time, Aboriginal groups in Australia are striving to preserve their heritage, which is embodied in the cultural landscapes the mining companies want to exploit. In general, mining companies pay for heritage surveys. The companies have a vested interest in recording as many heritage sites as possible because this will enable them to work in more areas, as they can say that the land has already been completely surveyed. The government's Department of Aboriginal Affairs also prefers to have as many sites as possible identified so they can protect sites under the law.

In practice, the mining industry and the Department "protect" sites by recording and studying them and then proceed to destroy them through mining processes. As a result, Indigenous groups typically seek to have the minimum number of sites recorded. By withholding information, they feel it gives them leverage in entering into dialogue with the Department and companies and also gives them more say about where and when mining can take place. Besides, there is some information that is not meant to be shared with the public, and other information that is only shared among certain members of the community at appropriate times. For heritage sites that are still at risk following this dialogue, the great majority of Aboriginal community members support detailed recording and salvaging. After all, a good handful of Aboriginal community members economically depend on mining.

William Buckman recently began working in the region. As he became aware of these issues, he felt increasingly torn. He is being constantly reminded by his colleagues at the Department and the mining companies that it is his duty to the archaeological record and as a professional archaeologist to record every archaeological site. But he is also being pressured by his Aboriginal friends and colleagues to only record sites that are certain to be destroyed by a pending project.

The mining company representative tells Buckman that these heritage sites are the intellectual property of all Australians; an Aboriginal leader tells him these sites are of primary significance to Aboriginal communities and are not necessarily part of the public record.

Themes: stewardship, records and preservation, Indigenous relations

5. The Violence of Heritage

In 2003, an ancient building complex was discovered in a small South Asian island-nation during the construction of the nation's new Capitol building. After a decade of violent civil war, the new Capitol building is being built to celebrate the recent truce and foster an emerging shared national identity. The archaeological site, however, has only fanned the flames of lingering animosities.

One hyper-nationalist group called The People's Movement, comprising a bare majority of the island's population, has claimed that the archaeological site is the island's first true Capitol, erected more than 800 years ago by their ancestors. The People's Movement, made up mostly of citizens whose families can be traced back centuries on the island, asserts that this site is their heritage and must be preserved at all costs. They are now demanding that the new Capitol building be moved. The opposing group, the National Democrats, is predominately made up of an ethnic group known to have migrated to the island some 200 years ago. They are claiming that the archaeological site is only a small trading outpost, settled closer to 300 years ago. They say it is too late to move the Capitol building, as it took two years of negotiations and millions of dollars to choose the location, purchase the land, and begin construction.

After several days of violent confrontations—dozens of people were hurt and several were killed in protests—both groups are insisting that archaeologists "reveal the truth." The People's Movement calls Professor A.R. Rai, the island's leading archaeologist from the nation's only university, pleading with him to excavate the site. When the National Democrats hear of this, they publicly demand that a "neutral" team of foreign archaeologists come and do the work.

Themes: ethnic violence, truth, accountability, conflict resolution

6. When Education Leads to Looting

You are an archaeologist running a survey with a crew of two others in an area about 10 km from a small fishing village on the Mediterranean coast. Once a week you take a group of local students from a career-education program who have shown an interest in archaeology out into the field with you. You walk the fields, pointing out features, drawing, photographing, and surface collecting materials with a permit from the regional archaeological agency. You spend quite a bit of time explaining the role of an archaeologist to the students and why it's important to document finds and leave objects in situ.

After a few weeks, you begin to notice that some of the places you have visited with students have subsequently been disturbed, some to a major extent, by digging. The pattern of destruction is the same that you've seen in other parts of the region where professional tomb robbers operate. You are very concerned that your interest in the archaeology of the area seems to have stimulated these activities. Could it be that one of the students is actually a digger or an informer? If you don't allow the students to accompany you any more, you are likely to offend people in your host community, as your participation in the career education program is part of the reason local authorities gave you permission to survey. As you ponder the future of the career-education program, you walk through a local market and see a new vendor selling local archaeological heritage for a reasonable price.

Themes: public education and outreach, stewardship, looting

7. The Road Not Taken

Ruins National Park is located in Utah, in a rural section of the state, which is part of the reason this spectacular park with dozens of ancient sites receives only 50,000 visitors a year. Another reason is that the road leading to the site is a 25-mile dirt road that resembles a beat up washboard. Sometimes during summer rains, the road washes out, even leaving visitors stranded in the park for a day or two. A number of accidents have also occurred on the road.

The county government has decided to pave the road leading to Ruins National Park, for which it is legally responsible. It has already secured $1,000,000 in Federal funding. County officials argue that after construction the road will be safer and will increase the number of visitors to one of the nation's prime national parks, which in turn will help the local, depressed economy.

In response, a citizen's group has formed, calling itself STOP! (Stop The Outrageous Paving!) The group agrees that paving the road will increase the number of visitors, but for them, this is the problem. They argue that the park is already maxed out and a number of the sites are already being damaged from too much foot and car traffic. They also say that the peace and quiet of the park is part of its value; its ability to "transport the visitor back to another time." Since getting to the park is so difficult, only the most dedicated visitors come, STOP! argues on its website, and hence nearly all the visitors are respectful and dedicated to the long-term preservation of the sites. Indeed, no looting has been documented in the park for 15 years.

The county responded that such opinions are anti-American and anti-democratic. "Our national parks are for everyone," one official was quoted in a local paper as saying, "Everyone should have the chance to see our national treasures—and to arrive there safely."

As a consequence of the controversy, STOP! has requested that the park's Superintendent write a white paper on the issues involved and provide an opinion on the matter.

Themes: stewardship, preservation, relations with host community, archaeotourism

8. *Archaeologist as Spy*

One day while surfing the Internet, Joe Trimble, an ABD in archaeology, was surprised to find several links from an archaeology organization's website to the top secret spying organization of the United States government. The spy organization's website disconcerted Joe in several ways.

One part of the website, clearly sponsored by the spying organization, was geared toward young adults (around ages 12–16), putatively to get them interested in cryptology. The website had several cartoon characters with different personalities. One of the characters, a cute weasel named Cunning Chris, apparently had a background in archaeology. The website explained that Cunning Chris has traveled all over the world, learning about the different cultures and languages, and this gave him the tools he needed to become a cryptologist. Cunning Chris' background was made clear enough by the trowel in his hand and the Indiana Jones-style hat he wore.

In another part of the organization's website, Joe came across a job advertisement for a position as a Cultural Analyst, which specifically mentioned that a background in anthropology or archaeology was desirable. There were few details about the position, except that the starting salary was $125,000 a year and the applicant had to be willing to travel. A salary like that would go a long way in paying off his student loans!

Themes: representation of archaeology, employment, secret research

9. A Late Night Massage

While hanging out in the graduate student lounge one day, Sara Carroll chatted with her acquaintance and fellow graduate student Isabel Rossini. Gossiping a bit about their advisors, Isabel told Sara a disconcerting story about Professor Tim Rogers, a very popular professor in the department.

One night, rather late, Isabel was working alone with Professor Rogers in his lab. As the two were talking, Isabel said how sore her shoulders were from bending over the microscope all day looking at ceramic tempers. Professor Rogers happened to be standing behind her and jokingly said to Isabel that he'd be happy to give her a little massage. Isabel made a sarcastic remark, and before she knew it, Professor Rogers was massaging her shoulders and neck. A bit uncomfortable, Isabel wriggled away after a few moments. Professor Rogers stopped immediately, and perhaps sensing the awkward moment, apologized to Isabel. The two went back to work and nothing more was said about the incident.

Isabel told Sara that she didn't want to make a bigger deal out of it than it was, but recognized that her main advisor had behaved somewhat inappropriately. Sara sometimes also worked late in the lab with Professor Rogers, and she realized that she now might feel uncomfortable being alone with him. Sara gently encouraged Isabel to tell someone, perhaps the department chair. Isabel responded absolutely not, saying that it is a private matter for her and that Sara should not tell anyone else either.

Themes: sexual harassment, student-professor relations, respect, trust

10. The Warriors' Mascot

Professor Sam Chan runs an archaeological field school outside of Phoenix, Arizona. Every year, to celebrate the end of the hot and dusty field season, Professor Chan sponsors a volleyball tournament and barbecue—a relaxing and fun highlight for many of the TAs and students. Typically, the students divide into two teams a week before the tournament, and select a team captain and mascot.

While driving into Phoenix one day on a supply run, Cheryl Albee, one of the team captains, passes the Phoenix Indian Boarding School, and sees on their marquee the school mascot—The Warriors—and their emblem represented by two crossed arrows. Earlier that day, Cheryl had excavated from a pithouse two arrows, placed in almost an identical position to the image on the marquee. Cheryl thought it almost fate that her volleyball team should be called The Warriors!

That night, Cheryl shared her idea with her teammates who readily agreed—except for one student, Brian Swain. Brian, although not against the mascot per se, asked his teammates if maybe it wasn't offensive to use an Indian moniker for their team mascot. Cheryl retorted that it was a mascot for the Indian boarding school after all, and since they used it, surely so could the volleyball team. Besides, Cheryl said, "I'm one-quarter Seminole, and I'm not offended by the mascot." Brian persisted, however, and explained that he was concerned several of the other students—perhaps especially the other Native American students attending the field school—might feel the name was inappropriate. Several students, after hearing the exchange, began to side with Brian. After further heated discussion, all agreed that in the morning they would take the issue to Professor Chan and let her decide.

Themes: Native American representation, mascots, student training, respect

11. Is Ethics Training an Ethical Obligation?

Professor Carlos Ortiz is the head of the Curricula Committee in his anthropology department. In recent months, the Committee has been debating a major overhaul of the department's requirements. A dispute has emerged over whether or not to have a required ethics course.

One Committee member, Professor Helen Guilliford, has been pushing for a class specifically devoted to studying the ethics of archaeological practice. She has been arguing that, given the complex social and political context of archaeological practice, it would be a grand disservice to their students to send them out from the university without ethics education. Furthermore, she claimed that ethics training is itself an ethical mandate. "Teaching archaeology students without teaching them the SAA Principles would be like training a police officer without mentioning the Miranda Rights," she exclaimed at one meeting.

Professor Abeje Nabila has been the most vocal and adamant challenger. He in turn argues that ethics is not anthropology, and thus should not be a part of an anthropology curriculum; it should be left to philosophy departments. Furthermore, he suggests that since ethical dilemmas are so context-dependent, it is not possible to teach general ethics anyway. Both professors have asked Professor Ortiz, as chairman, to make a decision about this contentious issue right away, as it has stymied all other discussion.

Themes: student training, ethics education

12. Contesting Plagiarism

Kay Smith-Jones is a full professor at Midwest State University. She is now a well-established scholar, having published three books and more than 100 journal articles. Some 25 years ago, Smith-Jones was a 21-year-old undergraduate student applying to graduate schools. As part of the application process, she submitted her senior honor's thesis to the graduate selections committees of five well-known universities. One chapter of Smith-Jones's honor thesis was a sophisticated quantitative analysis of artifact patterning among a suite of sites in the Arctic, an analysis funded by a small university grant. Four of the five graduate departments to which Smith-Jones applied accepted her.

Professor Tim Anders, a faculty member from Ivy University, the one department that rejected her application, went on to publish the key chapter of Smith-Jones' undergraduate honor's thesis in an international journal the following year. He collaborated with a statistician from his university and published her work under his own and his coauthor's names. Smith-Jones' thesis was not cited, and Smith-Jones did not give Anders permission to publish her work. Smith-Jones herself never published her thesis in a peer-reviewed journal, and her thesis was not archived at her alma mater.

For years, Smith-Jones has tried to forget this incident—which she feels was a clear case of plagiarism—recalling that her own undergraduate advisor told her that such appropriation is more common than people think, and that he too had his work taken by his professors. In recent months, Smith-Jones has begun to reconsider, however. Smith-Jones spoke with her department chair, and he encouraged her to publicly address the issue, even at this late stage in her career. However, a colleague in her department, after hearing the story, told Smith-Jones there is an "implicit statute of limitations on ethical violations." And still another colleague said that Smith-Jones should be glad that someone published her work—and that in fact Smith-Jones may have failed in her own professional responsibilities to publish funded research.

Smith-Jones was uncertain what she could do that would make a meaningful impact, and whether or not anyone would listen to her since she has been silent for more than two decades.

Themes: plagiarism, student training, publication, mediating conflict, honesty

Who Owns the Past?
Dilemmas of Collecting, Commercialization, and Collaboration

13. Locking Away Homo extensis

The discovery by a joint Chinese and Canadian team of the remains of some extremely tall humans with elongated arms and legs who lived during the last ice age in the mountains of southern China created a stir in the world of science last year. Soon after they were found, the remains were taken without warning and locked away by a scientist from the Chinese team, who refuses to let anyone else study them. The Chinese archaeologist is one of a small group of scientists that is highly critical of the theory that these elongated creatures are an early form of hominid, believing instead that their size is caused by a congenital disorder. He also has a number of other ancient and rare fossil hominid remains in his collection, and allows other scientists to see them only at his own discretion.

Media attention to this case has brought awareness of the fact that it is standard practice in many places to consider the data that may result from finds to be the intellectual property of the archaeologist who excavated them. Many archaeologists never get around to publishing finds or even handing over the data from their analysis to someone else. Just how much archaeological information is locked away in museums and laboratories, essentially lost, is unknown.

The Canadian scientists who helped excavate the remains of *Homo extensis* plead for a chance to look at the remains so they can perform DNA testing that would yield clues as to ancestry. When there is no sign that the remains will be released for study, the Canadians decide not to press the issue, which could risk inflaming the situation and lead to them not being able to return for further work in China.

Themes: records and preservation, intellectual property, international collaboration

14. An Invitation to Collaborate

After a dusty, bumpy daylong journey from the Salsa de Tomate International Airport, you jump out of the rented Toyota pick-up and land on the sidewalk, your feet swollen from the heat. It's early summer, high noon, and the town is fast asleep. It is the dry season, and that is why you are here—to excavate in dry soil so the cobble you expose doesn't slide apart before you can sketch it. You gulp a mouthful of heated air and head towards the cement-block house that has served as the project's home for the last ten years.

This is the last season of fieldwork in El Valle de La Rumba. On the one hand you feel a sense of urgency because you are ready to move on, to relocate and begin excavations in a more temperate climate with a more ornate archaeological record. But, you also wish for some sort of permanent, positive gift for the community where you've worked and sweated for ten years.

Don Ricardo, your faithful informant who spends the off-season tramping through cornfields, cow pastures, and jungles documenting potential sites for you, greets you excitedly. At first your Spanish is slow, but before long, your mind makes sense of it all. Don Ricardo has located a new site on the eroding side of a nearby mountain. Based on his description, you know that it is not a major site, but a peripheral cluster of residences. However, Don Ricardo says he has found evidence of a large ceramic kiln, one of the missing elements in the archaeological record of the valley. Amazing! You make plans to excavate the area with a few undergraduates after the six-week training period. You are sure to get a major publication or two from this new find.

Don Ricardo has arranged with the cooperative that owns the land to let your project dig on the site under one condition: you will work with them to preserve the ruins and help develop tourism in the area. The cooperative has already looked into the potential of receiving grant money from the government, which is pushing ecotourism as a primary focal point in economic development. Members of the cooperative, along with other community members, have agreed to pool what little resources they have to fund the project. They are asking you to stay on for three more years to aid them in excavating and preserving these eroding hillside mounds for tourism.

Later, alone in the cement-block house, you consider how the mazes of cobble lines that constitute the ruins in El Valle de La Rumba are little more than ambiguous cobble lines lying on eroding soil. Your mind drifts and you envision the nearest major site, almost 30 kilometers away, with scarlet macaws soaring around majestic towering temples, hordes of camera-clad tourists interpreting the ruins with a *National Geographic* issue that dons a picture of you on its cover. You think of the paved highway and tour buses leading to the outdoor museum, the trendy hotels, the airstrip, and the temples, which rendered jade burial masks and gold fishhooks.

Placing a pot of amoeba-infested water on your propane stove, you gaze out the window toward the endless stretch of dirt road and spiky grass, and wonder in which of the two local stores you will purchase your first load of plastic bags for the never-ending supply of sherds the site will surely produce—no gold or jade, no paramount architecture with parrots perching on the terraces, no *National Geographic* cover . . . You tell Don Ricardo you'll think about his project.

Themes: international collaboration, accountability, development, archaeotourism

15. War Torn Tablets

Three years ago, Persepolis, a country in the Near East, was invaded by the United Confederate and some of its allies. Immediately following the invasion, scores of local museums were looted—thousands of artifacts vanished from display cases and storage rooms. Presumably many objects were sold on the burgeoning black market. As the invasion turned into civil war, the social and political unrest allowed looters to dig into unguarded archaeological sites. Reportedly, nearly every one of the country's several dozen major sites has been almost completely obliterated by looters. Hundreds of smaller sites have also presumably been ransacked.

Dr. Satoko Murakami is a distinguished epigrapher who studies the ancient tablets and other writings that are quite famously found in this country's archaeological record. Shortly after the war began she noticed a few new tablets showing up on the international antiquities market, and then an undeniable surge of new objects in the subsequent years. Dr. Murakami became convinced that these artifacts could only be from the war-torn country—and that their purchase by unknown buyers is an incalculable loss to researchers.

Dr. Murakami wrote an open letter to Dr. E. B. Smith, the editor of the leading Near Eastern archaeology journal, that he should temporarily lift the prohibition against first publication of looted material. In her letter, Dr. Murakami argues that the journal's policy is valid in a general way but makes little sense for this particular and unforeseen crisis. Dr. Murakami indicates that she has studied many of the tablets and other artifacts that have recently surfaced on the antiquities market and would like to publish her results before they disappear (probably forever) into private collections. Furthermore, Dr. Murakami recognizes that one risk of publishing looted materials is that they might be fakes and therefore distort the archaeological record, but she contends that this particular region and its writings have been studied long enough that scholars can easily distinguish fakes from genuine artifacts.

Themes: publishing looted artifacts, records and preservation, stewardship

16. The Private Landowner and the #$!%^!&*^#! Government

Rebecca is a project director for a small CRM firm, which does work in Idaho, largely as a result of energy exploration and other similar activities on federal lands. Many of the jobs her firm performs are limited to lands under federal administration. Most ranchers and other private landowners in this region have never quite accepted the federal government's ownership and administration of vast amounts of land. Their distrust and sometimes animosity of the government is on occasion directed at archaeological consultants working on federal projects.

Several years ago Rebecca was conducting a survey, and at one point her crew had to take a road through private land to reach the project area. Rebecca's crew had permission to use the private road, but had been instructed not to examine private lands for the presence of cultural resources. Also, she knew that she would not be compensated for any time or expense for work done outside of federal lands. While driving through the private property to get to the project area, however, Rebecca discovered a large ancient site. Rebecca and her crew were curious and decided to record this "off project" site at their own time and expense.

Upon completion of the project, Rebecca contacted the private landowner, to ask about some recent structures observed near the site, so that the site forms would be as complete as possible, and also to see if he knew of any other sites on his land. The landowner became extremely uncooperative, bellowing that "the #$!%^!&*^#! government agencies had no business knowing what was on his land!" He was concerned that the government knowing of the site represented a threat to the future development and exploration of resources on his land.

Rebecca was faced with a dilemma about what to do with the information—field notes, maps, etc.—she had already collected. The landowner had made it very clear that he did not want a site form turned in to authorities. Rebecca felt that her permission to cross the land also meant permission to record the site. Although Rebecca wanted to honor the wishes of the legal owner, she also felt a responsibility to report the presence of this cultural resource to the appropriate agency.

Themes: records and preservation, stewardship, accountability

17. Archaeology Across Borders

An open letter written by the head of an archaeological project in Indonesia to an international archaeological association has accused Professor Mark Clark, a North American archaeologist at Big City University, of misappropriating the results of research performed by Indonesian archaeologists along the country's remote south. Extensive publications by the Indonesian archaeologist and project team document one decade of uninterrupted excavation in the region, with a number of important results concerning the origins of agriculture in Southeast Asia.

Professor Clark had completed his dissertation research in Indonesia, but had since moved on to conduct research in Cambodia and Laos. With these projects drawing to a close, he decided to return to Indonesia and explore the possibility of new work. Two years ago, while undertaking a preliminary research trip in Indonesia, Professor Clark had been invited to see the excavations being conducted by Dr. Dorrick Musa, an Indonesian archaeologist. While visiting the site, Professor Clark offered to have some radiocarbon tests done at the expense of his home institution. He intimated that more funding would be available to the project if it were bi-national and had his name associated with it. Dr. Musa, agreed and gave the samples to Professor Clark.

A few months later, however, information posted on Professor Clark's official Big City University website highlighted the discovery and dating of these important Indonesian sites without giving direct credit to Dr. Musa. Only a small logo from the Indonesian university that sponsored the work was included on the bottom of one webpage, creating the impression that the discovery had been made only by the North Americans. Because of this, the Indonesian team decided not to collaborate on further funding ventures. Professor Clark was genuinely disappointed.

Professor Clark then started his own research program in the next valley to the east. The growing feeling in Indonesia is that the North Americans have largely ignored the decade of work done by Indonesians in the adjacent valley but have gained international credit and funding because of the earlier accomplishments of the Indonesian team. Dr. Musa is calling for support from an international archaeological association and has asked the country's Ministry of Culture to sanction Professor Clark and his team for presenting the results of an Indonesian archaeologist's research as their own. Professor Clark, in his defense, has publicly argued that much of his funding was based on the continuation of his dissertation research, and that the dated samples provided by Dr. Musa were relatively unimportant.

Themes: international cooperation, intellectual property, publication

18. A Question of Open Access

Dr. Gomez is an Associate Professor of anthropology at Southern State University and President of the Southern Archaeological Organization (SAO), a regional society of avocational archaeologists, CRM professionals, and academic scholars dedicated to educating the interested public about archaeology. The SAO publishes *The Southern Archaeologist*, a peer-reviewed journal with field-based reports, typically resulting from federally funded CRM projects or NSF grants. Members of the SAO who pay the $55 membership fee per annum receive *The Southern Archaeologist* for free, one of the primary benefits of membership.

The Honorable James B. Jones is an Arkansas Senator, who has recently proposed a new law, America's Open Access Act, which would compel all recipients of a federal grant to publish their work on a designated government website, open to all Americans, and indeed, anyone with access to the Internet. More specifically, the law would require scholars to provide the government with a reprint of their published work no later than six months after it was published in a peer-reviewed journal. The reprint would then be scanned and made available as a PDF on the government website. If the researcher did not publish the federally funded work in a peer-reviewed journal, she or he would not need to submit anything to the government; but if a researcher failed to follow the law, the researcher would not be able to apply for a federal grant for five years.

Shortly after making his intentions public, the Hon. Jones called Dr. Gomez asking if he and the SAO would consider publicly supporting the proposed law.

Themes: intellectual property, public education and outreach, public reporting and publication

19. Salvaging a Shipwreck

Dr. Sandra Chen is an underwater archaeologist who works in the Caribbean on seventeenth- and eighteenth-century shipwrecks. Over the years, she has become increasingly vocal about trying to get her colleagues to work in collaboration with private salvage interests. Although Dr. Chen does not deny the differences between the groups, she genuinely believes that there is more to be gained by working together than working at odds. In sum, she believes that the underwater sites are heritage resources that need to be shared by all.

She has recently been approached by Mark Richards, the President of Salvage Inc.—a major private salvage company that has worked in the Caribbean for 10 years. Mr. Richards has proposed that Dr. Chen join him in a collaborative endeavor to locate and excavate the *La Rosa*, a shipwreck both of them have been researching (to-date independently) for decades. Mr. Richards will provide the money and Dr. Chen will provide the scholarly research. Mr. Richards will only keep and sell any coins that are found, and all other artifacts will go to Dr. Chen's university museum. Dr. Chen is aware that Richards has a reputation for always trying to make a fast buck and that he has never, to her knowledge, had any scientific work done on any of his previous finds or published their results. But even the UNESCO Convention exempts coins, and she would control the bulk of the scientific work.

Themes: stewardship, commercialization, new collaboration, underwater archaeology

20. Amateur Archaeology Collectors

The Midwestern United States boasts archaeological sites in every county, and Blackwater County is no exception. Local soil conditions and extensive agriculture ensure that people outside of the archaeological profession regularly find artifacts. Farmers often collect items accidentally encountered while working in their fields.

Bob Mann is an archaeologist employed in a curatorial facility that houses important collections from the surrounding area and states. Archaeological surveys conducted by Bob in recent years have brought him in contact with many amateur collectors, and the contacts have greatly increased the number of visitors to his facility. All types of collectors come to visit Bob, curious about the identity and age of objects they have found, or perhaps just wanting to show off what they believe to be a prized find. Some have collected artifacts from fields all over the area to add to family collections that have been passed down from generation to generation. Others have picked up an item with no idea of what it is. A very small minority of these people sells or swaps artifacts at relic shows, which have been held annually in Blackwater and adjoining counties for over a hundred years. Collectively, these amateurs know more about sites in the county, especially those located on private lands, than any professional archaeologist. Archaeologists like Bob have routinely identified artifacts for collectors for many years.

Bob routinely asks his visitors for the location of their finds, hoping to gain some information for the museum's records. Often the answers are ambiguous, or perhaps totally fabricated, from fear that someone will go dig up "his" or "her" site. Even when someone does locate an object on a map, it is impossible for Bob, due to lack of time, personnel, and funding, to investigate many of the locations he is given, and many of them are on private property. This task is also wearing on Bob's time and energy, although he uses it as a chance to explain why information about location and context is important.

Bob has recently been asked by the state archaeologist to contribute to a new policy statement about whether artifact identification for private individuals is something that archaeologists should do. The state archaeologist makes clear that she feels there is a risk that such identifications might encourage additional removal of artifacts from their archaeological contexts.

Themes: collecting, looting, ARPA, relations with host community

21. Putting Arrowheads to Use

Bill Sparks has lived in northern Arizona for all of his 78 years, working his family's large 15,000-acre ranch. Over the years, while tending cattle and mending fences, he has come across many archaeological sites dotting his ranch. Perennially fascinated by Native Americans and their histories, Bill has made a hobby of collecting artifacts, projectile points in particular. Bill, getting on in years, has begun to wonder what to do with his collection since none of his children or family members wants to inherit the artifacts.

One day while attending a public lecture given by Dr. Lisa Chavez, an archaeologist working with a CRM firm in Flagstaff, Arizona, Bill was surprised to hear that many of the area's Pueblo groups, such as the Hopi and Zuni, use projectile points in religious ceremonies. Dr. Chavez explained that the practitioners believe these ceremonies are central to the spiritual and physical well-being of the Pueblo communities, and in fact all life. Normally, religious leaders gather these projectile points in a ceremonial exchange of cornmeal from ancient pueblos in the region. However, Dr. Chavez said that several community leaders had recently told her that in recent years it has become increasingly difficult to find projectile points.

After the lecture, Bill approached Dr. Chavez with the idea that he would like to donate his collection of projectile points to the Pueblo Indian communities. He said that he had more than 300 points, most of them taken from the surface of his private ranch land. Bill was hoping Dr. Chavez might help facilitate this donation to some of the local tribes. Finally, Bill asked about the possibility of a tax-break if the donation was made. Dr. Chavez was sure that some of the Pueblo leaders would want and accept the donation, but she worried how acting as a go-between might conflict with some of her professional responsibilities.

Themes: stewardship, collecting, Native American relations, public outreach

22. *What is Commercialization? What are Data? Where's the Line?*

Professor Phillipa Delmotte is directing a new field project in a rural area of a Southern European country that has seen little archaeological exploration. The government has very strict standards for issuing excavation permits to citizens and foreigners alike, and forbids the export of all archaeological artifacts. Its citizens, however, may buy, sell, and maintain private collections of antiquities, provided the collections are registered with government authorities and do not leave the country.

Professor Delmotte's crew has located many sites, recognizable as low mounds, but most have been almost leveled by deep plowing and recent road building. Professor Delmotte and her crew chief Paul Bulard choose to excavate a site on slopes that appear to have been spared such destruction. The choice seems to be a good one: features are well preserved, the stratigraphy is clear, recovery from the water sieve is high, and artifacts are plentiful, although extremely fragmentary. Some artifacts suggest interaction with cultural groups to the north; others are different from anything known from the period. Especially tantalizing are fragments of what appear to be intricately made figurines. Things are going well. They have established a collegial relationship with their government supervisor, Dr. Efor, and, after an initially cool welcome, relations with the area residents are improving with the open invitation to visit the site on Thursday afternoons.

One Thursday, Ignacio, the biology teacher at the nearby school, requests a tour. He is charming, witty, and very interested. When they finally show him the day's figurine fragment and explain what they think it might have looked like, he modestly suggests reorienting the piece and makes a sketch of the missing parts. The implications—if his drawing is accurate—are profound, but there is no way the whole could be inferred from the small fragment. Ignacio explains that for years he has walked the valley after plowing and heavy rains, collecting exposed pieces that would otherwise be destroyed. He never actually digs, nor does he sell or buy artifacts. On occasion, he has even given a few pieces to the museum (50 miles away). He is a good friend of Efor's, who had encouraged him to visit the site, and to whom he reports all his best finds. Ignacio tells Delmotte and Bulard of his very large collection of nearly complete figurines and invites them to see them in his home. Professor Delmotte abruptly excuses herself to close things up for the night. She thanks Ignacio for his visit and interest, gives Bulard a meaningful glance, and leaves. Bulard gets directions to Ignacio's house before sending him off with a warm handshake.

As soon as Ignacio is out of earshot, Professor Delmotte tells Bulard that they must distance themselves from this man and wonders how to do so gracefully. Bulard, on the other hand, can't wait to see the collection to see what the fragmentary material might have looked like, and thinks they were very fortunate to have a local schoolteacher provide this connection to the community.

Themes: public outreach, records and preservation, commercialization

23. The Dirt People

When Spanish colonialists first entered what is now Florida, they named one group of Native people they encountered *Las Suciedades*, or the Dirt People, so called because of the earth-colored body paint they used. Through the centuries, government officials, local citizens, and still later anthropologists and archaeologists continued to use this name to describe the group. Members of the Native group, however, call themselves a word in their own language that translates simply as "The People." Because of the connotations of the term *suciedad*, and the fact that it was given to them by colonialists, The People have in recent years begun to protest its use.

Dr. Vernelda Blake is a curator at a major anthropology museum in Florida. She has been in charge of repatriation at the museum and has developed close personal and professional relationships with many Native Americans, including several members of The People. As might be expected given the tense history between Native peoples and museums in the area, however, many other Native communities and individuals remain suspicious of the museum.

On a visit by representatives of The People to work on developing a new collaborative exhibit, several elders go into the museum bookstore and notice the many archaeology and history books that refer to their ancestors as *Las Suciedades*. The elders immediately go upstairs and tell Dr. Blake that she had better remove any book with the phrase *Las Suciedades* in it from the museum bookstore. One elder is visibly upset while another suggests that the museum could face major protests from all the tribes in the area should the museum not acquiesce. Later in the day, Dr. Blake meets with the museum director, Dr. B.M. McGuire, who says that this request is a clear violation of academic freedom, and refuses to talk with Dr. Blake any further on the topic.

Themes: Native American relations, publication, censorship, respect, intellectual property

24. The Price of Sheep Hair

Almost twenty years ago, zooarchaeologist Zack Johnson was examining some sheep skins associated with Navajo pottery and weaving accoutrements found by colleagues during archaeological work in a cave in Arizona when he noticed that the fibers of the fleece of these creatures were many times slenderer and softer than that produced by sheep today. Woolens made from softer fiber command much higher prices on the market. Zack immediately saw this as a "golden egg" that could mean a major economic boost for Navajo herders and weavers, if they could begin to produce textiles of this quality again.

He began piecing together the story of the sheep through time; how animals once bred very selectively, possibly for ritual purposes, became the coarser-haired breeds of today. It took many years of writing grants and struggling for permissions and support, but Zack's persistence led him to work with experts to develop a sheep DNA bank and to isolate the gene responsible for the fine fiber. Finally, after almost two decades, he had developed viable methods of breeding herds to select for the genetically pure fine sheep fiber. Zack was just about ready to begin testing his methods with actual herds, but his funding sources had dried up for this final phase of his project, which promised to be expensive and take several more years.

A multinational woolen company heard about Zack's work and offered to fund all remaining steps of the project, in return for the patent on the sheep fiber and the condition that the project would, over time, become their own. Zack's intention always was to benefit local herders, and the company's involvement seemed to jeopardize the potential for local equity in the product of his work. On the other hand Zack had spent most of his career on this project, and the company's offer seemed to be the one sure way he could see his work to fruition.

Themes: commercialization, intellectual property

Who Makes History?
The Predicaments of Applied Archaeology and the Museum World

25. A Curation Crisis

A large, five-year CRM contract is being concluded in northern California, in preparation for the construction of Macrosoft World, a corporate interactive, birth-to-death life-care community. The archaeological work involves the survey of a 70,000-acre watershed and then testing and mitigation excavations of 30 pre-Columbian sites and 25 colonial-era sites.

During the course of the project, over 280 boxes of artifacts, soil samples, and paperwork were generated for curation. The designated curation facility does not have room for this massive collection. Standard curation fees are $750 for each box, making the project's costs $210,000 to store the materials. If the size of the collection could be reduced, Macrosoft World has committed to contributing any cost savings to the project's public interpretation program.

Noreen is a contract archaeologist with the large CRM firm that has been directing the mitigation program. She is a respected professional with a good publication record and has directed similar smaller projects for over a decade. She argues for allowing the project to develop guidelines to cull material with minimal research potential. She casts a practical and critical eye toward what is traditionally packed away for "future study" and believes that archaeologists generating collections should sort out the wheat from the chaff. Furthermore, she argues that any extra money that goes towards public programs will be money well spent.

Sandra is a 20-year veteran of the Bureau of Land Management and a nationally recognized advocate for cultural resources, charged with providing oversight for legal compliance with federal statutes. One of her jobs is to issue a permit for the projects, which requires her to sign off on the curation plans. Sandra is opposed to any culling of the collections, arguing her agency's point of view that research questions and technologies change over time and therefore all recovered materials must be kept in perpetuity.

Ned is the new collections manager of the university curatorial facility that committed to receiving the Macrosoft World collection five years ago. He is struggling with a statewide curation crisis that is reaching critical proportions because of the enormous increase in CRM projects over the past decade. Ned is overwhelmed by this obligation, as his available storage space is already crowded, and the condition of some of the boxes can only be described as deplorable. He has applied to the dean to raise the curation fee to $1,000 per box, but even this will not cover "in perpetuity" storage, nor does it solve his growing space problems.

Themes: records and preservation, stewardship, curation crisis

26. Developing Sav-Mart

A group of developers, BD Partners, is planning a major shopping area with a Sav-Mart in Albuquerque, New Mexico. The developers hired Phillip Chow, owner of a small CRM firm, to investigate the vacant 65-acre lot. The developers told Chow that they were quite certain his team wouldn't find anything at all. The contract stipulated that Chow would receive "a base fee of $5,000 if no significant archaeology was found or, in the alternative, $200 an hour." Furthermore, the contract included an ownership clause that stated, "All studies and reports made, developed, or created, in whole or in part, by the CRM firm in the course of its research shall be the property of BD Partners."

Chow and his crew recorded seven sites, including an Archaic site. Feeling that the sites were important—especially the Archaic site, a relatively rare find for the area—Chow tested all seven sites. The messages Chow left for the developers went unanswered. At several points in the fieldwork, Chow and his team were confronted by a group of protestors who objected to the planned Sav-Mart. After discussing their work, the protestors grew to support Chow, thinking that the identification of archaeological sites could slow the development process. After four weeks of work, Chow sent a bill to the developers for $20,000, and stated that the written report would follow shortly.

A day later, the developers contacted Chow and told him that they were only going to pay him $5,000. They recently found a 1994 archaeological report, archived in the state land offices, which cleared the area of archaeological resources and specifically stated that no archaeological sites were located on the 65-acre parcel in question. The developers informed Chow matter-of-factly that they have decided to use the 1994 report, and that the services of his company were no longer needed. Since the 1994 report stated that there was no archaeology on the parcel, he would not be paid more than the originally contracted amount. Furthermore, Chow was told that he should turn over all studies and reports produced from the project to the company, and not publish or distribute any of them to anyone.

Themes: CRM contract, public reporting, accountability

27. Gender Matters

Sam Hardy is in charge of a Native American government crew—composed entirely of Native Americans—that stabilizes old Pueblo ruins, Athapaskan ruins, and Anglo homesteads. This summer he has been allocated some extra funding to provide summer employment for additional crewmembers. The applicants are few; all are individuals who know the existing crew in some way. One of the applicants is a young woman named Trudy Lujan, the daughter of a local Native American man who worked for many years with archaeologists at Chaco Canyon. Sam hires Trudy, but the all-male crew reacts in an unexpected manner. They do not want a woman working in certain areas, nor do they think she should be taught to do masonry work on the old ruins.

Trudy turns out to be a highly competent laboratory assistant, and she ends up doing most of the conservation work on the many artifacts that turn up as part of the stabilization project. She is well motivated, good at artifact analysis, and can be credited with a number of improvements to the project. Word spreads across the reservation, and several other women begin to show an interest in archaeological work. Rumors also spread; false rumors about improper behavior among Trudy and several members of the stabilization crew, causing her husband to visit the field site and complain. The crew wants her out. Angry words are exchanged. Government administrators back in town hear of the problems within the project and declare that they never thought a woman should be hired in the first place.

At the end of the year the stabilization crew is disbanded. Sam takes a full-time archaeology job at another federal agency. Hiring proceeds for a new head of the stabilization project. All of the top applicants are women.

Themes: gender rights and local norms, accountability

28. Building Upon Burials

A proposed residential development in southern California will destroy several large coastal midden sites. The development is quite controversial. Public hearings on the development plan have gone on for more than a decade, with legal challenges forwarded on a variety of issues including transportation, air quality, housing density, and the loss of open space. As part of the environmental review process, the archaeological sites have been thoroughly documented, and a treatment plan to mitigate the adverse effects of the development has been approved by all appropriate federal, state, and local agencies. The area lies within the traditional territory of a nonfederally recognized Indian tribe that is divided into multiple, divisive factions. Several factions have agreed with the treatment plan; members of these groups have been hired by the developer to monitor construction activities for cultural remains.

Upon completion of the data recovery excavation, the remainder of the midden deposits were graded during construction. At this time, archaeologists discovered multiple burials. Members of Native American groups that were not chosen as monitors, backed by other groups opposing the development, including other archaeologists, have requested that all construction halt. These groups want time to re-evaluate the development plan and suggest ways to redesign around the areas with burials. The archaeologists, however, have not found a pattern to the burials, which appear to be randomly dispersed throughout the midden deposits. The developer insists that they have the appropriate approvals and the right to continue.

Themes: CRM controversy, Native American relations, NAGPRA, burials

29. An ARPA Dilemma

Dr. Julie Heron, a project director at a major CRM company in Nevada, was recently approached by James McPhee, an attorney defending a man accused of violating the Archaeological Resources Protection Act. McPhee asked if she would be interested in helping with the case, for which she would be well compensated. McPhee explained that his client was caught digging into middens on federal land in southern Nevada, but the 23-year-old client erroneously believed that as a member of the public he was free to dig on public lands—a foolish mistake for which he now feels deep remorse.

The lawyer said that that during "discovery" phase of the case, he learned that an assessment of $38,000 in damages had been made. Following the procedures established by the ARPA Uniform Regulations (43 CFR Part 7), an archaeologist, hired by the federal prosecutor, examined the looted site, and determined a figure of $27,000 for archaeological value, $8,000 for cost of restoration and repair, and $3,000 for commercial value of the artifacts taken. McPhee said that he recently found a damage assessment for a similar site with similar damage, and the total damage figure was only $9,000. The lawyer emphasized to Dr. Heron that her investigation should be objective, but that a five-year prison sentence for the accused is on the line, and if a lower assessment could be found, it would likely result in a stiff fine, but no jail time.

Themes: ARPA, stewardship, justice

30. Problematic Repatriation

Allyson Carson is on her first dig as a crew member since receiving her B.A. in anthropology, from Northwest State University. The 5,000-year-old village site she is working on is in Washington, in the path of a major highway re-alignment. The excavation is being conducted by a medium-sized CRM firm, and about half of the crew members and all of the field assistants are Native Americans from surrounding communities.

After several weeks of work, Allyson and the Native American field assistant assigned to help her, Paul Chaplin, come across a burial. Per the Memorandum of Agreement (MOA) between the CRM firm and the local tribe, the archaeologists stop and temporarily cover the burial. The tribe is notified, and the archaeologists are given permission to excavate the burial, conduct in-field analyses, and then turn over the human remains and associated artifacts to the tribe for reburial.

As Allyson begins working with her dental pick—Paul is standing, waiting at the screen—the human bone practically disintegrates upon being touched. Allyson does her best to be careful and gingerly places small batches of dirt in the eighth-inch screen Paul is using. However, as Paul gently shakes the screen, it is easy to see white bits of bone falling through the mesh and into the back dirt. Paul becomes visibly upset. Allyson stops and goes over to the Project Director for advice. He tells Allyson that the MOA expressly states that the archaeologists must use eighth-inch screens, and so it is not their fault if a few fragments slip through; he also says that the discovery of the burial has already put them behind schedule and he wants her to finish the burial as quickly as possible, especially since the tribe will only let them do "token" analyses. Another crew member, overhearing the exchange, asks the Project Director if it might be possible to use Rhoplex 24 to preserve the remains in situ. The Project Director counters that he's not familiar with such techniques and, anyway, using them to keep human bones in place might raise too many ethical problems and is not mentioned in the MOA.

Allyson returns to work, although somewhat uncomfortable with her Project Director's direction. Paul says nothing. After another half hour of work, Paul suddenly stops screening and tells Allyson that he can't work on the site anymore and that he is going to have to call his tribal office to tell them what's going on.

Themes: repatriation, Native American relations, NAGPRA, CRM

31. Ethical Borders

A well-known physical anthropologist visited Mexico in 1902. He went to see a battlefield where combat had taken place just three weeks before between Mexican troops and the Yaqui. At least 64 Yaqui, including women and children, had died in the mêlée.

The anthropologist collected skulls and artifacts from the battlefield. On the same trip, he encountered the body of a Yaqui in another part of Sonora and removed the head from this body. He sent all of this material to a major museum in the United States. The catalogue of the museum lists 12 Yaqui skulls and one complete skeleton were received, along with 37 objects including arrows, bows, and blankets. There are complete catalogue listings and photos for all of the human remains and the objects from the battlefield, including some illustrations. The anthropologist's journal offers a more detailed description of his activities, and additional photos.

The museum did not include the collection in their NAGPRA inventory despite the fact that the Yaqui are a federally recognized tribe in the United States, because the materials were from Mexico and therefore not covered by United States law. An archaeologist who has been working with the Yaqui is asked to help them repatriate the materials.

Themes: repatriation, international relations, preservation

32. A Political Display

In a well-known department of anthropology, Professor Thomas Ipswich (who specializes in art and anthropology) and Professor Veronica Cordova (who specializes in visual anthropology) invite George Baroff, an antiquities dealer, to contribute material for a student-installed show of Cambodian art held at the University's small but prestigious anthropology museum. All of the objects the dealer plans to offer were at one point taken from temples and other old sites in Cambodia, but he has submitted a handwritten statement that there is nothing illegal about them; he can prove that they all entered the country before the U.S. ratified the UNESCO Convention in 1981. The dealer hopes to use the University museum show as proof of his own status and reputation. Indeed, Baroff has already begun advertising the show, describing his role as providing the clues to the mystery of lost Cambodian civilizations.

The anthropology museum director, Dr. Gloria Ortiz, contacts the chair of the department, Professor Vern Raburn, and meets with him to express her concern over Baroff's involvement and his contribution of patently looted material. She points out that displaying the dealer's objects in a museum setting both condones the antiquities market and increases the market value of the objects, potentially causing more looting in the future.

Chair Raburn says he has already addressed the matter by calling the director of the University's art museum, John Dendahl, who has assured him that this kind of thing happens all the time, and that as long as the objects came into the U.S. before a certain date, everything is fine. Dendahl also knows the dealer well, as he has sold objects to several of the museum's donors. The art museum also owns two or three fabulous ancient objects from Cambodia (also potentially looted material) that Dendahl would like to see in the exhibition. Not only would this please donors, it would get them and many others to visit the anthropology museum (which is rarely visited) to see the exhibition.

Chair Raburn tells Dr. Ortiz that the issue is settled and not to bring it up again, at the risk of getting censured. But Dr. Ortiz ends up discussing the dilemma with several of the students who are organizing the exhibition. Some of them talk about meeting with Chair Raburn themselves, and if that doesn't work, making an official complaint. One student contacts the local Cambodian Peoples Association (CPA), which is quite active in the community. The museum has a good relationship with Cambodian residents in the area, having previously constructed an exhibition in collaboration with the CPA about Cambodian culture and immigration experiences. Instead of being upset about the presence of Cambodian antiquities in the exhibition, members of the association express a sense of pride that cultural artifacts from their homeland's ancient past will be included in the display. In fact, they are excited about a chance to come and see them.

Meanwhile, Dr. Ortiz calls several other anthropology faculty members that she knows to share her concern, in the hope that they will support her at the next faculty meeting. All of them commiserate, but they each feel it is a waste of time and energy to try to get Chair Raburn and his cohorts to understand the issues and don't want to stick their necks out over something like this.

Themes: UNESCO Convention, antiquities trade, looting, public outreach

33. The Out-of-Date Diorama

A museum in British Columbia, Canada has long displayed a diorama of a First Nation gatherer-hunter encampment. The diorama is populated by body casts, made a century ago, by a meticulous scientist who even captured the variable suntan on his models (giving lie to the fact that, though clad in traditional gatherer-hunter garb in the diorama, they were already wearing Western clothes at the time of casting). The making of these casts required the subject to, sometimes forcibly, be covered in plaster for hours in a series of humiliating poses. The diorama is one of the museum's most famous and visited exhibitions. There are other displays of this particular gatherer-hunter group's history in the museum, including a rock painting that appears on the provincial coat of arms.

A decade or so ago the museum's archaeologists persuaded the museum's management to allow them to place a revisionist display flanking the diorama in which the pros and cons of the casting project are explained, including photographs showing how the gatherer-hunters really looked at the time of casting and how they look today.

A change in museum management recently occurred and a new director, not native to the country and keen to curry favor with local and national politicians, decides the diorama should be closed so as not to cause offense to the gatherer-hunters displayed or their descendants. After much protest, the diorama is closed. Some of the most vociferous and pro-diorama protests comes from the majority of the descendants of the gatherer-hunters displayed. They argue that the diorama displays a major part of their history. If it is okay for modern Britons to dress as sixteenth-century Puritans in theme parks and museums, why can't the gatherer-hunter part of their history be displayed? The descendant's wishes are not listened to because the closure makes contemporary politicians happy, and this means more money will go to the museum for public outreach and other core functions.

In this case, the initiative of a well-meaning, "progressive" museum is at odds with the more "conservative" stance of the people being displayed. What to do?

Themes: museum display, public education and outreach, Native American relations

34. Paying for Terrorism

In 1992, a suicide bomber killed 127 people at the ancient site of Tuminia, a popular tourist destination in the Near East. Among those killed were 12 Americans. Several years later, the families of the bombing victims sued the Republic of Qumar in an American court, arguing that the state sponsored this act of terrorism. The families won the lawsuit, and a $200 million award. Since Qumar rejected the American court's decision and refused to pay, the court gave the families the right to collect Qumar assets in the United States.

In 1970, the Qumar government had made a long-term loan of hundreds of ancient artifacts, including the famous Gold Cache of Tuminia, to the Museum of Antiquities, located in New York City. The families of the bombing victims recently asserted in the press that their lawyer advised them to seek a court order that would compel the museum to turn over the artifacts, which could then be auctioned off and the money used as part of the compensation awarded to them.

One morning, while sipping coffee at her desk, Dr. Cynthia Alberto, the director of the Museum of Antiquities, reads the article about the families' intention to sue. As the sweat breaks from her brow, she begins to think about all the different issues: Doesn't the country of Qumar have certain property rights? What would happen to the museum if suddenly hundreds of the museum's prized artifacts disappeared from the display cases? Would donors still want to donate artifacts to the museum if they knew the museum would hand them over for liquidation? Even with sympathies to the families, wouldn't putting the museum's collections up for auction mean abetting in the commercialization of the collections?

Themes: museum loans, property rights, commercialization, archaeology and terrorism

35. The Leaking Memorial

The USS Washington was one of the major battleships struck during the attack on Pearl Harbor on December 7, 1941. Today, the ship is an underwater war memorial maintained by the National Park Service; it is also a tomb. Some 800 sailors were trapped in the attack and, because of the damage to the vessel, their bodies were never recovered.

Although a symbol of national valor and a powerful historical artifact, the USS Washington has begun to leak oil into the harbor. Scientists have estimated that a half million gallons of oil are trapped in the hull. Several studies warn that the hull is rapidly deteriorating, and if it breaks apart, which is a distinct possibility, there will be an oil spill in the harbor of catastrophic proportions. Because the hull was so mangled in the attack, a simple extraction of the oil is not possible.

The National Park Service, responsible for the stewardship of the USS Washington, has been receiving numerous calls—primarily from environmentalists that want the ship dismantled and from war veterans who demand the ship's preservation. The NPS decides to hire a preservationist-oriented archaeologist, Dr. Verity Rather, to give them a report that offers ethical guidance on how to approach the problem.

Themes: underwater archaeology, stewardship, memorials, environmental concerns

36. Museums in Nation Building

The country of Kandi is in the midst of a horrifying civil war, brought about in part by the invasion of the United Republic, a large and powerful Western nation. The National Museum of Kandi holds the nation's most treasured archaeological objects, including tens of thousands of objects excavated over the last century throughout the country. When the country was first invaded in 2000, the museum was one of the first buildings looted. While some of these artifacts moved into the international art market, other objects were taken to different areas of the country, where ethnic factions claimed they were safeguarding their heritage for their own people.

The Interim President of Kandi has recently said that to help quell the country's ethnic tensions, the collections of the National Museum of Kandi should be divided and placed into three regional museums. The President argued that this would allow the three main ethnic groups in the country to control their own heritage, while ensuring that all the collections remain in the country. Furthermore, he strongly feels that this gesture will result in an immediate reduction in ethnic violence.

In response, a group of 100 archaeologists—including many from the United Republic—have signed a letter pleading with the President of Kandi to reconsider. They ask that the collection be kept intact because a dispersed collection impedes productive research; moreover, they make a case that the antiquities of Kandi have already been scattered far too widely by the seven-year war. They argue that for the sake of national unity and the well being of humanity's heritage, the government should instead strive to redouble—not reduce—its power over Kandi's cultural heritage. The archaeologists write: "separating the collections will reify and perpetuate ethnic division, whereas a national repository celebrates and enhances national unity." Specific recommendations include using the Army to protect archaeological sites from looters, stiff prison terms for prosecuted looters, the creation of a Secretary of National Heritage (a cabinet-level position), and increasing the National Museum's budget. "It is only the nation that can protect and preserve national heritage," the letter concludes.

Themes: museum goals, records and preservation, archaeology and war

References Cited

Ames, Michael
   1992 *Cannibal Tours and Glass Boxes: The Anthropology of Museums.* University of
      British Columbia Press, Vancouver.

Anderson, David G.
   2000 Archaeologists as Anthropologists: The Question of Training. In *Teaching Archae-
      ology in the Twenty-First Century*, edited by Susan J. Bender and George S. Smith,
      pp. 141–146. Society for American Archaeology, Washington, D.C.

Anderson, Duane
   1996 Reburial: Is it Reasonable? In *Archaeological Ethics*, edited by Karen D. Vitelli, pp.
      200–208. AltaMira Press, Walnut Creek, CA.

Aristotle
   1985 *Nicomachean Ethics.* Translated by Terence Irwin. Hackett Publishing, Indianapo-
      lis.

Arnold, Bettina
   1990 The Past as Propaganda: Totalitarian Archaeology in Nazi Germany. *Antiquity*
      64(244):464–478.

Baker, Alexi S.
   2003 Selling the Past: *United States v. Frederick Schultz. Archaeology* (online features)
      www.archaeology.org/online/features/schultz/. Accessed: 20 March 2007.

Banks, James (editor)
   2004 *Diversity and Citizenship Education: Global Perspectives.* John Wiley and Sons,
      Inc., San Francisco.

Barkan, Elazar, and Ronald Bush (editors)
   2002 *Claiming the Stones/Naming the Bones: Cultural Property and the Negotiation of
      National and Ethnic Identity.* Getty Research Institute, Los Angeles.

Bassett, Carol Ann
   1986 The Culture Thieves. *Science* 86(July/August):23–29.

Bender, Susan J., and George S. Smith (editors)
   2000 *Teaching Archaeology in the Twenty-First Century.* Society for American Archaeol-
      ogy, Washington, D.C.

Bendremer, Jeffrey C., and Kenneth A. Richman
   2006 Human Subjects Review and Archaeology: A View from Indian Country. In *The
      Ethics of Archaeology: Philosophical Perspectives on Archaeological Practice*, edited by
      Chris Scarre and Geoffrey F. Scarre, pp. 97–114. Cambridge University Press,
      Cambridge.

Benjamin, Martin
   2001 Between Subway and Spaceship: Practical Ethics at the Outset of the Twenty-
      First Century. *Hastings Center Report* 31(4):24–31.

Bonnichsen, Robson, Bradley T. Lepper, Dennis Stanford, and Michael R. Waters (editors)
   2005 *Paleoamerican Origins: Beyond Clovis.* Texas A&M University Press, College Sta-
      tion.

Borrego, Anne Marie
   2004 Ethics Bowls Exercise Students' Moral Muscles. *The Chronicle of Higher Educa-
      tion* 50(26):A31.

Breglia, Lisa
  2006 Complicit Agendas: Ethnography of Archaeology as Ethical Research Practice. In
        *Ethnographies of Archaeological Practice: Cultural Encounters, Material Transforma-
        tions*, edited by Matt Edgeworth, pp. 173–184. AltaMira Press, Walnut Creek, CA.
Brainard, Jeffrey
  2006 Universities Experiment with Classes in Scientific Ethics. *The Chronicle of Higher
        Education* 52(12):A2.
Brodie, Neil, Jennifer Doole, and Colin Renfrew (editors)
  2001 *Trade in Illicit Antiquities: The Destruction of the World's Archaeological Heritage.*
        The McDonald Institute, Cambridge.
Brodie, Neil J., and Colin Renfrew
  2005 Looting and the World's Archaeological Heritage: The Inadequate Response.
        Annual Review of Anthropology 34:343–361.
Brugge, Doug, and Mariam Missaghian
  2006 Protecting the Navajo People through Tribal Regulation of Research. *Science and
        Engineering Ethics* 12(3):491–507.
Burke, Heather, and Claire Smith
  2007 *Archaeology to Delight and Instruct: Active Learning in the University Classroom.*
        Left Coast Press, Walnut Creek, CA.
Callahan, Daniel, and Sissela Bok
  1980 *Ethics Teaching in Higher Education.* The Hastings Center Series in Ethics.
        Springer, New York.
Caplan, Patricia
  2003 *The Ethics of Anthropology: Debates and Dilemmas.* Routledge, London.
Carman, John
  2005 *Against Cultural Property: Archaeology, Heritage and Ownership.* Duckworth, Lon-
        don.
Carver, Martin
  1996 On Archaeological Value. *Antiquity* 70(267):45–56.
Cassell, Joan, and Sue-Ellen Jacobs
  1987 *Handbook on Ethical Issues in Anthropology.* American Anthropological Associa-
        tion, Washington, D.C.
Castles, Stephen
  2004 Migration, Citizenship and Education. In *Diversity and Citizenship Education:
        Global Perspectives*, edited by James A. Banks, pp. 17–48. John Wiley and Sons,
        Inc., San Francisco.
Champe, John L., Douglas S. Byers, Clifford Evans, A. K. Guthe, Henry W. Hamilton,
Edward B. Jelks, Clement W. Meighan, Sigfus Olafson, George I. Quimby, Watson
Smith, and Fred Wendorf
  1961 Four Statements for Archaeology. *American Antiquity* 27(2):137–138.
Clark, Geoffrey A.
  1999 NAGPRA, Science, and the Demon-Haunted World. *Skeptical Inquirer*
        23(3):44–48.
Climent, Etienne
  1994 Some Recent Practical Experience in the Implementation of the 1954 Hague
        Convention. *International Journal of Cultural Property* 3(1):11–25.

Coe, Michael D.
  1993   From Huaquero to Connoisseur: The Early Market in Pre-Columbian Art. In *Collecting the Pre-Columbian Past*, edited by Elizabeth H. Boone, pp. 271–90. Dumbarton Oaks Research Library and Collection, Washington, D.C.

Coggins, Clemency
  1969   Illicit Traffic of Pre-Columbian Antiquities. *Art Journal* 29(1):94–98, 114.

Colwell-Chanthaphonh, Chip
  2003   Dismembering / Disremembering the Buddhas: Renderings on the Internet during the Afghan Purge of the Past. *Journal of Social Archaeology* 3(1):75–98.
  2005   The Incorporation of the Native American Past: Cultural Extermination, Archaeological Protection, and the Antiquities Act of 1906. *International Journal of Cultural Property* 12(2):375–391.
  2006   Dreams at the Edge of the World and Other Evocations of O'odham History. *Archaeologies* 2(1):20–44.

Colwell-Chanthaphonh, Chip, and T. J. Ferguson
  2004   Virtue Ethics and the Practice of History: Native Americans and Archaeologists along the San Pedro Valley of Arizona. *Journal of Social Archaeology* 4(1):5–27.

Colwell-Chanthaphonh, Chip, and T. J. Ferguson (editors)
  2008   *Collaboration in Archaeological Practice: Engaging Descendant Communities.* AltaMira Press, Lanham, MD.

Colwell-Chanthaphonh, Chip, and John Piper
  2001   War and Cultural Property: The 1954 Hague Convention and the Status of U.S. Ratification. *International Journal of Cultural Property* 10(2):217–245.

Colley, Sarah
  2004   University-based Archaeology Teaching and Learning and Professionalism in Australia. *World Archaeology* 36(2):189–202.

Conkey, Margaret W.
  2005   Dwelling at the Margins, Action at the Intersection? Feminist and Indigenous Archaeologies, 2005. *Archaeologies* 1(1):9–80.

Conkey, Margaret W., and Joan Gero
  1997   Programme to Practice: Gender and Feminism in Archaeology. *Annual Review of Anthropology* 26: 411–437.

Cooper, David E.
  2004   *Ethics for Professionals in a Multicultural World.* Prentice Hall, NJ.

Council of Graduate Schools
  2006   *Graduate Education for the Responsible Conduct of Research.* CGS Publications, Washington, D.C.

Craib, Donald Forsyth
  2000   *Topics in Cultural Resource Law.* Society for American Archaeology, Washington, D.C.

Cultural Policy Center
  2006   Protecting Cultural Heritage: International Law after the War in Iraq. Cultural Policy Center Conference (University of Chicago, February 3, 2006). Papers online at http://culturalpolicy.uchicago.edu/protectingculturalheritage/papers.shtml. Accessed: 20 March 2007.

Cunningham, Richard B.
   2006   *Archaeology, Relics, and the Law.* 2nd ed. Carolina Academic Press, Durham.
Darvill, Timothy
   1993   *Valuing Britain's Archaeological Resource.* Bournemouth University, Bournemouth.
David, Nick, and Carol Kramer
   2001   *Ethnoarchaeology in Action.* Cambridge University Press, Cambridge.
Davis, Hester A.
   1984   Approaches to Ethical Problems by Archaeological Organizations. In *Ethics and Values in Archaeology*, edited by Ernestene L. Green, pp. 13–21. Free Press, New York.
de Bono, Edward
   1990   *Six Thinking Hats.* Penguin Books, London.
   1993   *Water Logic.* Penguin Books, New York
Deming, N., K. Fryer-Edwards, D. Dudzinski, H. Starks, J. Culver, E. Hopley, L. Robins, and W. Burke
   2007   Incorporating Principles and Practical Wisdom in Research Ethics Education: A Preliminary Study. *Academic Medicine* 82(1):18–23.
Derry, Linda, and Maureen Malloy (editors)
   2003   *Archaeologists and Local Communities: Partners in Exploring the Past.* Society for American Archaeology, Washington, D.C.
Dongoske, Kurt E., Mark Aldenderfer, and Karen Doehner (editors)
   2000   *Working Together: Native Americans and Archaeologists.* Society for American Archaeology, Washington, D.C.
Dowdall, Katherine, and Otis Parrish
   2002   A Meaningful Disturbance of the Earth. *Journal of Social Archaeology* 3(1):99–113.
Drower, Margaret S.
   1995   *Flinders Petrie: A Life in Archaeology.* University of Wisconsin, Madison.
Dunnell, Robert C.
   1984   The Ethics of Archeological Significance Decisions. In *Ethics and Values in Archeology*, edited by Ernestene L. Green, pp. 45–56. Free Press, New York.
Edgeworth, Matt (editor)
   2006   *Ethnographies of Archaeological Practice: Cultural Encounters, Material Transformations.* AltaMira Press, Lanham, MD.
Elia, Ricardo J.
   1993   U.S. Cultural Resource Management and the ICAHM Charter. *Antiquity* (67):426–38.
Fagan, Brian M.
   1975   *The Rape of the Nile: Tomb Robbers, Tourists, and Archaeologists in Egypt.* Scribner's, New York.
   1977   *Elusive Treasure: The Story of Early Archaeologists in the Americas.* Scribner's, New York.
Fawcett, Clare
   1986   Politics of Assimilation in Japanese Archaeology. *Archaeological Review of Cambridge* 5(1):43–57.

Ferguson, T. J.
1990   The Repatriation of Ahayu:da Zuni War Gods: An Interview with the Zuni Tribal Council on April 25, 1990. *Museum Anthropology* 14(2):7–14.
2000   NHPA: Changing the Role of Native Americans in the Archaeological Study of the Past. In *Working Together: Native Americans and Archaeologists*, edited by Kurt E. Dongoske, Mark Aldenderfer and Karen Doehner, pp. 25–36. Society for American Archaeology, Washington, D.C.
2003   Anthropological Archaeology Conducted by Tribes: Traditional Cultural Properties and Cultural Affiliation. In *Archaeology Is Anthropology*, edited by Susan D. Gillespie and Deborah L. Nichols, pp. 137–144. Archaeological Papers of the American Anthropological Association No. 13. American Anthropological Association, Washington, D.C.
Ferguson, T. J., and Chip Colwell-Chanthaphonh
2006   *History Is in the Land: Multivocal Tribal Traditions in Arizona's San Pedro Valley.* University of Arizona Press, Tucson.
Ferrett, Sharon K.
2002   *Peak Performance: Success in College and Beyond.* McGraw-Hill, New York.
FitzGibbon, Kate (editor)
2005   *Who Owns the Past? Cultural Policy, Cultural Property, and the Law.* Rutgers University Press and Council for Cultural Policy, New Brunswick, NJ.
Fluehr-Lobban, Carolyn (editor)
2003   *Ethics and the Profession of Anthropology: Dialogue for Ethically Conscious Practice.* 2nd ed. AltaMira Press, Walnut Creek, CA.
Garen, Micah
2006   The War within the War. In *Archaeological Ethics*, edited by Karen D. Vitelli and Chip Colwell-Chanthaphonh, pp. 91–95. 2nd ed. AltaMira Press, Walnut Creek, CA.
Gero, Joan M.
2000   The Social World of Prehistoric Facts: Gender and Power in Palaeoindian Research. In *Interpretive Archaeology*, edited by Julian Thomas, pp. 304–316. Leicester University Press, London.
Gerstenblith, Patty
1995   Identity and Cultural Property: The Protection of Cultural Property in the United States. *Boston University Law Review* 75:559–688.
2002   United States v. Schultz. *Culture without Context* 10(Spring):27–31.
Gerstenblith, Patty (editor)
1998   Ethical Considerations and Cultural Property. *International Journal of Cultural Property* 7(1).
Goldstein, Lynne, and Keith Kintigh
1990   Ethics and the Reburial Controversy. *American Antiquity* 55(3):585–591.
Green, Lesley F., David R. Green, and Eduardo G. Neves
2003   Indigenous Knowledge and Archaeological Science: The Challenges of Public Archaeology in the Reserva Uaça. *Journal of Social Archaeology* 3(3):366–398
Greenawalt, Kent
1998   Thinking in Terms of Law and Morality. *International Journal of Cultural Property* 7(1):7–20.

Greenfield, Jeanette
   1989   *The Return of Cultural Treasures.* Cambridge University Press, Cambridge.
Groarke, Leo, and Gary Warrick
   2006   Stewardship Gone Astray? Ethics and the SAA. In *The Ethics of Archaeology: Philosophical Perspectives on Archaeological Practice*, edited by Chris Scarre and Geoffrey F. Scarre, pp. 163–177. Cambridge University Press, Cambridge.
Hall, Martin
   2005   Situational Ethics and Engaged Practice: The Case of Archaeology in Africa. In *Embedding Ethics*, edited by Lynn Meskell and Peter Pels, pp. 169–194. Berg, Oxford.
Hamilakis, Yannis
   1999   La Trahison des Archeologues? Archaeological Practice as Intellectual Activity in Postmodernity. *Journal of Mediterranean Archaeology* 12(1):60–79.
   2003   Iraq, Stewardship and the "Record": An Ethical Crisis for Archaeology *Public Archaeology* 3(2):104–111.
   2004   Archaeology and the Politics of Pedagogy. *World Archaeology* 36(2):287–309.
   2005   Whose World and Whose Archaeology? The Colonial Present and the Return of the Political. *Archaeologies* 1(2):94–101.
Harmon, David, Francis P. McManamon, and Dwight T. Pitcaithley (editors)
   2006   *The Antiquities Act: A Century of American Archaeology, Historic Preservation, and Nature Conservation.* University of Arizona Press, Tucson.
Helms, Mary W.
   1993   *Craft and the Kingly Ideal: Art, Trade, Power.* University of Texas Press, Austin.
Hill, Rick
   1988   Mining the Dead. *Daybreak* Summer:10–14.
Hodder, Ian
   1986   *Reading the Past.* Cambridge University Press, Cambridge.
   1997   "Always Momentary, Fluid and Flexible": Towards a Reflexive Excavation Methodology. *Antiquity* 71(273):691–700.
   1998   The Past as Passion and Play: Çatalhöyük as a Site of Conflict in the Construction of Multiple Pasts. In *Archaeology Under Fire: Nationalism, Politics, and Heritage in the Eastern Mediterranean and Middle East*, edited by Lynn Meskell, pp. 124–139. Routledge Press, London.
   2002   Ethics and Archaeology: The Attempt at Çatalhöyük. *Near Eastern Archaeology* 65(3):174–181.
Hollowell, Julie
   2003   Digging in the Dirt: Ethics and "Low-End Looting." In *Ethical Issues in Archaeology*, edited by Larry J. Zimmerman, Karen D. Vitelli and Julie Hollowell-Zimmer, pp. 45–56. AltaMira Press, Walnut Creek, CA.
   2006   St. Lawrence Island's Legal Market in Archaeological Goods. In *Archaeology, Cultural Heritage, and the Antiquities Trade*, edited by Neil Brodie, Morag M. Kersel, Christina Luke, and Kathryn Walker Tubb, pp. 98–132. University Press of Florida, Gainesville.
Hutt, Sherry, Elwood W. Jones, and Martin E. McAllister
   1992   *Archaeological Resource Protection.* Preservation Press, Washington, D.C.

Jameson, John H., Jr. (editor)
1997 *Presenting Archaeology to the Public.* AltaMira Press, Walnut Creek, CA.
Johnson, Richard
1990 The Bones of Their Fathers. *Sunday Denver Post, Contemporary Section* (February 4):12–17, 21.
Jones, James H.
1992 *Bad Blood: The Tuskegee Syphilis Experiment.* Simon & Schuster, New York.
Kant, Immanuel
1963[1785] *Groundwork of the Metaphysic of Morals.* Translated by H. J. Paton. Hutchinson University Library, London.
1994[1797] On the Supposed Right to Lie from Altruistic Reasons. In *Ethics,* edited by Peter Singer, pp. 280. Oxford University Press, Oxford.
Karlsson, Håkan (editor)
2004 *Swedish Archaeologists on Ethics.* Bricoleur Press, Lindome.
Kehoe, Alice B., and Mary Beth Emmerichs (editors)
1999 *Assembling the Past: Studies in the Professionalization of Archaeology.* University of New Mexico Press, Albuquerque.
Kerber, Jordan E. (editor)
2006 *Cross-Cultural Collaboration: Native Peoples and Archaeology in the Northeastern United States.* University of Nebraska Press, Lincoln.
King, Thomas
1983 Professional Responsibility in Public Archaeology. *Annual Review of Anthropology* 12:143–164.
King, Thomas F., and Margaret M. Lyneis
1978 Preservation: A Developing Focus of American Archaeology. *American Anthropologist* 80(4):873–893.
Kleiner, Fred S.
1990 On the Publication of Recent Acquisitions of Antiquities. *American Journal of Archaeology* 94:525–527.
Klesert, Anthony, and Alan Downer (editors)
1990 *Preservation on the Reservation: Native Americans, Native American Lands, and Archaeologists.* Navajo Nation Papers in Anthropology 26, Window Rock.
Klesert, Anthony L. and Shirley Powell
1993 A Perspective on Ethics and the Reburial Controversy. *American Antiquity* 58(2): 348–354.
Klugman, Craig, and Benjamin Stump
2006 The Effect of Ethics Training upon Individual Choice. *Journal of Further and Higher Education* 30(2):181–192.
Kouroupas, Maria Papageorge
1995 United States Efforts to Protect Cultural Property: Implementation of the 1970 UNESCO Convention. In *Antiquities Trade or Betrayed: Legal, Ethical and Conservation Issues,* edited by Kathryn W. Tubb, pp. 83–90. Archetype Publications, London.
Ladd, John (editor)
2002 *Ethical Relativism.* University Press of America, Lanham, MD.

Layton, Robert (editor)

1989 *Conflict in the Archaeology of Living Tradition.* Routledge, London.

1994 *Who Needs the Past? Indigenous Values and Archaeology.* Routledge, London.

Layton, Robert, Peter Stone, and Julian Thomas (editors)

2001 *Destruction and Conservation of Cultural Property.* Routledge, London.

Leask, Nigel

2002 *Curiosity and the Aesthetics of Travel Writing, 1770–1840: "From an Antique Land."* Oxford University Press, Oxford.

LeBlanc, Steven

1979 A Proposal for an Archaeological Conservancy. *Journal of Field Archaeology* 6(3):360–365.

Levy, Janet E.

2006 Preparing for the SAA Ethics Bowl. www.saa.org/aboutSAA/committees/ethics/eBowlPrep.html. Accessed: 20 March 2007.

Lilley, Ian (editor)

2000 *Native Title and the Transformation of Archaeology in the Postcolonial World.* Oceania Monographs 50. University of Sydney, Sydney.

Lipe, William D.

1974 A Conservation Model for American Archaeology. *The Kiva* 39(3–4):213–245.

1984 Value and Meaning in Cultural Resources. In *Approaches to the Archaeological Heritage,* edited by Henry Cleere, pp. 1–11. Cambridge University Press, Cambridge.

Little, Barbara J. (editor)

2002 *Public Benefits of Archaeology.* University Press of Florida, Gainesville.

Lo, Bernard

1993 Skepticism about Teaching Ethics. In *Ethics, Values, and the Promise of Science,* edited by George Bugliarello, pp. 151–153. Sigma Xi, The Scientific Research Society, Research Triangle Park, N.C.

Lynott, Mark J.

1997 Ethical Principles and Archaeological Practice: Development of an Ethics Policy. *American Antiquity* 62(4):589–599.

2003 The Development of Ethics in Archaeology. In *Ethical Issues in Archaeology* edited by Larry J. Zimmerman, Karen D. Vitelli, and Julie Hollowell-Zimmer, pp. 17–27. AltaMira Press, Walnut Creek, CA.

Lynott, Mark J., and Vincas P. Steponaitis

2000 Training Students in Archaeological Ethics. In *Teaching Archaeology in the Twenty-First Century,* edited by Susan J. Bender and George S. Smith, pp. 53–57. Society for American Archaeology, Washington, D.C.

Lynott, Mark J., and Alison Wylie (editors)

1995a *Ethics in American Archaeology: Challenges for the 1990s.* Society for American Archaeology Special Report, Washington, D.C.

Lynott, Mark J., and Alison Wylie

1995b Foreword. In *Ethics in American Archaeology: Challenges for the 1990's,* edited by Mark J. Lynott and Alison Wylie, pp. 7–9. Society for American Archaeology Special Report, Washington, D.C.

McDavid, Carol
   2002 Archaeologies that Hurt; Descendants that Matter: A Pragmatic Approach to Collaboration in the Public Interpretation of African-American Archaeology. *World Archaeology* 34(2):303–314.

McGimsey, Charles R., III
   1972 *Public Archaeology*. Seminar Press, New York.
   1995 Standards, Ethics, and Archaeology: A Brief History. In *Ethics in American Archaeology: Challenges for the 1990s*, edited by Mark J. Lynott and Alison Wylie, pp. 11–13. Society for American Archaeology Special Report, Washington, D.C.

McGimsey, Charles R., III, and Hester A. Davis (editors)
   1977 *The Management of Archeological Resources: The Airlie House Report.* Special Publication of the Society for American Archaeology, Washington, D.C.

McGuire, Randall
   1993 *A Marxist Archaeology.* Academic Press, San Diego.

McLaughlin, Robert H.
   1998 The Antiquities Act of 1906: Politics and the Framing of an American Anthropology and Archaeology. *Oklahoma City University Law Review* 25(1&2):61–91.

McManamon, Frank P.
   1991 The Many Publics for Archaeology. *American Antiquity* 56(1):121–130.

Making Archaeology Teaching Relevant for the Twenty-First Century (M.A.T.R.I.X.)
   2003 The M.A.T.R.I.X. Project. www.indiana.edu/~arch/saa/matrix/homepage.html. Accessed: 21 March 2007.

Marino, Gordon
   2004 Before Teaching Ethics, Stop Kidding Yourself. *Chronicle of Higher Education* 50(24):B5.

Marshall, Eliot
   1989 Smithsonian, Indian Leaders Call a Truce. *Science* 245:1184–1186.

Martin, Mike W.
   2000 *Meaningful Work: Rethinking Professional Ethics.* Oxford University Press, New York.

Matsuda, David
   1998 The Ethics of Archaeology, Subsistence Digging, and Artifact Looting in Latin America: Point, Muted Counterpoint. *International Journal of Cultural Property* 7(1):87–97.

Meighan, Clement W.
   2006 Burying American Archaeology. In *Archaeological Ethics*, edited by Karen D. Vitelli and Chip Colwell-Chanthaphonh, pp. 167–170. 2nd ed. AltaMira Press, Lanham, MD.

Merriman, Nick (editor)
   2004 *Public Archaeology.* Routledge, London.

Meskell, Lynn
   2005 Archaeological Ethnography: Conversations around Kruger National Park. *Archaeologies* 1(1):81–100.

Messenger, Phyllis (editor)
   1999 *The Ethics of Collecting Cultural Property: Whose Culture? Whose Property?* University of New Mexico Press, Albuquerque.

Meyer, David A.
  1993 The 1954 Hague Cultural Property Convention and Its Emergence Into Cus-
        tomary International Law. *Boston University International Law Journal*
        11(2):349–388.
Meyer, Karl
  1973 *The Plundered Past: The Story of the Illegal International Traffic in Works of Art.*
        Atheneum, New York.
Mihesuah, Devon A. (editor)
  2000 *Repatriation Reader: Who Owns American Indian Remains?* University of Nebraska
        Press, Lincoln.
Mill, John Stuart
  1956[1859] *On Liberty.* Liberal Arts Press, New York.
  1987[1863] *Utilitarianism.* Prometheus, Buffalo.
Momeyer, Richard W.
  1995 Teaching Ethics to Student Relativists. *Teaching Philosophy* 18(4):301–311.
Moody-Adams, Michele
  1997 *Fieldwork in Familiar Places: Morality, Culture, and Philosophy.* Harvard Univer-
        sity Press, Cambridge.
Muskavitch, Karen M. T.
  2005 Cases and Goals for Ethics Education. *Science and Engineering Ethics*
        11(3):431–434.
Nicholas, George P.
  2007 Native Americans and Archaeology. *The Encyclopedia of Archaeology*, vol. 3, pp.
        1660–1669. Edited by Deborah M. Pearsall. Elsevier, Oxford.
Nicholas, George P., and Thomas D. Andrews (editors)
  1997 *At a Crossroads: Archaeology and First Peoples in Canada.* Archaeology Press, Burn-
        aby.
O'Keefe, Patrick J.
  1998 Codes of Ethics: Form and Function in Cultural Heritage Management. *Interna-
        tional Journal of Cultural Property* 7(1):32–51.
Parezo, Nancy J.
  2006 Collecting Diné Culture in the 1880s: Two Army Physicians and Their Ethno-
        graphic Approaches. *Museum Anthropology* 29(2):95–117.
Parker, Patricia L., and Thomas F. King
  1998 *Guidelines for Evaluating and Documenting Traditional Cultural Properties.*
        National Register Bulletin 38. U.S. Government Printing Office, Washington,
        D.C.
Parker, Walter C.
  2004 Diversity, Globalization, and Democratic Education: Curriculum Possibilities. In
        Diversity and Citizenship Education: Global Perspectives, edited by James Banks,
        pp. 433–458. John Wiley and Sons, Inc., San Francisco.
Patton, Paul
  2006 Foucault, Critique and Rights. In *Critical Theory Today*, edited by Robert Sinner-
        brink, Jean-Philippe Deranty, Nicholas H. Smith, and Peter Schmiedgen, pp.
        267–287. Brill, Leiden.

Paul, Richard, A.J.A. Binker, Douglas Martin, and Ken Adamson
  1995 *Critical Thinking: High School, A Guide for Redesigning Instruction.* Foundation for Critical Thinking, Santa Rosa, California.
Pavao-Zuckerman, Mitchell A.
  2000 The Conceptual Utility of Models in Human Ecology. *Journal of Ecological Anthropology* 4:31–56.
Pence, Gregory
  2000 *A Dictionary of Common Philosophical Terms.* McGraw-Hill, Boston.
Pendergast, David M.
  1994 Looting the Maya World: The Other Losers. *Public Archaeology Review* 2(2):2–4.
Perry, William
  1970 *Forms of Intellectual and Ethical Development in the College Years: A Scheme.* Holt, Rinehart, and Winston, New York.
Pringle, Heather
  2006 *The Master Plan: Himmler's Scholars and the Holocaust.* Hyperion, New York.
Prott, Lyndel V., and Patrick J. O'Keefe
  1984 *Law and the Cultural Heritage.* 3 vols. Professional Books, Abingdon.
Preucel, Robert (editor)
  1991 *Processual and Post-processual Archaeologies: Multiple Ways of Knowing the Past.* Occasional Paper No. 10. Center for Archaeological Investigations, Carbondale, IL.
Pyburn, K. Anne
  2003 Archaeology for a New Millennium: The Rules of Engagement. In *Archaeologists and Local Communities: Partners in Exploring the Past*, edited by Linda Derry and Maureen Malloy, pp. 167–184. Society for American Archaeology, Washington, D.C.
Pyburn, K. Anne, and Richard R. Wilk
  1995 Responsible Archaeology is Applied Anthropology. In *Ethics in American Archaeology: Challenges for the 1990's*, edited by Mark J. Lynott and Alison Wylie, pp. 71–76. Society for American Archaeology Special Report, Washington, D.C.
Raab, L. Mark, Timothy C. Klinger, Michael B. Schiffer, and Albert C. Goodyear
  1980 Clients, Contracts, and Profits: Conflicts in Public Archaeology. *American Anthropologist* 82(3):539–551.
Rachels, James
  2003 *The Elements of Moral Philosophy.* 4th ed. McGraw-Hill, Boston.
Renfrew, Colin
  2000 *Loot, Legitimacy, and Ownership.* Duckworth, London.
Richman, Jennifer R., and Marion P. Forsyth
  2004 *Legal Perspectives on Cultural Resources.* AltaMira Press, Walnut Creek, CA.
Ritter, David
  2006 Many Bottles for Many Flies: Managing Conflict over Indigenous Peoples' Cultural Heritage in Western Australia. *Public History Review* 13:125–142.
Rose, Jerome C., Thomas J. Green, and Victoria D. Green
  1996 NAGPRA is Forever: Osteology and the Repatriation of Skeletons. *Annual Review of Anthropology* 25:81–103.
Rosenswig, Robert M.
  1997 Ethics in Canadian Archaeology: An International, Comparative Analysis. *Canadian Journal of Archaeology* 21(2):99–114.

Salmon, Merrilee H.
  1997 Ethical Considerations in Anthropology and Archaeology, or Relativism and Justice For All. *Journal of Anthropological Research* 53(1):47–63.
Schmidt, Peter R., and Thomas C. Patterson (editors)
  1995 *Making Alternative Histories: The Practice of Archaeology and History in Non-Western Settings.* School of American Research Press, Santa Fe, NM.
Schrag, Brian (editor)
  2006 *Research Ethics: Cases and Commentaries*, vol. 7. Association for Practical and Professional Ethics, Bloomington, IN.
Shackel, Paul A., and Erve J. Chambers (editors)
  2004 *Places in Mind: Public Archaeology as Applied Anthropology.* Routledge, London.
Smardz, Karolyn, and Shelley Smith (editors)
  2000 *The Archaeology Education Handbook: Sharing the Past with Kids.* AltaMira Press, Walnut Creek, CA.
Smith, Claire, and Heather Burke
  2003 In the Spirit of the Code. In *Ethical Issues in Archaeology*, edited by Larry J. Zimmerman, Karen D. Vitelli, and Julie Hollowell-Zimmer, pp. 177–200. AltaMira Press, Walnut Creek, CA.
Smith, Claire, and H. Martin Wobst (editors)
  2005 *Indigenous Archaeologies: Decolonizing Theory and Practice.* Routledge, London.
Smith, Laurajane
  2004 *Archaeological Theory and the Politics of Cultural Heritage*, Routledge, London.
Society for American Archeology (SAA)
  1990 *Save the Past for the Future: Actions for the 90s.* Final Report, Taos Working Conference on Preventing Archeological Looting and Vandalism (May 7–12, 1989). Report on file, SAA Office of Government Relations, Washington, D.C.
Spector, Janet
  1993 *What This Awl Means: Feminist Archaeology at a Wahpeton Dakota Village.* Minnesota Historical Society Press, St. Paul, MN.
Stone, Peter
  2005 "All Smoke and Mirrors": The World Archaeological Congress, 1987–2004. *Archaeologies* 1(1):101–110.
Swazey, Judith P., and Stephanie J. Bird
  1997 Teaching and Learning Research Ethics. In *Research Ethics: A Reader*, edited by Deni Elliott and Judy E. Stern, pp. 1–19. University Press of New England, Hanover, NH.
Swidler, Nina, Kurt E. Dongoske, Roger Anyon, and Alan S. Downer (editors)
  1997 *Native Americans and Archaeologists: Stepping Stones to Common Ground.* AltaMira Press, Walnut Creek, CA.
Thomas, David Hurst
  2000 *Skull Wars: Kennewick Man, Archaeology, and the Battle for Native American Identity.* Basic Books, New York.
Trigger, Bruce G.
  1984 Alternative Archaeologies: Nationalist, Colonialist, Imperialist. *Man* 19(3):355–370.

1995   Romanticism, Nationalism, and Archaeology. In *Nationalism, Politics, and the Practice of Archaeology*, edited by Philip L. Kohl and Clare Fawcett, pp. 263–279. Cambridge University Press, Cambridge.

Tubb, Kathryn W. (editor)
1995   *Antiquities: Trade or Betrayed.* Archetype Publications, London.

Turner, Ernest
1994   The Souls of My Dead Brothers. In *Conflict in the Archaeology of Living Traditions*, edited by Robert Layton, pp. 189–194. Routledge, London.

Turner, Trudy
2005   *Biological Anthropology and Ethics: From Repatriation to Genetic Identity.* State University of New York Press, Albany.

Ucko, Peter J.
1987   *Academic Freedom and Apartheid: The Story of the World Archaeological Congress.* Duckworth, London.

VanderVeen, James M.
2004   Site Preservation or Self Preservation? The Issue of Stewardship and Control. *The SAA Archaeological Record* 4(1):30–33.

Vitelli, Karen D. (editor)
1996   *Archaeological Ethics.* AltaMira Press, Walnut Creek, CA.

Vitelli, Karen D., and Chip Colwell-Chanthaphonh (editors)
2006   *Archaeological Ethics.* 2nd ed. AltaMira Press, Lanham, MD.

Vitelli, Karen D., and K. Anne Pyburn
1997   Past Imperfect, Future Tense: Archaeology and Development. *Nonrenewable Resources* 6(2):71–84.

Vrdoljak, Ana F.
2006   *International Law, Museums and the Return of Cultural Objects.* Cambridge University Press, Cambridge.

Watkins, Joe
1999   Conflicting Codes: Professional, Ethical, and Legal Obligations in Archaeology. *Science and Engineering Ethics* 5(3):337–345.
2000   *Indigenous Archaeology: American Indian Values and Scientific Practice.* AltaMira Press, Walnut Creek, CA.

Watkins, Joe E., and T. J. Ferguson
2005   Working with and Working for Indigenous Communities. In *Handbook of Archaeological Methods*, vol. II, edited by Herbert Mashner and Christopher Chippindale, pp. 1372–1406. AltaMira Press, Lanham, MD.

Welch, John R., Mark Altaha, Doreen Gatewood, Karl A. Hoerig, and Ramon Riley
2006   Archaeology, Stewardship, and Sovereignty. *The SAA Archaeological Record* 6(4):17–20, 57.

Wildesen, Leslie E.
1984   The Search for an Ethic in Archeology: An Historical Perspective. In *Ethics and Values in Archeology*, edited by Ernestene L. Green, pp. 3–12. Free Press, New York.

Wilcox, Michael
2000   Dialogue or Diatribe? Indians and Archaeologists in the Post-NAGPRA Era. In *Spirit Wars: Native North American Religions in the Age of Nation Building*, edited by Ronald Niezen, pp. 190–193. University of California Press, Berkeley.

Winter, Joseph C.
1984   The Way to Somewhere: Ethics in American Archaeology. In *Ethics and Values in Archaeology*, edited by Ernestene L. Green, pp. 36–47. Free Press, New York.

Wood, John J., and Shirley Powell
1993   An Ethos for Archaeological Practice. *Human Organization* 52(4):405–413.

Wylie, Alison
1995   Archaeology and the Antiquities Market: The Use of 'Looted' Data. In *Ethics in American Archaeology: Challenges for the 1990s*, edited by Mark J. Lynott and Alison Wylie, pp. 17–21. Society for American Archaeology Special Report, Washington, D.C.

1996   Ethical Dilemmas in Archaeological Practice: Looting, Repatriation, Stewardship, and the (Trans)formation of Disciplinary Identity. *Perspectives on Science* 4(2):154–194.

1997   Contextualizing Ethics: Comments on Ethics in Canadian Archaeology by Robert Rosenswig. *Canadian Journal of Archaeology* 21(2):115–120.

1999   Science, Conservation, and Stewardship: Evolving Codes of Conduct in Archeology. *Science and Engineering Ethics* 5(3):319–336.

2003   On Ethics. In *Ethical Issues in Archaeology*, edited by Larry J. Zimmerman, Karen D. Vitelli, and Julie Hollowell-Zimmer, pp. 3–16. AltaMira Press, Walnut Creek, CA.

2005   The Promises and Perils of Stewardship. In *Embedding Ethics: Shifting Boundaries of the Anthropological Profession*, edited by Lynn Meskell and Peter Pels, pp. 47–68. Berg Press, Oxford.

Zimmerman, Larry J.
1995   Regaining Our Nerve: Ethics, Values, and the Transformation of Archaeology. In *Ethics in American Archaeology: Challenges for the 1990s*, edited by Mark J. Lynott and Alison Wylie, pp. 64–67. Society for American Archaeology Special Report, Washington, D.C.

1998   When Data Become People: Archaeological Ethics, Reburial, and the Past as Public Heritage. *International Journal of Cultural Property* 7(1):69–86.

2006   Sharing Control of the Past. In *Archaeological Ethics*, edited by Karen D. Vitelli and Chip Colwell-Chanthaphonh, pp. 170–175. 2nd ed. AltaMira Press, Lanham, MD.

Zimmerman, Larry J., and Leonard Bruguier
1994   Indigenous Peoples and the World Archaeological Congress Code of Ethics. *Public Archaeology Review* 2(1):5–8.

Zimmerman, Larry J., Karen D. Vitelli, and Julie Hollowell-Zimmer (editors)
2003   *Ethical Issues in Archaeology*. AltaMira Press, Walnut Creek, CA.

Appendix 1
Ethics Bowl Competition Guidelines[1]

Ethics Bowl Rules and Procedures

1. In an Ethics Bowl match, each 3 to 5 member team—representing no more than two universities—will be questioned by a moderator on a case. Although the cases are made available ahead of time, none of the participants will know in advance which of the cases they will be asked to address in the Ethics Bowl competition, nor will they know the questions. Books and notes will not be allowed. However, blank scrap paper to jot down thoughts is permitted.

2. At the beginning of each match, the moderator will flip a coin. The winner of the coin toss will choose to go first or second.

3. The moderator will read aloud the case and a question about the case.

4. The team will have one (1) minute to confer, after which one spokesperson for the team may use up to five (5) minutes to respond to the moderator's question.

5. The opposing team receives one (1) minute to confer, after which it may choose to present a response to the other team's answer which may include a question to the other team. The opposing team's response/question may not exceed five (5) minutes.

6. The first team will have one (1) minute to confer, after which it may have up to two (2) minutes to respond to the opposing team's statement or question.

7. The judges have one (1) minute to confer. Each judge asks one question, with the option of one brief immediate follow-up question. The entire period for the judges' questions should not exceed sixteen (16) minutes.

---

1. These rules and procedures can be accessed from a drop-down menu on the Ethics Bowl page of the SAA website, along with former sets of case studies, some tips for preparing for the competition, and many other ethics resources. See http://www.saa.org/aboutSAA/committees/ethics/ebowl.html.

8. The first team has one (1) minute to confer after each question and two (2) minutes to respond to each question. Different team members may respond to the questions of different judges. However, only one team member may respond to a judge's question.

9. When the first team is done answering the judges' questions, the opposing team will have one (1) minute to confer, and then have two (2) minutes to make a closing statement or rebuttal.

10. Scoring. Each team will be evaluated on the basis of four (4) criteria:

　　i. **Intelligibility**—Has the team stated and defended its position in a way that is logically consistent? Has the team expressed its responses with enough clarity and precision so that the judges can understand them?

　　ii. **Depth**—To what extent does the team's statement and defense of its position indicate an awareness and understanding of the issues that the judge views as ethically central to the case.

　　iii. **Focus**—To what extent does the team's statement and defense of its position avoid issues that are ethically irrelevant to the case?

　　iv. **Judgment**—To what extent, in the judge's view, has the team made a careful and reasonable comparative assessment of considerations it identifies as ethically relevant to the case.

11. Each of the four criteria will be rated on a scale from one to five, five being the highest score, one being the lowest. When the scores for the four criteria are tallied, a team may receive as many as twenty (20) points per judge or as few as four (4). A perfect score for a panel of three judges would be sixty (60) points. Each judge will give the opposing team an overall score of one to five—five (5) being the highest score—based on the same criteria.

12. Teams switch roles, and steps 3—9 are repeated with a different case.

13. The winner is announced (although the scores are not). The team with the most points wins the match, and continues on to the next round of competition until it either wins the tournament or is defeated. Judges are invited to make any final comments to the participating teams.

Ethics Bowl Guidelines

Ethics Bowl Judges' Guidelines in Considering Outside Research of Ethics Bowl Teams (taken in part from a handout developed for the 9th Intercollegiate Ethics Bowl of the Association of Professional and Practical Ethics)

1. When a team makes use of factual information based on outside research, the judges should pay special attention to whether the team has presented a clear, well-focused (i.e., not too narrow and not overly broad), and deliberately thoughtful analysis to explain why the team considers the independent factual information it presents in a case as ethically relevant.

2. When a team makes use of factual information based on outside research, the judge should pay special attention to whether the team has identified its

sources, and presented reasonable grounds for considering the information worthy of being given significant weight.

3. If a team bases its response to a question on independently obtained information that conflicts with information presented in a case then:

i. The judge should consider the team as required to present clear and convincing reasons (beyond a mere preponderance of the evidence) for its reliance upon the conflicting information, and

ii. The judge should not, in any case, penalize a team for relying on information provided in the case.

4. If a team makes use of factual information not provided in a case, the volume of such information that the team acquired through research, as reflected in its presentation, should not be considered, in itself, as a factor in favor of the team's presentation.

5. Teams and all event participants should be sensitive to the diversity of opinions and concerns of the SAA and the many constituencies it represents. Teams will be identified by the formal name of their institution, and should be encouraged to conduct themselves as representatives of their school, college or university.

Judge's Score Sheet

Criteria:

   i. **Intelligibility**—Has the team stated and defended its position in a way that is logically consistent? Has the team expressed its responses with enough clarity and precision that the judges can understand it?

   ii. **Depth**—To what extent does the team's statement and defense of its position indicate an awareness and understanding of the issues that the judge views as ethically central to the case?

   iii. **Focus**—To what extent does the team's statement and defense of its position avoid issues that are ethically irrelevant to the case?

   iv. **Judgment**—To what extent, in the judge's view, has the team made a careful and reasonable comparative assessment of considerations it identifies as ethically relevant to the case?

First Team: Rate 0–5 in each category:
(5 = high)

I. Intelligibility	
II. Depth	
III. Focus	
IV. Judgment	
TOTAL (add I–IV)	

Opposing Team's Response: Rate 0–5
(One composite score)

Appendix 2
Codes and Principles of Ethics

C odes of archaeological ethics differ significantly from one organization to the next depending on the primary interests and objectives of the group and the social and political contexts in which they are written. A similar situation could have a very different outcome depending on which code is followed, as Claire Smith and Heather Burke (2003) clearly illustrate in their comparison of the treatments of Kennewick Man and Lake Mungo Lady.

Alison Wylie (1997:117) has identified three categories describing the different kinds of ethics documents developed by archaeological associations. The first includes standards and codes of conduct formulated by organizations such as the Register of Professional Archaeologists (RPA) in the United States (previously the Society of Professional Archaeologists or SOPA), the Institute of Field Archaeology (IFA) of the United Kingdom, and the Australia's Association of Consulting Archaeologists (AACAI). These organizations all have grievance procedures as mechanisms of enforcing their professional codes. The second category is comprised of codes or statements adopted by national and international societies that lay out the special responsibilities of archaeologists to Indigenous peoples. The Archaeological Associations of Canada, Australia, and New Zealand all have statements to this effect, as well as the World Archaeological Congress (WAC). The third kind of ethics documents are general statements of goals, principles, and responsibilities such as the SAA Principles, the Code of Ethics of the Archaeological Institute of America (AIA), or the Society for Historical Archaeology (SHA).

As Wylie points out, some organizations have codes in more than one category. The Canadian Archaeological Association has a set of general ethical goals in addition to its Statement of Principles for Ethical Conduct Pertaining to Aboriginal Peoples (CAA 1997). The AIA, with its mixed membership of professional archaeologists and interested individuals, has both a Code of Ethics, strongly focused on the global antiquities trade, and a Code of Professional Standards that applies only to its professional members and is backed up by a detailed grievance procedure.[1] The real question that Wylie and others have raised is why the SAA has yet to develop a statement, similar to the CAA or WAC, on the special responsibilities archaeologists have to Indigenous populations (see also Rosenswig 1997). Perhaps this will happen yet, since as of 2007 the SAA's Committee on Native American Relations has drafted several proposed amendments to the Principles on this very topic for consideration by the Committee on Ethics.

Many subdisciplines and specialized roles within archaeology now have their own associations and ethics codes, from museums and conservationists to underwater archaeologists and rock art researchers. The quasi-legal role of international charters and associations such as the International Council of Archaeological Heritage Management (ICAHM), the International Council on Monuments and Sites (ICOMOS), and the Burra Charter (adopted in 1999 by Australia ICOMOS to create a standard of practice for those working in places of cultural significance) is less clear and seems to depend on how or whether other institutions and organizations recognize them. The SAA has turned to the Code of Ethics of the International Council on Museums for guidance in forming its own statements on museum-related issues before.

In the U.S., archaeology is traditionally one of four fields of anthropology. Does this mean that the American Anthropological Association's (AAA) Code of Ethics should apply to archaeologists who are members of the AAA? The AAA framed its Principles of Social Responsibility in 1971, declaring that a researcher's primary responsibility is to the people being studied. In 1998, these principles were incorporated into a Code of Ethics that expanded on this primary responsibility, clearly stating that obligations to those studied could in some situations supersede other research goals or responsibilities. Another question that has recently entered discussions on ethics is whether archaeologists should consider themselves exempt from Human Subjects Review, since their work obviously affects living peoples (Bendremer and Richman 2006). These are just a few of the many questions you must have in mind when using codes, principles, and charters in solving ethical dilemmas.

Founded in 1879, the Archaeological Institute of America (AIA) has established several institutes for archaeological research around the world and has provided assistance to scholarly excavations since the 1880s.

Codes, Principles, Statements, and Accords

American Anthropological Association (AAA)

Reprinted by permission of the American Anthropological Association
http://aaanet.org/committees/ethics/ethcode.htm
Code of Ethics
Last amended 1998

I. Preamble

Anthropological researchers, teachers and practitioners are members of many different communities, each with its own moral rules or codes of ethics. Anthropologists have moral obligations as members of other groups, such as the family, religion, and community, as well as the profession. They also have obligations to the scholarly discipline, to the wider society and culture, and to the human species, other species, and the environment. Furthermore, fieldworkers may develop close relationships with persons or animals with whom they work, generating an additional level of ethical considerations

In a field of such complex involvements and obligations, it is inevitable that misunderstandings, conflicts, and the need to make choices among apparently incompatible values will arise. Anthropologists are responsible for grappling with such difficulties and struggling to resolve them in ways compatible with the principles stated here. The purpose of this Code is to foster discussion and education. The American Anthropological Association (AAA) does not adjudicate claims for unethical behavior.

The principles and guidelines in this Code provide the anthropologist with tools to engage in developing and maintaining an ethical framework for all anthropological work.

II. Introduction

Anthropology is a multidisciplinary field of science and scholarship, which includes the study of all aspects of humankind—archaeological, biological, linguistic, and sociocultural. Anthropology has roots in the natural and social sciences and in the humanities, ranging in approach from basic to applied research and to scholarly interpretation.

As the principal organization representing the breadth of anthropology, the American Anthropological Association (AAA) starts from the position that generating and appropriately utilizing knowledge (i.e., publishing, teaching, developing programs, and informing policy) of the peoples of the world, past and present, is a worthy goal; that the generation of anthropological knowledge is a dynamic process using many different and ever-evolving approaches; and that for moral and practical reasons, the generation and utilization of knowledge should be achieved in an ethical manner.

The mission of American Anthropological Association is to advance all aspects of anthropological research and to foster dissemination of anthropological knowledge through publications, teaching, public education, and application. An important part of that mission is to help educate AAA members about ethical obligations and challenges involved in the generation, dissemination, and utilization of anthropological knowledge.

The purpose of this Code is to provide AAA members and other interested persons with guidelines for making ethical choices in the conduct of their anthropological work. Because anthropologists can find themselves in complex situations and subject to more than one code of ethics, the AAA Code of Ethics provides a framework, not an ironclad formula, for making decisions.

Persons using the Code as a guideline for making ethical choices or for teaching are encouraged to seek out illustrative examples and appropriate case studies to enrich their knowledge base.

Anthropologists have a duty to be informed about ethical codes relating to their work, and ought periodically to receive training on current research activities and ethical issues. In addition, departments offering anthropology degrees should include and require ethical training in their curriculums.

No code or set of guidelines can anticipate unique circumstances or direct actions in specific situations. The individual anthropologist must be willing to make carefully considered ethical choices and be prepared to make clear the assumptions, facts and issues on which those choices are based. These guidelines therefore address *general* contexts, priorities and relationships which should be considered in ethical decision making in anthropological work.

III. Research

In both proposing and carrying out research, anthropological researchers must be open about the purpose(s), potential impacts, and source(s) of support for research projects with funders, colleagues, persons studied or providing information, and with relevant parties affected by the research. Researchers must expect to utilize the results of their work in an appropriate fashion and disseminate the results through appropriate and timely activities. Research fulfilling these expectations is ethical, regardless of the source of funding (public or private) or purpose (i.e., "applied," "basic," "pure," or "proprietary").

Anthropological researchers should be alert to the danger of compromising anthropological ethics as a condition to engage in research, yet also be alert to proper demands of good citizenship or host-guest relations. Active contribution and leadership in seeking to shape public or private sector actions and policies may be as ethically justifiable as inaction, detachment, or noncooperation, depending on circumstances. Similar principles hold for anthropological researchers employed or otherwise affiliated with nonanthropological institutions, public institutions, or private enterprises.

A. Responsibility to people and animals with whom anthropological researchers work and whose lives and cultures they study.

1. Anthropological researchers have primary ethical obligations to the people, species, and materials they study and to the people with whom they work. These obligations can supersede the goal of seeking new knowledge, and can lead to decisions not to undertake or to discontinue a research project when the primary obligation conflicts with other responsibilities, such as those owed to sponsors or clients. These ethical obligations include:

• To avoid harm or wrong, understanding that the development of knowledge can lead to change which may be positive or negative for the people or animals worked with or studied

• To respect the well-being of humans and nonhuman primates

• To work for the long-term conservation of the archaeological, fossil, and historical records

• To consult actively with the affected individuals or group(s), with the goal of establishing a working relationship that can be beneficial to all parties involved

2. Anthropological researchers must do everything in their power to ensure that their research does not harm the safety, dignity, or privacy of the people with whom they work, conduct research, or perform other professional activities. Anthropological researchers working with animals must do everything in their power to ensure that the research does not harm the safety, psychological well-being or survival of the animals or species with which they work.

3. Anthropological researchers must determine in advance whether their hosts/providers of information wish to remain anonymous or receive recognition, and make every effort to comply with those wishes. Researchers must present to their research participants the possible impacts of the choices, and make clear that despite their best efforts, anonymity may be compromised or recognition fail to materialize.

4. Anthropological researchers should obtain in advance the informed consent of persons being studied, providing information, owning or controlling access to material being studied, or otherwise identified as having interests which might be impacted by the research. It is understood that the degree and breadth of informed consent required will depend on the nature of the project and may be affected by requirements of other codes, laws, and ethics of the country or community in which the research is pursued. Further, it is understood that the informed consent process is dynamic and continuous; the process should be initiated in the project design and continue through implementation by way of dialogue and negotiation with those studied. Researchers are responsible for identifying and complying with the various informed consent codes, laws and regulations affecting their projects. Informed consent, for the purposes of this code, does not necessarily imply or require a particular written or signed form. It is the quality of the consent, not the format, that is relevant.

5. Anthropological researchers who have developed close and enduring relationships (i.e., covenantal relationships) with either individual persons providing information or with hosts must adhere to the obligations of openness and informed consent, while carefully and respectfully negotiating the limits of the relationship.

6. While anthropologists may gain personally from their work, they must not exploit individuals, groups, animals, or cultural or biological materials. They should recognize their debt to the societies in which they work and their obligation to reciprocate with people studied in appropriate ways.

B. Responsibility to scholarship and science

1. Anthropological researchers must expect to encounter ethical dilemmas at every stage of their work, and must make good-faith efforts to identify potential ethical claims and conflicts in advance when preparing proposals and as projects proceed. A section raising and responding to potential ethical issues should be part of every research proposal.

2. Anthropological researchers bear responsibility for the integrity and reputation of their discipline, of scholarship, and of science. Thus, anthropological researchers are subject to the general moral rules of scientific and scholarly conduct: they should not deceive or knowingly misrepresent (i.e., fabricate evidence, falsify, plagiarize), or attempt to prevent reporting of misconduct, or obstruct the scientific/scholarly research of others.

3. Anthropological researchers should do all they can to preserve opportunities for future fieldworkers to follow them to the field.

4. Anthropological researchers should utilize the results of their work in an appropriate fashion, and whenever possible disseminate their findings to the scientific and scholarly community.

5. Anthropological researchers should seriously consider all reasonable requests for access to their data and other research materials for purposes of research. They should also make every effort to insure preservation of their fieldwork data for use by posterity.

C. Responsibility to the public

1. Anthropological researchers should make the results of their research appropriately available to sponsors, students, decision makers, and other nonanthropologists. In so doing, they must be truthful; they are not only responsible for the factual content of their statements but also must consider carefully the social and political implications of the information they disseminate. They must do everything in their power to insure that such information is well understood, properly contextualized, and responsibly utilized. They should make clear the empirical bases upon which their reports stand, be candid about their qualifications and philosophical or political biases, and recognize and make clear the lim-

its of anthropological expertise. At the same time, they must be alert to possible harm their information may cause people with whom they work or colleagues.

2. Anthropologists may choose to move beyond disseminating research results to a position of advocacy. This is an individual decision, but not an ethical responsibility.

IV. Teaching
Responsibility to students and trainees
While adhering to ethical and legal codes governing relations between teachers/mentors and students/trainees at their educational institutions or as members of wider organizations, anthropological teachers should be particularly sensitive to the ways such codes apply in their discipline (for example, when teaching involves close contact with students/trainees in field situations). Among the widely recognized precepts which anthropological teachers, like other teachers/mentors, should follow are:

1. Teachers/mentors should conduct their programs in ways that preclude discrimination on the basis of sex, marital status, "race," social class, political convictions, disability, religion, ethnic background, national origin, sexual orientation, age, or other criteria irrelevant to academic performance.

2. Teachers'/mentors' duties include continually striving to improve their teaching/training techniques; being available and responsive to student/trainee interests; counseling students/ trainees realistically regarding career opportunities; conscientiously supervising, encouraging, and supporting students'/trainees' studies; being fair, prompt, and reliable in communicating evaluations; assisting students/trainees in securing research support; and helping students/trainees when they seek professional placement.

3. Teachers/mentors should impress upon students/trainees the ethical challenges involved in every phase of anthropological work; encourage them to reflect upon this and other codes; encourage dialogue with colleagues on ethical issues; and discourage participation in ethically questionable projects.

4. Teachers/mentors should publicly acknowledge student/trainee assistance in research and preparation of their work; give appropriate credit for coauthorship to students/trainees; encourage publication of worthy student/trainee papers; and compensate students/trainees justly for their participation in all professional activities.

5. Teachers/mentors should beware of the exploitation and serious conflicts of interest which may result if they engage in sexual relations with students/trainees. They must avoid sexual liaisons with students/trainees for whose education and professional training they are in any way responsible.

V. Application

1. The same ethical guidelines apply to all anthropological work. That is, in both proposing and carrying out research, anthropologists must be open with funders, colleagues, persons studied or providing information, and relevant parties affected by the work about the purpose(s), potential impacts, and source(s) of support for the work. Applied anthropologists must intend and expect to utilize the results of their work appropriately (i.e., publication, teaching, program and policy development) within a reasonable time. In situations in which anthropological knowledge is applied, anthropologists bear the same responsibility to be open and candid about their skills and intentions, and monitor the effects of their work on all persons affected. Anthropologists may be involved in many types of work, frequently affecting individuals and groups with diverse and sometimes conflicting interests. The individual anthropologist must make carefully considered ethical choices and be prepared to make clear the assumptions, facts and issues on which those choices are based.

2. In all dealings with employers, persons hired to pursue anthropological research or apply anthropological knowledge should be honest about their qualifications, capabilities, and aims. Prior to making any professional commitments, they must review the purposes of prospective employers, taking into consideration the employer's past activities and future goals. In working for governmental agencies or private businesses, they should be especially careful not to promise or imply acceptance of conditions contrary to professional ethics or competing commitments.

3. Applied anthropologists, as any anthropologist, should be alert to the danger of compromising anthropological ethics as a condition for engaging in research or practice. They should also be alert to proper demands of hospitality, good citizenship and guest status. Proactive contribution and leadership in shaping public or private sector actions and policies may be as ethically justifiable as inaction, detachment, or noncooperation, depending on circumstances.

VI. Epilogue

Anthropological research, teaching, and application, like any human actions, pose choices for which anthropologists individually and collectively bear ethical responsibility. Since anthropologists are members of a variety of groups and subject to a variety of ethical codes, choices must sometimes be made not only between the varied obligations presented in this code but also between those of this code and those incurred in other statuses or roles. This statement does not dictate choice or propose sanctions. Rather, it is designed to promote discussion and provide general guidelines for ethically responsible decisions.

American Association of Museums (AAM)

Reprinted by permission of the American Association of Museums
Code of Ethics
Adopted 1993

Introduction

Ethical codes evolve in response to changing conditions, values, and ideas. A professional code of ethics must, therefore, be periodically updated. It must also rest upon widely shared values. Although the operating environment of museums grows more complex each year, the root value for museums, the tie that connects all of us together despite our diversity, is the commitment to serving people, both present and future generations. This value guided the creation of and remains the most fundamental principle in the following *Code of Ethics for Museums*.

Code of Ethics for Museums

Museums make their unique contribution to the public by collecting, preserving, and interpreting the things of this world. Historically, they have owned and used natural objects, living and nonliving, and all manner of human artifacts to advance knowledge and nourish the human spirit. Today, the range of their special interests reflects the scope of human vision. Their missions include collecting and preserving, as well as exhibiting and educating with materials not only owned but also borrowed and fabricated for these ends. Their numbers include both governmental and private museums of anthropology, art history and natural history, aquariums, arboreta, art centers, botanical gardens, children's museums, historic sites, nature centers, planetariums, science and technology centers, and zoos. The museum universe in the United States includes both collecting and noncollecting institutions. Although diverse in their missions, they have in common their nonprofit form of organization and a commitment of service to the public. Their collections and/or the objects they borrow or fabricate are the basis for research, exhibits, and programs that invite public participation.

Taken as a whole, museum collections and exhibition materials represent the world's natural and cultural common wealth. As stewards of that wealth, museums are compelled to advance an understanding of all natural forms and of the human experience. It is incumbent on museums to be resources for humankind and in all their activities to foster an informed appreciation of the rich and diverse world we have inherited. It is also incumbent upon them to preserve that inheritance for posterity.

Museums in the United States are grounded in the tradition of public service. They are organized as public trusts, holding their collections and information as a benefit for those they were established to serve. Members of their governing authority, employees, and volunteers are committed to the interests of these beneficiaries. The law provides the basic framework for museum operations. As non-profit institutions, museums comply with applicable local, state, and federal laws and international conventions, as well as with the specific legal standards governing trust responsibilities. This *Code of Ethics for Museums* takes that compliance as given. But legal standards are a minimum. Museums and those responsible for them must do more than avoid legal liability, they must take affirmative steps to maintain their integrity so as to warrant public confidence. They must act not only legally but also ethically. This *Code of Ethics for Museums*, therefore, outlines ethical standards that frequently exceed legal minimums.

Loyalty to the mission of the museum and to the public it serves is the essence of museum work, whether volunteer or paid. Where conflicts of interest arise—actual, potential, or perceived—the duty of loyalty must never be compromised. No individual may use his or her position in a museum for personal gain or to benefit another at the expense of the museum, its mission, its reputation, and the society it serves.

For museums, public service is paramount. To affirm that ethic and to elaborate its application to their governance, collections, and programs, the American Association of Museums promulgates this *Code of Ethics for Museums*. In subscribing to this code, museums assume responsibility for the actions of members of their governing authority, employees, and volunteers in the performance of museum-related duties. Museums, thereby, affirm their chartered purpose, ensure the prudent application of their resources, enhance their effectiveness, and maintain public confidence. This collective endeavor strengthens museum work and the contributions of museums to society—present and future.

Governance

Museum governance in its various forms is a public trust responsible for the institution's service to society. The governing authority protects and enhances the museum's collections and programs and its physical, human, and financial resources. It ensures that all these resources support the museum's mission, respond to the pluralism of society, and respect the diversity of the natural and cultural common wealth.

Thus, the governing authority ensures that:
- all those who work for or on behalf of a museum understand and support its mission and public trust responsibilities
- its members understand and fulfill their trusteeship and act corporately, not as individuals
- the museum's collections and programs and its physical, human, and financial resources are protected, maintained, and developed in support of the museum's mission
- it is responsive to and represents the interests of society

- it maintains the relationship with staff in which shared roles are recognized and separate responsibilities respected
- working relationships among trustees, employees, and volunteers are based on equity and mutual respect
- professional standards and practices inform and guide museum operations
- policies are articulated and prudent oversight is practiced
- governance promotes the public good rather than individual financial gain.

Collections

The distinctive character of museum ethics derives from the ownership, care, and use of objects, specimens, and living collections representing the world's natural and cultural common wealth. This stewardship of collections entails the highest public trust and carries with it the presumption of rightful ownership, permanence, care, documentation, accessibility, and responsible disposal.

Thus, the museum ensures that:

- collections in its custody support its mission and public trust responsibilities
- collections in its custody are lawfully held, protected, secure, unencumbered, cared for, and preserved
- collections in its custody are accounted for and documented
- access to the collections and related information is permitted and regulated
- acquisition, disposal, and loan activities are conducted in a manner that respects the protection and preservation of natural and cultural resources and discourages illicit trade in such materials
- acquisition, disposal, and loan activities conform to its mission and public trust responsibilities
- disposal of collections through sale, trade, or research activities is solely for the advancement of the museum's mission. Proceeds from the sale of nonliving collections are to be used consistent with the established standards of the museum's discipline, but in no event shall they be used for anything other than acquisition or direct care of collections
- the unique and special nature of human remains and funerary and sacred objects is recognized as the basis of all decisions concerning such collections
- collections-related activities promote the public good rather than individual financial gain
- competing claims of ownership that may be asserted in connection with objects in its custody should be handled openly, seriously, responsively and with respect for the dignity of all parties involved.

Programs

Museums serve society by advancing an understanding and appreciation of the natural and cultural common wealth through exhibitions, research, scholarship, publications, and educational activities. These programs further the museum's mission and are responsive to the concerns, interests, and needs of society.

Thus, the museum ensures that:

- programs support its mission and public trust responsibilities
- programs are founded on scholarship and marked by intellectual integrity
- programs are accessible and encourage participation of the widest possible audience consistent with its mission and resources
- programs respect pluralistic values, traditions, and concerns
- revenue-producing activities and activities that involve relationships with external entities are compatible with the museum's mission and support its public trust responsibilities
- programs promote the public good rather than individual financial gain.

Promulgation

This *Code of Ethics for Museums* was adopted by the Board of Directors of the American Association of Museums on November 12, 1993. The AAM Board of Directors recommends that each nonprofit museum member of the American Association of Museums adopt and promulgate its separate code of ethics, applying the *Code of Ethics for Museums* to its own institutional setting.

A Committee on Ethics, nominated by the president of the AAM and confirmed by the Board of Directors, will be charged with two responsibilities:

- establishing programs of information, education, and assistance to guide museums in developing their own codes of ethics
- reviewing the *Code of Ethics for Museums* and periodically recommending refinements and revisions to the Board of Directors.

Afterword

In 1987 the Council of the American Association of Museums determined to revise the association's 1978 statement on ethics. The impetus for revision was recognition throughout the American museum community that the statement needed to be refined and strengthened in light of the expanded role of museums in society and a heightened awareness that the collection, preservation, and interpretation of natural and cultural heritages involve issues of significant concern to the American people.

Following a series of group discussions and commentary by members of the AAM Council, the Accreditation Commission, and museum leaders throughout the country, the president of AAM appointed an Ethics Task Force to prepare a code of ethics. In its work, the Ethics Task Force was committed to codifying the common understanding of ethics in the museum profession and to establishing a framework within which each institution could develop its own code. For guidance, the task force looked to the tradition of museum ethics and drew inspiration from AAM's first code of ethics, published in 1925 as Code of Ethics for Museum Workers, which states in its preface:

Museums, in the broadest sense, are institutions which hold their possessions in trust for mankind and for the future welfare of the [human] race. Their value is in direct proportion to the service they render the emotional and intellectual life of the people. The life of a museum worker is essentially one of service.

This commitment to service derived from nineteenth-century notions of the advancement and dissemination of knowledge that informed the founding documents of America's museums. George Brown Goode, a noted zoologist and first head of the United States National Museum, declared in 1889:

The museums of the future in this democratic land should be adapted to the needs of the mechanic, the factory operator, the day laborer, the salesman, and the clerk, as much as to those of the professional man and the man of leisure. . . . In short, the public museum is, first of all, for the benefit of the public.

John Cotton Dana, an early twentieth-century museum leader and director of the Newark Museum, promoted the concept of museum work as public service in essays with titles such as "Increasing the Usefulness of Museums" and "A Museum of Service." Dana believed that museums did not exist solely to gather and preserve collections. For him, they were important centers of enlightenment.

By the 1940s, Theodore Low, a strong proponent of museum education, detected a new concentration in the museum profession on scholarship and methodology. These concerns are reflected in Museum Ethics, published by AAM in 1978, which elaborated on relationships among staff, management, and governing authority.

During the 1980s, Americans grew increasingly sensitive to the nation's cultural pluralism, concerned about the global environment, and vigilant regarding the public institutions. Rapid technological change, new public policies relating to nonprofit corporations, a troubled educational system, shifting patterns of private and public wealth, and increased financial pressures all called for a sharper delineation of museums' ethical responsibilities. In 1984 AAM's Commission on Museums for a New Century placed renewed emphasis on public service and education, and in 1986 the code of ethics adopted by the International Council of Museums (ICOM) put service to society at the center of museum responsibilities. ICOM defines museums as institutions "in the service of society and of its development" and holds that "employment by a museum, whether publicly or privately supported, is a public trust involving great responsibility."

Building upon this history, the Ethics Task Force produced several drafts of a Code of Ethics for Museums. These drafts were shared with the AAM Executive Committee and Board of Directors, and twice referred to the field for comment. Hundreds of individuals and representatives of professional organizations and museums of all types and sizes submitted thoughtful critiques. These critiques were instrumental in shaping the document submitted to the AAM Board of

Directors, which adopted the code on May 18, 1991. However, despite the review process, when the adopted code was circulated, it soon became clear that the diversity of the museum field prevented immediate consensus on every point.

Therefore, at its November 1991 meeting, the AAM Board of Directors voted to postpone implementation of the Code of Ethics for at least one year. At the same meeting an Ethics Commission nominated by the AAM president was confirmed. The newly appointed commission—in addition to its other charges of establishing educational programs to guide museums in developing their own code of ethics and establishing procedures for addressing alleged violations of the code—was asked to review the code and recommend to the Board changes in either the code or its implementation.

The new Ethics Commission spent its first year reviewing the code and the hundreds of communications it had generated, and initiating additional dialogue. AAM institutional members were invited to comment further on the issues that were most divisive—the mode of implementation and the restrictions placed on funds from deaccessioned objects. Ethics Commission members also met in person with their colleagues at the annual and regional meetings, and an ad hoc meeting of museum directors was convened by the board president to examine the code's language regarding deaccessioning.

This process of review produced two alternatives for the board to consider at its May meeting: (1) to accept a new code developed by the Ethics Commission, or (2) to rewrite the sections of the 1991 code relating to use of funds from deaccessioning and mode of implementation. Following a very lively and involved discussion, the motion to reinstate the 1991 code with modified language was passed and a small committee met separately to make the necessary changes.

In addition, it was voted that the Ethics Commission be renamed the Committee on Ethics with responsibilities for establishing information and educational programs and reviewing the Code of Ethics for Museums and making periodic recommendations for revisions to the board. These final changes were approved by the board in November 1993 and are incorporated into this document, which is the AAM *Code of Ethics for Museums*.

Each nonprofit museum member of the American Association of Museums should subscribe to the AAM *Code of Ethics for Museums*. Subsequently, these museums should set about framing their own institutional codes of ethics, which should be in conformance with the AAM code and should expand on it through the elaboration of specific practices. This recommendation is made to these member institutions in the belief that engaging the governing authority, staff, and volunteers in applying the AAM code to institutional settings will stimulate the development and maintenance of sound policies and procedures necessary to understanding and ensuring ethical behavior by institutions and by all who work for them or on their behalf.

With these steps, the American museum community expands its continuing effort to advance museum work through self-regulation. The *Code of Ethics for Museums* serves the interests of museums, their constituencies, and society. The primary goal of AAM is to encourage institutions to regulate the ethical behavior of members of their governing authority, employees, and volunteers. Formal adoption of an institutional code promotes higher and more consistent ethical standards. To this end, the Committee on Ethics will develop workshops, model codes, and publications. These and other forms of technical assistance will stimulate a dialogue about ethics throughout the museum community and provide guidance to museums in developing their institutional codes.

American Association of Physical Anthropologists (AAPA)

Reprinted by permission of the American Association of Physical Anthropologists
Code of Ethics
Approved 2003

I. Preamble
Physical anthropologists are part of the anthropology community and members of many other different communities each with its own moral rules or codes of ethics. Physical anthropologists have obligations to their scholarly discipline, the wider society, and the environment. Furthermore, field workers may develop close relationships with the people with whom they work, generating an additional level of ethical considerations.

In a field of such complex involvement and obligations, it is inevitable that misunderstanding, conflicts, and the need to make choices among apparently incompatible values will arise. Physical anthropologists are responsible for grappling with such difficulties and struggling to resolve them in ways compatible with the principles stated here. The purpose of this Code is to foster discussion and education. The American Association of Physical Anthropologists (AAPA) does not adjudicate claims of unethical behavior.

The principles and guidelines in this Code provide physical anthropologists with the tools to engage in developing and maintaining an ethical framework, as they engage in their work. This Code is based on the Code developed and approved by the American Anthropological Association (AAA). The AAPA has the permission of the AAA to use and modify the AAA Code as needed. In sections III, IV, V, VI, VII, and VIII anthropology or anthropologists refers to physical anthropology or physical anthropologists.

II. Introduction
Physical anthropology is a multidisciplinary field of science and scholarship, which includes the study of biological aspects of humankind and nonhuman primates. Physical anthropology has roots in the natural and social sciences, ranging in approach from basic to applied research and to scholarly interpretation. The purpose of the AAPA is the advancement of the science of physical anthropology. The Code holds the position that generating and appropriately utilizing knowledge (i.e., publishing, teaching, developing programs, and informing policy) of the peoples of the world, past and present, is a worthy goal; that general knowledge is a dynamic process using many different and ever-evolving approaches; and that for moral and practical reasons, the generation and utilization of knowledge should be achieved in an ethical manner.

The purpose of this Code is to provide AAPA members and other interested persons with guidelines for making ethical choices in the conduct of their physical anthropological work. Because physical anthropologists can find themselves in complex situations and subject to more than one code of ethics, the AAPA Code of Ethics provides a framework, not an ironclad formula, for making decisions.

Physical anthropologists have a duty to be informed about ethical codes relating to their work and ought periodically to receive training on ethical issues. In addition, departments offering anthropology degrees should include and require ethical training in their curriculums.

No code or set of guidelines can anticipate unique circumstances or direct actions required in any specific situation. The individual physical anthropologist must be willing to make carefully considered ethical choices and be prepared to make clear the assumptions, facts and issues on which those choices are based. These guidelines therefore address general contexts, priorities and relationships that should be considered in ethical decision making in physical anthropological work.

III. Research

In both proposing and carrying out research, anthropological researchers must be open about the purpose(s), potential impacts, and source(s) of support for research projects with funders, colleagues, persons studied or providing information, and with relevant parties affected by the research. Researchers must expect to utilize the results of their work in an appropriate fashion and disseminate the results through appropriate and timely activities. Research fulfilling these expectations is ethical, regardless of the source of funding (public or private) or purpose (i.e., "applied," "basic," "pure," or "proprietary").

Anthropological researchers should be alert to the danger of compromising anthropological ethics as a condition to engage in research, yet also be alert to proper demands of good citizenship or host-guest relations. Active contribution and leadership in seeking to shape public or private sector actions and policies may be as ethically justifiable as inaction, detachment, or noncooperation, depending on circumstances. Similar principles hold for anthropological researchers employed or otherwise affiliated with nonanthropological institutions, public institutions, or private enterprises.

A. Responsibility to people and animals with whom anthropological researchers work and whose lives and cultures they study.
1. Anthropological researchers have primary ethical obligations to the people, species, and materials they study and to the people with whom they work. These obligations can supersede the goal of seeking new knowledge, and can lead to decisions not to undertake or to discontinue a research project when the primary obligation conflicts with other responsibilities, such as those owed to sponsors or clients. These ethical obligations include:
- To respect the well-being of humans and nonhuman primates

- To work for the long-term conservation of the archaeological, fossil, and historical records
- To consult actively with the affected individuals or group(s), with the goal of establishing a working relationship that can be beneficial to all parties involved

2. Anthropological researchers must do everything in their power to ensure that their research does not harm the safety, dignity, or privacy of the people with whom they work, conduct research, or perform other professional activities

3. Anthropological researchers must determine in advance whether their hosts/providers of information wish to remain anonymous or receive recognition, and make every effort to comply with those wishes. Researchers must present to their research participants the possible impacts of the choices, and make clear that despite their best efforts, anonymity may be compromised or recognition fail to materialize.

4. Anthropological researchers should obtain in advance the informed consent of persons being studied, providing information, owning or controlling access to material being studied, or otherwise identified as having interests which might be impacted by the research. It is understood that the degree and breadth of informed consent required will depend on the nature of the project and may be affected by requirements of other codes, laws, and ethics of the country or community in which the research is pursued. Further, it is understood that the informed consent process is dynamic and continuous; the process should be initiated in the project design and continue through implementation by way of dialogue and negotiation with those studied. Researchers are responsible for identifying and complying with the various informed consent codes, laws and regulations affecting their projects. Informed consent, for the purposes of this code, does not necessarily imply or require a particular written or signed form. It is the quality of the consent, not the format, that is relevant.

5. Anthropological researchers who have developed close and enduring relationships (i.e., covenantal relationships) with either individual persons providing information or with hosts must adhere to the obligations of openness and informed consent, while carefully and respectfully negotiating the limits of the relationship.

6. While anthropologists may gain personally from their work, they must not exploit individuals, groups, animals, or cultural or biological materials. They should recognize their debt to the societies in which they work and their obligation to reciprocate with people studied in appropriate ways.

B. Responsibility to scholarship and science

1. Anthropological researchers must expect to encounter ethical dilemmas at every stage of their work, and must make good-faith efforts to identify potential ethical claims and conflicts in advance when preparing proposals and as projects proceed.

2. Anthropological researchers bear responsibility for the integrity and reputation of their discipline, of scholarship, and of science. Thus, anthropological researchers are subject to the general moral rules of scientific and scholarly conduct: they should not deceive or knowingly misrepresent (i.e., fabricate evidence, falsify, plagiarize), or attempt to prevent reporting of misconduct, or obstruct the scientific/scholarly research of others.

3. Anthropological researchers should do all they can to preserve opportunities for future fieldworkers to follow them to the field.

4. Anthropological researchers should utilize the results of their work in an appropriate fashion, and whenever possible disseminate their findings to the scientific and scholarly community.

5. Anthropological researchers should seriously consider all reasonable requests for access to their data and other research materials for purposes of research. They should also make every effort to ensure preservation of their fieldwork data for use by posterity.

C. Responsibility to the public

1. Anthropological researchers should make the results of their research appropriately available to sponsors, students, decision makers, and other nonanthropologists. In so doing, they must be truthful; they are not only responsible for the factual content of their statements but also must consider carefully the social and political implications of the information they disseminate. They must do everything in their power to insure that such information is well understood, properly contextualized, and responsibly utilized. They should make clear the empirical bases upon which their reports stand, be candid about their qualifications and philosophical or political biases, and recognize and make clear the limits of anthropological expertise. At the same time, they must be alert to possible harm their information may cause people with whom they work or colleagues.

2. Anthropologists may choose to move beyond disseminating research results to a position of advocacy. This is an individual decision, but not an ethical responsibility.

IV. Teaching
Responsibility to students and trainees.

While adhering to ethical and legal codes governing relations between teachers/mentors and students/trainees at their educational institutions or as members of wider organizations, anthropological teachers should be particularly sensitive to the ways such codes apply in their discipline (for example, when teaching involves close contact with students/trainees in field situations). Among the widely recognized precepts which anthropological teachers, like other teachers/mentors, should follow are:

1. Teachers/mentors should conduct their programs in ways that preclude discrimination on the basis of sex, marital status, "race," social class, political convictions, disability, religion, ethnic background, national origin, sexual orientation, age, or other criteria irrelevant to academic performance.

2. Teachers'/mentors' duties include continually striving to improve their teaching/training techniques; being available and responsive to student/trainee interests; counseling students/ trainees realistically regarding career opportunities; conscientiously supervising, encouraging, and supporting students'/trainees' studies; being fair, prompt, and reliable in communicating evaluations; assisting students/trainees in securing research support; and helping students/trainees when they seek professional placement.

3. Teachers/mentors should impress upon students/trainees the ethical challenges involved in every phase of anthropological work; encourage them to reflect upon this and other codes; encourage dialogue with colleagues on ethical issues; and discourage participation in ethically questionable projects.

4. Teachers/mentors should publicly acknowledge student/trainee assistance in research and preparation of their work; give appropriate credit for coauthorship to students/trainees; encourage publication of worthy student/trainee papers; and compensate students/trainees justly for their participation in all professional activities.

5. Teachers/mentors should beware of the exploitation and serious conflicts of interest which may result if they engage in sexual relations with students/trainees. They must avoid sexual liaisons with students/trainees for whose education and professional training they are in any way responsible.

V. Application

1. The same ethical guidelines apply to all anthropological work. That is, in both proposing and carrying out research, anthropologists must be open with funders, colleagues, persons studied or providing information, and relevant parties affected by the work about the purpose(s), potential impacts, and source(s) of support for the work. Applied anthropologists must intend and expect to utilize the results of their work appropriately (i.e., publication, teaching, program and policy development) within a reasonable time. In situations in which anthropological knowledge is applied, anthropologists bear the same responsibility to be open and candid about their skills and intentions, and monitor the effects of their work on all persons affected. Anthropologists may be involved in many types of work, frequently affecting individuals and groups with diverse and sometimes conflicting interests. The individual anthropologist must make carefully considered ethical choices and be prepared to make clear the assumptions, facts and issues on which those choices are based.

2. In all dealings with employers, persons hired to pursue anthropological research or apply anthropological knowledge should be honest about their quali-

fications, capabilities, and aims. Prior to making any professional commitments, they must review the purposes of prospective employers, taking into consideration the employer's past activities and future goals. In working for governmental agencies or private businesses, they should be especially careful not to promise or imply acceptance of conditions contrary to professional ethics or competing commitments.

3. Applied anthropologists, as any anthropologist, should be alert to the danger of compromising anthropological ethics as a condition for engaging in research or practice. They should also be alert to proper demands of hospitality, good citizenship and guest status. Proactive contribution and leadership in shaping public or private sector actions and policies may be as ethically justifiable as inaction, detachment, or noncooperation, depending on circumstances.

VI. Epilogue

Anthropological research, teaching, and application, like any human actions, pose choices for which anthropologists individually and collectively bear ethical responsibility. Since anthropologists are members of a variety of groups and subject to a variety of ethical codes, choices must sometimes be made not only between the varied obligations presented in this code but also between those of this code and those incurred in other statuses or roles. This statement does not dictate choice or propose sanctions. Rather, it is designed to promote discussion and provide general guidelines for ethically responsible decisions.

Archaeological Institute of America (AIA)

Reprinted by permission of the Archaeological Institute of America
Code of Ethics
Approved 1990, Amended 1997

The Archaeological Institute of America is dedicated to the greater understanding of archaeology, to the protection and preservation of the world's archaeological resources and the information they contain, and to the encouragement and support of archaeological research and publication.

In accordance with these principles, members of the AIA should:

1. Seek to ensure that the exploration of archaeological sites be conducted according to the highest standards under the direct supervision of qualified personnel, and that the results of such research be made public;

2. Refuse to participate in the trade in undocumented antiquities and refrain from activities that enhance the commercial value of such objects. Undocumented antiquities are those which are not documented as belonging to a public or private collection before December 30, 1970, when the AIA Council endorsed the UNESCO Convention on Cultural Property, or which have not been excavated and exported from the country of origin in accordance with the laws of that country;

3. Inform appropriate authorities of threats to, or plunder of archaeological sites, and illegal import or export of archaeological material.

Code of Professional Standards
Approved 1994, Amended 1997[1]

Preamble
This Code applies to those members of the AIA who play an active, professional role in the recovery, care, study, or publication of archaeological material, including cultural resources located under water. Within the Institute they enjoy the privileges of organizing sessions and submitting papers for the Annual Meetings, of lecturing to local societies, participating in the AIA committees that shape and direct the discipline, participating in the placement service, and of being listed in the Directory of Professionals in Archaeology.

Along with those privileges come special responsibilities. Our members should inform themselves about and abide by the laws of the countries in which they live and work. They should treat others at home and in the field with respect and sensitivity. As primary stewards of the archaeological record, they

---

At the time of publication, the AIA Code of Professional Standards was being revised. For the most current version of the code, please visit the AIA Web site at: http://www.archaeological.org/

should work actively to preserve that record in all its dimensions and for the long term; and they should give due consideration to the interests of others, both colleagues and the lay public, who are affected by the research.

The AIA recognizes that archaeology is a discipline dealing, in all its aspects, with the human condition, and that archaeological research must often balance competing ethical principles. This Code of Professional Standards does not seek to legislate all aspects of professional behavior and it realizes the conflicts embedded in many of the issues addressed. The Code sets forth three broad areas of responsibility and provides examples of the kinds of considerations called for by each. It aims to encourage all professional archaeologists to keep ethical considerations in mind as they plan and conduct research.

I. Responsibilities to the Archaeological Record

Professional archaeologists incur responsibilities to the archaeological record—the physical remains and all the associated information about those remains, including those located under water.

1. Professional archaeologists should adhere to the Guidelines of the AIA general Code of Ethics concerning illegal antiquities in their research and publications.

2. The purposes and consequences of all archaeological research should be carefully considered before the beginning of work. Approaches and methods should be chosen that require a minimum of damage to the archaeological record. Although excavation is sometimes the appropriate means of research, archaeological survey, study of previously excavated material, and other means should be considered before resort is made to excavation.

3. The recovery and study of archaeological material from all periods should be carried out only under the supervision of qualified personnel.

4. Archaeologists should anticipate and provide for adequate and accessible long-term storage and curatorial facilities for all archaeological materials, records, and archives, including machine-readable data, which require specialized archival care and maintenance.

5. Archaeologists should make public the results of their research in a timely fashion, making evidence available to others if publication is not accomplished within a reasonable time.

6. All research projects should contain specific plans for conservation, preservation, and publication from the very outset, and funds should be secured for such purposes.

II. Responsibilities to the Public

Because the archaeological record represents the heritage of all people, it is the responsibility of professional archaeologists to communicate with the general public about the nature of archaeological research and the importance of archaeological resources. Archaeologists also have specific responsibilities to the local communities where they carry out research and field work, as well as to their home institutions and communities.

Archaeologists should be sensitive to cultural mores and attitudes, and be aware of the impact research and fieldwork may have on a local population, both during and after the work. Such considerations should be taken into account in designing the project's strategy.

1. Professional archaeologists should be actively engaged in public outreach through lecturing, popular writing, school programs, and other educational initiatives.

2. Plans for field work should consider the ecological impact of the project and its overall impact on the local communities.

3. Professional archaeologists should not participate in projects whose primary goal is private gain.

4. For field projects, archaeologists should consult with appropriate representatives of the local community during the planning stage, invite local participation in the project, and regularly inform the local community about the results of the research.

5. Archaeologists should respect the cultural norms and dignity of local inhabitants in areas where archaeological research is carried out.

6. The legitimate concerns of people who claim descent from, or some other connection with, cultures of the past must be balanced against the scholarly integrity of the discipline. A mutually acceptable accommodation should be sought.

III. Responsibilities to Colleagues

Professional archaeologists owe consideration to colleagues, striving at all times to be fair, never plagiarize, and give credit where due.

1. Archaeologists involved in cooperative projects should strive for harmony and fairness; those in positions of authority should behave with consideration toward those under their authority, while all team members should strive to promote the success of the broader undertaking.

2. The Principal Investigator(s) of archaeological projects should maintain acceptable standards of safety and ascertain that staff members are adequately insured.

3. Professional archaeologists should maintain confidentiality of information gleaned in reviewing grant proposals and other such privileged sources.

4. Professional archaeologists should not practice discrimination or harassment based on sex, religion, age, race, national origin, disability, or sexual orientation; project sponsors should establish the means to eliminate and/or investigate complaints of discrimination or harassment.

5. Archaeologists should honor reasonable requests from colleagues for access to materials and records, preserving existing rights to publication, but sharing information useful for the research of others. Scholars seeking access to unpublished information should not expect to receive interpretive information if that is also unpublished and in progress.

6. Before studying and/or publishing any unpublished material archaeologists should secure proper permission, normally in writing, from the appropriate project director or the appointed representative of the sponsoring institution and/or the antiquities authorities in the country of origin.

7. Scholars studying material from a particular site should keep the project director informed of their progress and intentions; project directors should return the courtesy.

8. Members of cooperative projects should prepare and evaluate reports in a timely and collegial fashion.

Australian Archaeological Association (AAA)

Reprinted by permission of the Australian Archaeological Association
Code of Ethics
Last Amended 2004

1. Foreword

1.1 Members will serve the interests of the Association by adhering to its objects and purposes as defined by this Code of Ethics and the Constitution, specifically:

- to promote the advancement of archaeology;
- to provide an organisation for the discussion and dissemination of archaeological information and ideas in archaeology;
- to convene meetings at regular intervals;
- to publicise the need for the study and conservation of archaeological sites and collections; and
- to publicise the work of the Association.

1.2 Members will negotiate and make every reasonable effort to obtain the informed consent of representatives of the communities of concern whose cultural heritage is the subject of investigation. Members cannot assume that there is no community of concern.

1.3 Members recognise that there are many interests in cultural heritage, but they specifically acknowledge the rights and interests of Indigenous peoples. AAA endorses and directs members to the current guidelines for ethical research with Indigenous parties published by the Australian Institute of Aboriginal and Torres Strait Islander Studies (www.aiatsis.gov.au/data/assets/pdf_file/3512/Ethics-GuideA4.pdf).

1.4 Members whose actions are detrimental to the interests of the Association may be subject to disciplinary procedures as defined by the Constitution.

2. Principles Relating to the Archaeological Record

2.1 Consonant with their obligations arising from government and international agreements, legislation and regulations, members will advocate the conservation, curation and preservation of archaeological sites, assemblages, collections and archival records.

2.2 Members will endeavour to ensure that archaeological sites and materials which they investigate are managed in a manner which conserves the archaeological and cultural heritage values of the sites and materials.

2.3 Members will neither engage in nor support the illicit trade in cultural heritage.

2.4 Members recognise the importance of repatriation of archaeological materials for both Indigenous and non-Indigenous communities of concern and they support and advocate the necessity to properly manage archaeological materials in accordance with agreements with communities of concern.

3. Principles Relating to Indigenous Archaeology

3.1 Members acknowledge the importance of cultural heritage to Indigenous communities.

3.2 Members acknowledge the special importance to Indigenous peoples of ancestral remains and objects and sites associated with such remains. Members will treat such remains with respect.

3.3 Members acknowledge Indigenous approaches to the interpretation of cultural heritage and to its conservation.

3.4 Members will negotiate equitable agreements between archaeologists and the Indigenous communities whose cultural heritage is being investigated. AAA endorses and directs members to the current guidelines regarding such agreements published by the Australian Institute of Aboriginal and Torres Strait Islander Studies

4. Principles Relating to Conduct

4.1 Members will treat each other in a professional manner.

4.2 Members will disseminate the results of their work as widely as possible using plain language where appropriate.

4.3 Any person can notify the Executive Committee of a member's conduct which they believe to be detrimental to the interests of the Association. Complaints may activate procedures outlined in Section 32 (Expulsion of Members) of the Constitution, including rights of appeal.

4.4 Personal information provided to the Association by members will be kept confidential.

Canadian Archaeological Association (CAA)
Reprinted by permission of the Canadian Archaeological Association
Principles of Ethical Conduct
Approved 2000

Preamble
The objectives of the Canadian Archaeological Association include promoting, protecting and conserving the archaeological heritage of Canada, and the dissemination of archaeological knowledge. Canadian archaeologists conduct their activities according to the principles of scholarly practice and recognize the interests of groups affected by their research.

Stewardship
We expect that the members of the CAA will exercise respect for archaeological remains and for those who share an interest in these irreplaceable and non-renewable resources now and in the future. The archaeological record includes in-situ materials and sites, archaeological collections, records and reports. Stewardship involves having care for and promoting the conservation of the archaeological record. This record is unique, finite and fragile. CAA members should acknowledge:
- access to knowledge from the past is an essential part of the heritage of everyone;
- conservation is a preferred option;
- where conservation is not an option, ensure accurate recording and dissemination of results;
- excavations should be no more invasive/destructive than determined by mitigation circumstances or comprehensive research goals;
- the commodification of archaeological sites and artifacts through selling and trading is unethical.

Aboriginal Relationships
Recognizing that the heritage of Aboriginal Peoples constitutes the greater part of the Canadian archaeological record, the Canadian Archaeological Association has accepted the Statement of Principles for Ethical Conduct Pertaining to Aboriginal Peoples. Members of the Association have agreed to abide by those Principles.

Professional Responsibilities
Archaeological remains are finite, fragile, non-renewable and unique. Before undertaking responsibility for any excavation that destroys a portion of the archaeological record, members of the Canadian Archaeological Association must:

- keep abreast of developments in their specializations;
- possess adequate training, support, resources and facilities to undertake excavation and analysis;
- produce an adequate document worthy of the destruction of the archaeological remains;
- present archaeology and research results in a timely and responsible manner;
- preserve documentation in such a way that it is of value to future researchers;
- comply with all legislation and local protocols with Aboriginal Peoples, as described in the Statement of Principles for Ethical Conduct Pertaining to Aboriginal Peoples, as appropriate in each province and/or territory;
- respect colleagues, and cooperate with them;
- allow the expression of alternative views of the past;
- exercise the right to defend our own scholarship;
- recognize documentation of an archaeological record should, within a reasonable period of time, become available to others with legitimate research interests;
- present archaeological information in an objective and well informed manner in all contexts.

Public Education and Outreach

A fundamental commitment to stewardship is the sharing of knowledge about archaeological topics to a broader public and to enlist public support for stewardship. Members of the CAA are encouraged to:

- communicate the results of archaeological work to a broad audience;
- encourage the public to support and involvement in archaeological stewardship;
- actively cooperate in stewardship of archaeological remains with aboriginal peoples;
- promote public interest in, and knowledge of, Canada's past;
- explain appropriate archaeological methods and techniques to interested people;
- promote archaeology through education in the K—12 school systems;
- support and be accessible to local archaeological and other heritage groups;
- contribute to the CAA Web Page, and promote where appropriate electronic publication of archaeological materials.

Statement of Principles for Ethical Conduct Pertaining to Aboriginal Peoples
Approved 1997

Preamble
The objectives of the Canadian Archaeological Association include the promotion, protection and conservation of the archaeological heritage of Canada, and the dissemination of archaeological knowledge. Canadian archaeologists conduct their activities according to the principles of scholarly practice and recognize the interests of groups affected by their research. Whereas the heritage of First Nations Peoples constitutes the greater part of the Canadian archaeological record, this document presents a Statement of Principles that guides members of the Association in their relationships with Aboriginal peoples.

Principles
Members of the CAA/ACA agree to abide by the following principles:
I. Consultation:
   1. To recognize the cultural and spiritual links between Aboriginal peoples and the archaeological record.
   2. To acknowledge that Aboriginal people have a fundamental interest in the protection and management of the archaeological record, its interpretation and presentation.
   3. To recognize and respect the role of Aboriginal communities in matters relating to their heritage.
   4. To negotiate and respect protocols, developed in consultation with Aboriginal communities, relating to the conduct of archaeological activities dealing with Aboriginal culture.

II. Aboriginal Involvement:
   1. To encourage partnerships with Aboriginal communities in archaeological research, management and education, based on respect and mutual sharing of knowledge and expertise.
   2. To support formal training programs in archaeology for Aboriginal people.
   3. To support the recruitment of Aboriginal people as professional archaeologists.

III. Sacred Sites and Places:
   1. To recognize and respect the spiritual bond that exists between Aboriginal peoples and special places and features on the landscape.
   2. To acknowledge the cultural significance of human remains and associated objects to Aboriginal peoples.
   3. To respect protocols governing the investigation, removal, curation and reburial of human remains and associated objects.

IV. Communication and Interpretation:

1. To respect the cultural significance of oral history and traditional knowledge in the interpretation and presentation of the archaeological record of Aboriginal peoples.

2. To communicate the results of archaeological investigations to Aboriginal communities in a timely and accessible manner.

European Association of Archaeologists (EAA)

Reprinted by permission of the European Association of Archaeologists
Code of Practice
Approved 1997

Preamble

The archaeological heritage, as defined in Article 1 of the 1992 *European Convention on the Protection of the Archaeological Heritage*, is the heritage of all humankind. Archaeology is the study and interpretation of that heritage for the benefit of society as a whole. Archaeologists are the interpreters and stewards of that heritage on behalf of their fellow men and women. The object of this Code is to establish standards of conduct for the members of the European Association of Archaeologists to follow in fulfilling their responsibilities, both to the community and to their professional colleagues.

1. Archaeologists and society

1.1 All archaeological work should be carried out in the spirit of the *Charter for the management of the archaeological heritage* approved by ICOMOS (International Council on Monuments and Sites) in 1990.

1.2 It is the duty of every archaeologist to ensure the preservation of the archaeological heritage by every legal means.

1.3 In achieving that end archaeologists will take active steps to inform the general public at all levels of the objectives and methods of archaeology in general and of individual projects in particular, using all the communication techniques at their disposal.

1.4 Where preservation is impossible, archaeologists will ensure that investigations are carried out to the highest professional standards.

1.5 In carrying out such projects, archaeologists will wherever possible, and in accordance with any contractual obligations that they may have entered into, carry out prior evaluations of the ecological and social implications of their work for local communities.

1.6 Archaeologists will not engage in, or allow their names to be associated with, any form of activity relating to the illicit trade in antiquities and works of art, covered by the 1970 UNESCO *Convention on the means of prohibiting and preventing the illicit import, export, and transfer of ownership of cultural property*.

1.7 Archaeologists will not engage in, or allow their names to be associated with, any activity that impacts the archaeological heritage which is carried out for commercial profit which derives directly from or exploits the archaeological heritage itself.

1.8 It is the responsibility of archaeologists to draw the attention of the competent authorities to threats to the archaeological heritage, including the plundering of sites and monuments and illicit trade in antiquities, and to use all the means at their disposal to ensure that action is taken in such cases by the competent authorities.

2. Archaeologists and the Profession

2.1 Archaeologists will carry out their work to the highest standards recognised by their professional peers.

2.2 Archaeologists have a duty to keep themselves informed of developments in knowledge and methodology relating to their field of specialisation and to techniques of fieldwork, conservation, information dissemination, and related areas.

2.3 Archaeologists should not undertake projects for which they are not adequately trained or prepared.

2.4 A research design should be formulated as an essential prelude to all projects. Arrangements should also be made before starting projects for the subsequent storage and curation of finds, samples, and records in accessible public repositories (museums, archive collections, etc).

2.5 Proper records, prepared in a comprehensible and durable form, should be made of all archaeological projects.

2.6 Adequate reports on all projects should be prepared and made accessible to the archaeological community as a whole with the minimum delay through appropriate conventional and/or electronic publishing media, following an initial period of confidentiality not exceeding six calendar months.

2.7 Archaeologists will have prior rights of publication in respect of projects for which they are responsible for a reasonable period, not exceeding ten years. During this period they will make their results as widely accessible as possible and will give sympathetic consideration to requests for information from colleagues and students, provided that these do not conflict with the primary right of publication. When the ten-year period has expired, the records should be freely available for analysis and publication by others.

2.8 Written permission must be obtained for the use of original material and acknowledgement to the source included in any publication.

2.9 In recruiting staff for projects, archaeologists shall not practise any form of discrimination based on sex, religion, age, race, disability, or sexual orientation.

2.10 The management of all projects must respect national standards relating to conditions of employment and safety.

Principles of Conduct
Approved 1998

The membership of the EAA voted to approve and adopt a set of Principles of Conduct for archaeologists involved in contract archaeological work. These had been prepared by the EAA's Working Party on Commercial Archaeology, were aired at the Ravenna meeting in 1997, and were published in draft in The European Archaeologist 8 (Winter 1997). The draft principles were further discussed at a well attended and lively round table held at the Göteborg meeting.

The text that was approved by the membership is reproduced below. The Principles of Conduct help to define the standards of conduct expected of professional archaeologists in Europe.

Two important changes were made as a result of the discussions at Göteborg. First, the earlier phrase "commercial archaeological work" was replaced with "contract archaeological work." This reflects the view that archaeology is not, in the end, a commercial activity (even though it is often carried out under contracts, of various kinds). Secondly, a new principle (No 14) was added. This reflects the importance of promoting both the principles and the means to make them work in practice. The need for adequate regulation of contract archaeology (normally by state or municipal authorities, but with professional associations also having a crucial role to play) is especially important.

Note: many of these principles apply equally to all kinds of archaeological work, but this code deals especially with issues arising from a contract system of funding.

1. Archaeologists should ensure that they understand, and operate within, the legal framework within which the regulation of archaeological work takes place in that country.

2. Archaeologists should ensure that they give the best possible advice to developers and planners, and should not advise on matters beyond their knowledge or competence.

3. Archaeologists should ensure that they understand the structure of archaeological roles and responsibilities, the relationships between these roles, and their place in this structure.

4. Archaeologists should avoid conflicts of interest between the role of giving advice in a regulatory capacity and undertaking (or offering to undertake) work in a contract capacity.

5. Archaeologists should not offer to undertake contract work for which they or their organizations are not suitably equipped, staffed or experienced.

6. Archaeologists should maintain adequate project control systems (academic, financial, quality, time) in relation to the work which they are undertaking.

7. Archaeologists should adhere to recognized professional standards for archaeological work.

8. Archaeologists should adhere both to the relevant law and to ethical standards in the area of competition between archaeological organizations.

9. Archaeologists involved in contract archaeological work should ensure that the results of such work are properly completed and made publicly available.

10. Archaeologists involved in contract archaeological work should ensure that archaeological information is not suppressed unreasonably or indefinitely (by developers or by archaeological organizations) for commercial reasons.

11. Archaeologists involved in contract archaeological work should be conscious of the need to maintain the academic coherence of archaeology, in the face of a tendency towards fragmentation under a contract system of organization.

12. Archaeologists involved in managing contract archaeological work should be conscious of their responsibilities towards the pay, conditions of employment and training, and career development opportunities of archaeologists, in relation to the effects of competition between archaeological organizations on these aspects of life.

13. Archaeologists involved in contract archaeological work should recognize the need to demonstrate, to developers and to the public at large, the benefits of support for archaeological work.

14. Where contract archaeology exists, all archaeologists (especially in positions of influence) should promote the application of this code, and promote development of the means to make it work effectively, especially adequate systems of regulation.

Institute of Field Archaeologists (IFA)

Reprinted by permission of the Institute of Field Archaeologists
Code of Conduct
Adopted 1985, Last Revised 2006

Introduction

The object of the Code is to promote those standards of conduct and self-discipline required of an archaeologist in the interests of the public and in the pursuit of archaeological research. Archaeology is the study of the nature and past behaviour of human beings in their environmental setting. It is carried out through the investigation and interpretation of the material remains of human activities, which together constitute the archaeological heritage. The archaeological heritage is a finite, vulnerable and diminishing resource. The fuller understanding of our past provided by archaeology is part of society's common heritage and it should be available to everyone. Because of this, and because the archaeological heritage is an irreplaceable resource, archaeologists both corporately and individually have a responsibility to help conserve the archaeological heritage, to use it economically in their work, to conduct their studies in such a way that reliable information may be acquired, and to disseminate the results of their studies.

Subscription to this *Code of conduct* for individuals engaged in archaeology assumes acceptance of these responsibilities. Those who subscribe to it and carry out its provisions will thereby be identified as persons professing specific standards of competence, responsibility and ethical behaviour in the pursuit of archaeological work.

The Code indicates the general standard of conduct to which members of the Institute are expected to adhere, failing which its governing body may judge them guilty of conduct unbecoming to a member of the Institute and may either reprimand, suspend or expel them. The Institute from time to time produces written standards and guidance for the execution of archaeological projects, and policy statements. All members are advised to respect such standards, guidance and policy statements in the interests of good professional practice.

Principle 1

The archaeologist shall adhere to the highest standards of ethical and responsible behaviour in the conduct of archaeological affairs.

Rules

1.1 An archaeologist shall conduct himself or herself in a manner which will not bring archaeology or the Institute into disrepute.

1.2 An archaeologist shall present archaeology and its results in a responsible manner and shall avoid and discourage exaggerated, misleading or unwarranted statements about archaeological matters.

1.3 An archaeologist shall not offer advice, make a public statement, or give legal testimony involving archaeological matters, without being as thoroughly informed on the matters concerned as might reasonably be expected.

1.4 An archaeologist shall not undertake archaeological work for which he or she is not adequately qualified. He or she should ensure that adequate support, whether of advice, personnel or facilities, has been arranged.

Note: It is the archaeologist's duty to have regard to his/her skills, proficiencies and capabilities and to the maintenance and enhancement of these through appropriate training and learning experiences.

It is the archaeologist's responsibility to inform current or prospective employers or clients of inadequacies in his/her qualifications for any work which may be proposed; he/she may of course seek to minimise such inadequacies by acquiring additional expertise, by seeking the advice or involvement of associates or consultants, or by arranging for modifications of the work involved; similar considerations apply where an archaeologist, during the course of a project, encounters problems which lie beyond his/her competence at that time.

It is also the archaeologist's responsibility to seek adequate support services for any project in which he/she may become involved, either directly or by way of recommendation.

1.5 An archaeologist shall give appropriate credit for work done by others, and shall not commit plagiarism in oral or written communication, and shall not enter into conduct that might unjustifiably injure the reputation of another archaeologist.

1.6 An archaeologist shall know and comply with all laws applicable to his or her archaeological activities whether as employer or employee, and with national and international agreements relating to the illicit import, export or transfer of ownership of archaeological material. An archaeologist shall not engage in, and shall seek to discourage, illicit or unethical dealings in antiquities.

Note: (a) The archaeologist should also consider his/her position in respect of seeking or accepting financial benefit on his/her own behalf or that of relatives in relation to the recovery or disposal of objects or materials recovered during archaeological work.

(b) Archaeologists working on the foreshore and underwater may at times find themselves in difficulty regarding their association with commercial salvors and others engaged in exploiting the underwater cultural heritage. The underlying principles are 1) conserving the seabed heritage, 2) using it economically and in such a way that reliable information may be acquired, 3) dissemination of the results and 4) professional permanent curation of the total site archive.

It may be a legitimate part of the archaeologist's duty to work with commercial salvage organisations or individuals, in respect of recording sites and material, including possible museum acquisitions, and assessing sites and the work that takes place on them. In such dealings, however, archaeologists must ensure that: 1) they do not knowingly permit their names or services to be used in a manner which may promote the recovery of archaeological material unless the primary objective of their work is to preserve the scientific integrity of the total site archive in a permanent professionally curated and publicly accessible collection, and unless provision is made for its study, interpretation and publication; 2) they do not enter into any contract or agreement whereby archaeological or curatorial standards may be compromised in deference to commercial interests; 3) so far as excavated material is concerned, they do not encourage the purchase of objects in any case where they have reasonable cause to believe that their recovery involved the deliberate unscientific destruction or damage of archaeological sites, and that they discourage the sale and consequent dispersal of excavated material; 4) they do not encourage the purchase of objects where there is reasonable cause to believe that recovery involved the failure to disclose the finds to the proper legal or governmental authorities.

1.7 An archaeologist shall abstain from, and shall not sanction in others, conduct involving dishonesty, fraud, deceit or misrepresentation in archaeological matters, nor knowingly permit the use of his/her name in support of activities involving such conduct.

1.8 An archaeologist, in the conduct of his/her archaeological work, shall not offer or accept inducements which could reasonably be construed as bribes.

1.9 [deleted]

1.10 An archaeologist shall not reveal confidential information unless required by law; nor use confidential or privileged information to his/her own advantage or that of a third person.

Note: The archaeologist should also exercise care to prevent employees, colleagues, associates and helpers from revealing or using confidential information in these ways. Confidential information means information gained in the course of the project which the employer or client has for the time being requested be held inviolate, or the disclosure of which would be potentially embarrassing or detrimental to the employer or client. Information ceases to be confidential when the employer or client so indicates, or when such information becomes publicly known. Where specifically archaeological information is involved, it is however the responsibility of the archaeologist to inform the employer or client of any conflict with his/her own responsibilities under Principle 4 of the Code (dissemination of archaeological information) and to seek to minimise or remove any such conflict.

1.11 An archaeologist shall take account of the legitimate concerns of groups whose material past may be the subject of archaeological investigation.

1.12 An archaeologist has a duty to ensure that this Code is observed throughout the membership of the Institute, and also to encourage its adoption by others (see note on Rule 1.12).

Note: From time to time the Institute receives formal or informal complaints about members and allegations of breaches of its by-laws. An archaeologist's duty to ensure that the Code of Conduct is observed includes providing information in response to a request from the Chair or a Vice Chair, and/or giving evidence to such panels and hearings as may be established for the purposes of investigating an alleged breach of the Institute's by-laws. This requirement is without prejudice to the provisions of Rule 1.10 regarding confidential information.

1.13 An archaeologist shall ensure, as far as is reasonably practical, that all work for which he/she is directly or indirectly responsible by virtue of his/her position in the organization undertaking the work, is carried out in accordance with this Code.

1.14 An archaeologist may find himself/herself in an ethical dilemma where he/she is confronted by competing loyalties, responsibilities or duties. In such circumstances an archaeologist shall act in accordance with the Principles of the *Code of Conduct.*

Principle 2
The archaeologist has a responsibility for the conservation of the archaeological heritage.

Rules

2.1 An archaeologist shall strive to conserve archaeological sites and material as a resource for study and enjoyment now and in the future and shall encourage others to do the same. Where such conservation is not possible he/she shall seek to ensure the creation and maintenance of an adequate record through appropriate forms of research, recording and dissemination of results.

Note: Dissemination in these rules is taken to include the deposition of primary records and unpublished material in an accessible public archive.

2.2 Where destructive investigation is undertaken the archaeologist shall ensure that it causes minimal attrition of the archaeological heritage consistent with the stated objects of the project.

Note: Particular attention should be paid to this injunction in the case of projects carried out for purposes of pure research. In all projects, whether prompted by pure research or the needs of rescue, consideration should be given to the legitimate interests of other archaeologists; for example, the upper levels of a site should be conscientiously excavated and recorded, within the exigencies of the project, even if the main focus is on the underlying levels.

2.3 An archaeologist shall ensure that the objects of a research project are an adequate justification for the destruction of the archaeological evidence which it will entail.

Principle 3
The archaeologist shall conduct his/her work in such a way that reliable information about the past may be acquired, and shall ensure that the results be properly recorded.

Rules

3.1 The archaeologist shall keep himself/herself informed about developments in his/her field or fields of specialisation.

3.2 An archaeologist shall prepare adequately for any project he/she may undertake.

3.3 An archaeologist shall ensure that experimental design, recording, and sampling procedures, where relevant, are adequate for the project in hand.

3.4 An archaeologist shall ensure that the record resulting from his/her work is prepared in a comprehensible, readily usable and durable form.

3.5 An archaeologist shall ensure that the record, including artefacts and specimens and experimental results, is maintained in good condition while in his/her charge and shall seek to ensure that it is eventually deposited where it is likely to receive adequate curatorial care and storage conditions and to be readily available for study and examination.

3.6 An archaeologist shall seek to determine whether a project he/she undertakes is likely detrimentally to affect research work or projects of other archaeologists. If there is such likelihood, he/she shall attempt to minimise such effects.

Principle 4

The archaeologist has responsibility for making available the results of archaeological work with reasonable dispatch.

Rules

4.1 An archaeologist shall communicate and cooperate with colleagues having common archaeological interests and give due respect to colleagues' interests in, and rights to information about sites, areas, collections or data where there is a shared field of concern, whether active or potentially so.

4.2 An archaeologist shall accurately and without undue delay prepare and properly disseminate an appropriate record of work done under his/her control.

Note: Dissemination in these rules is taken to include the deposition of primary records and unpublished material in an accessible public archive. This rule carries with it the implication that an archaeologist should not initiate, take part in or support work which materially damages the archaeological heritage unless reasonably prompt and appropriate analysis and reporting can be expected. Where results are felt to be substantial contributions to knowledge or to the advancement of theory, method or technique, they should be communicated as soon as reasonably possible to colleagues and others by means of letters, lectures, reports to meetings or interim publications, especially where full publication is likely to be significantly delayed.

4.3 An archaeologist shall honour requests from colleagues or students for information on the results of research or projects if consistent with his/her prior rights to publication and with his/her other archaeological responsibilities.

Note: Archaeologists receiving such information shall observe such prior rights, remembering that laws of copyright may also apply.

4.4 An archaeologist is responsible for the analysis and publication of data derived from projects under his/her control. While the archaeologist exercises this responsibility he/she shall enjoy consequent rights of primacy. However, failure to prepare or publish the results within 10 years of completion of the fieldwork shall be construed as a waiver of such rights, unless such failure can reasonably be attributed to circumstances beyond the archaeologist's control.

Note: It is accepted that the movement of archaeologists from one employment to another raises problems of responsibility for the publication of projects. This ultimate responsibility for publication of a piece of work must be determined either by the contract of employment through which the work was undertaken, or by agreement with the original promoter of the work. It is the responsibility of the archaeologist, either as employer or employee, to establish a satisfactory agreement on this issue at the outset of work.

4.5 An archaeologist, in the event of his/her failure to prepare or publish the results within 10 years of completion of the fieldwork and in the absence of countervailing circumstances, or in the event of his/her determining not to publish the results, shall if requested make data concerning the project available to other archaeologists for analysis and publication.

4.6 An archaeologist shall accept the responsibility of informing the public of the purpose and results of his/her work and shall accede to reasonable requests for information for dispersal to the general public.

Note: The archaeologist should be prepared to allow access to sites at suitable times and under controlled conditions, within limitations laid down by the funding agency or by the owners or the tenants of the site, or by considerations of safety or the well-being of the site.

4.7 An archaeologist shall respect contractual obligations in reporting but shall not enter into a contract which prohibits the archaeologist from including his/her own interpretations or conclusions in the resulting record, or from a continuing right to use the data after completion of the project.

Note: Adherence to this rule may on occasion appear to clash with the requirements of rule 1.10. A client employer may legitimately seek to impose whatever conditions of confidentiality he/she wishes. An archaeologist should not accept conditions which require the permanent suppression of archaeological discoveries or interpretations.

Principle 5

The archaeologist shall recognise the aspirations of employees, colleagues and helpers with regard to all matters relating to employment, including career development, health and safety, terms and conditions of employment and equality of opportunity.

Rules

5.1 An archaeologist shall give due regard to the requirements of employment legislation relating to employees, colleagues or helpers.

5.2 An archaeologist shall give due regard to the requirements of health and safety legislation relating to employees or to other persons potentially affected by his or her archaeological activities.

5.3 An archaeologist shall give due regard to the requirements of legislation relating to employment discrimination on grounds of race, sex, disability, sexual orientation or religious belief.

5.4 An archaeologist shall ensure that adequate insurance cover is maintained for persons or property which may be affected by his or her archaeological activities.

5.5 An archaeologist shall give due regard to the welfare of employees, colleagues and helpers in relation to terms and conditions of service. He or she shall give reasonable consideration to any IFA recommended pay minima and conditions of employment.

5.6 An archaeologist shall give reasonable consideration to cumulative service and proven experience of employees, colleagues or helpers when deciding rates of remuneration and other employment benefits, such as leave.

5.7 An archaeologist shall have due regard to the rights of individuals who wish to join or belong to a trade union, professional or trade association.

5.8 An archaeologist shall give due regard and appropriate support to the training and development of employees, colleagues or helpers to enable them to execute their duties.

Register of Professional Archaeologists (RPA)

Reprinted by permission of the Register of Professional Archaeologists
Code of Conduct
Last Revised 2007

Archaeology is a profession, and the privilege of professional practice requires professional morality and professional responsibility, as well as professional competence, on the part of each practitioner.

I. The Archaeologist's Responsibility to the Public

1.1 An archaeologist shall:

a. Recognize a commitment to represent Archaeology and its research results to the public in a responsible manner;

b. Actively support conservation of the archaeological resource base;

c. Be sensitive to, and respect the legitimate concerns of, groups whose culture histories are the subjects of archaeological investigations;

d. Avoid and discourage exaggerated, misleading, or unwarranted statements about archaeological matters that might induce others to engage in unethical or illegal activity;

e. Support and comply with the terms of the UNESCO Convention on the means of prohibiting and preventing the illicit import, export, and transfer of ownership of cultural property, as adopted by the General Conference, 14 November 1970, Paris.

1.2 An archaeologist shall not:

a. Engage in any illegal or unethical conduct involving archaeological matters or knowingly permit the use of his/her name in support of any illegal or unethical activity involving archaeological matters;

b. Give a professional opinion, make a public report, or give legal testimony involving archaeological matters without being as thoroughly informed as might reasonably be expected;

c. Engage in conduct involving dishonesty, fraud, deceit or misrepresentation about archaeological matters;

d. Undertake any research that affects the archaeological resource base for which she/he is not qualified.

e. Knowingly be involved in the recovery or excavation of artifacts for commercial exploitation, or knowingly be employed by or knowingly contract with an individual or entity who recovers or excavates archaeological artifacts for commercial exploitation.

II. The Archaeologist's Responsibility to Colleagues, Employees, and Students

2.1 An archaeologist shall:

a. Give appropriate credit for work done by others;

b. Stay informed and knowledgeable about developments in her/his field or fields of specialization;

c. Accurately, and without undue delay, prepare and properly disseminate a description of research done and its results;

d. Communicate and cooperate with colleagues having common professional interests;

e. Give due respect to colleagues' interests in, and rights to, information about sites, areas, collections, or data where there is a mutual active or potentially active research concern;

f. Know and comply with all federal, state, and local laws, ordinances, and regulations applicable to her/his archaeological research and activities;

g. Report knowledge of violations of this Code to proper authorities.

h. Honor and comply with the spirit and letter of the Register of Professional Archaeologist's Disciplinary Procedures.

2.2 An archaeologist shall not:

a. Falsely or maliciously attempt to injure the reputation of another archaeologist;

b. Commit plagiarism in oral or written communication;

c. Undertake research that affects the archaeological resource base unless reasonably prompt, appropriate analysis and reporting can be expected;

d. Refuse a reasonable request from a qualified colleague for research data;

e. Submit a false or misleading application for registration by the Register of Professional Archaeologists.

III. The Archaeologist's Responsibility to Employers and Clients

3.1 An archaeologist shall:

a. Respect the interests of her/his employer or client, so far as is consistent with the public welfare and this Code and Standards;

b. Refuse to comply with any request or demand of an employer or client which conflicts with the Code and Standards;

c. Recommend to employers or clients the employment of other archaeologists or other expert consultants upon encountering archaeological problems beyond her/his own competence;

d. Exercise reasonable care to prevent her/his employees, colleagues, associates and others whose services are utilized by her/him from revealing or using confidential information. Confidential information means information of a non-archaeological nature gained in the course of employment which the employer or client has requested be held inviolate, or the disclosure of which would be embarrassing or would be likely to be detrimental to the employer or client. Information ceases to be confidential when the employer or client so indicates or when such information becomes publicly known.

3.2 An archaeologist shall not:

a. Reveal confidential information, unless required by law;

b. Use confidential information to the disadvantage of the client or employer;

c. Use confidential information for the advantage of herself/himself or a third person, unless the client consents after full disclosure;

d. Accept compensation or anything of value for recommending the employment of another archaeologist or other person, unless such compensation or thing of value is fully disclosed to the potential employer or client;

e. Recommend or participate in any research which does not comply with the requirements of the Standards of Research Performance.

Standards of Research Performance
Last Revised 2007
The research archaeologist has a responsibility to attempt to design and conduct projects that will add to our understanding of past cultures and/or that will develop better theories, methods, or techniques for interpreting the archaeological record, while causing minimal attrition of the archaeological resource base. In the conduct of a research project, the following minimum standards should be followed:

I. The archaeologist has a responsibility to prepare adequately for any research project, whether or not in the field. The archaeologist must:

1.1 Assess the adequacy of her/his qualifications for the demands of the project, and minimize inadequacies by acquiring additional expertise, by bringing in associates with the needed qualifications, or by modifying the scope of the project;

1.2 Inform herself/himself of relevant previous research;

1.3 Develop a scientific plan of research which specifies the objectives of the project, takes into account previous relevant research, employs a suitable methodology, and provides for economical use of the resource base (whether such base consists of an excavation site or of specimens) consistent with the objectives of the project;

1.4 Ensure the availability of adequate and competent staff and support facilities to carry the project to completion, and of adequate curatorial facilities for specimens and records;

1.5 Comply with all legal requirements, including, without limitation, obtaining all necessary governmental permits and necessary permission from landowners or other persons;

1.6 Determine whether the project is likely to interfere with the program or projects of other scholars and, if there is such a likelihood, initiate negotiations to minimize such interference.

II. In conducting research, the archaeologist must follow her/his scientific plan of research, except to the extent that unforeseen circumstances warrant its modification.

III. Procedures for field survey or excavation must meet the following minimal standards:

3.1 If specimens are collected, a system for identifying and recording their proveniences must be maintained.

3.2 Uncollected entities such as environmental or cultural features, depositional strata, and the like, must be fully and accurately recorded by appropriate means, and their location recorded.

3.3 The methods employed in data collection must be fully and accurately described. Significant stratigraphic and/or associational relationships among artifacts, other specimens, and cultural and environmental features must also be fully and accurately recorded.

3.4 All records should be intelligible to other archaeologists. If terms lacking commonly held referents are used, they should be clearly defined.

3.5 Insofar as possible, the interests of other researchers should be considered. For example, upper levels of a site should be scientifically excavated and recorded whenever feasible, even if the focus of the project is on underlying levels.

IV. During accessioning, analysis, and storage of specimens and records in the laboratory, the archaeologist must take precautions to ensure that correlations between the specimens and the field records are maintained, so that provenience contextual relationships and the like are not confused or obscured.

V. Specimens and research records resulting from a project must be deposited at an institution with permanent curatorial facilities, unless otherwise required by law.

VI. The archaeologist has responsibility for appropriate dissemination of the results of her/his research to the appropriate constituencies with reasonable dispatch.

6.1 Results reviewed as significant contributions to substantive knowledge of the past or to advancements in theory, method or technique should be disseminated to colleagues and other interested persons by appropriate means such as publications, reports at professional meetings, or letters to colleagues.

6.2 Requests from qualified colleagues for information on research results directly should be honored, if consistent with the researcher's prior rights to publication and with her/his other professional responsibilities.

6.3 Failure to complete a full scholarly report within 10 years after completion of a field project shall be construed as a waiver of an archaeologist's right of primacy with respect to analysis and publication of the data. Upon expiration of such 10-year period, or at such earlier time as the archaeologist shall determine not to publish the results, such data should be made fully accessible to other archaeologists for analysis and publication.

6.4 While contractual obligations in reporting must be respected, archaeologists should not enter into a contract which prohibits the archaeologist from including her or his own interpretations or conclusions in the contractual reports, or from a continuing right to use the data after completion of the project.

6.5 Archaeologists have an obligation to accede to reasonable requests for information from the news media.

Society for American Archaeology (SAA)

Reprinted by permission of the Society for American Archaeology
Four Statements for Archaeology
Published 1961

1. The Field of Archaeology

Archaeology, a branch of the science of anthropology, is that area of scholarship concerned with the reconstruction of past human life and culture. Its primary data lie in material objects and their relationships; of equal importance may be ancillary data from other fields, including geology, biology, and history.

2. Methods in Archaeology

Archaeological research depends on systematic collection of material objects together with adequate records of the circumstances of the finds and relationships among objects and their surroundings. Value attaches to objects so collected because of their status as documents, and is not intrinsic. Therefore, collecting practices which destroy data and thus prevent the scholarly goal of archaeology are censured.

Explicit permission of the property owner must be secured before excavation is undertaken. State and federal statutes regarding preservation of antiquities and permits for excavation must be scrupulously observed.

Field techniques aim at preserving all recoverable information by means of adequate descriptive records and diagrams. Although archaeologists may take only a limited sample from a site, the collection should include all classes of artifacts encountered, not excluding any category; all pertinent data, including relationships and associations; samples of faunal remains; and other data to be interpreted by scientists in other fields. The archaeologist does not discard classes of information in favor of a special interest.

Certain basic field records must be kept, including the following: (1) A map of the site showing the surface features of the site and environs as well as the location and extent of the digging. (2) Detailed written records and maps of burials, houses, and other structural or natural features, known or assumed to have significance in the cultural history of the site. (3) Stratigraphic relationships of data must be noted and preserved, either through separation in natural soil layers or by arbitrary levels established during digging. (4) A catalogue of all the specimens found indicating their location, stratum of origin, and cultural association. Specimens should be labeled, numbered, and catalogued to preserve their identity as scientific data. (5) Photographs, drawings, and other documentation necessary to clarify the technique of the work and the context and associations of the finds.

Disregard of proper archaeological methods provides grounds for expulsion from the Society for American Archaeology, at the discretion of the Executive Committee.

3. Ethics for Archaeology

Collections made by competent archaeologists must be available for examination by qualified scholars; relevant supporting data must also be accessible for study whether the collection is in a museum or other institution or in private hands.

It is the scholarly obligation of the archaeologist to report his findings in a recognized scientific medium. In the event that significance of the collection does not warrant publication, a manuscript report should be prepared and be available.

Inasmuch as the buying and selling of artifacts usually results in the loss of context and cultural associations, the practice is censured.

An archaeological site presents problems which must be handled by the excavator according to a plan. Therefore, members of the Society for American Archaeology do not undertake excavations on any site being studied by someone without the prior knowledge and consent of that person.

Willful destruction, distortion, or concealment of the data of archaeology is censured, and provides grounds for expulsion from the Society for American Archaeology, at the discretion of the Executive Committee.

4. Recommendations for Training in Archaeology

Archaeology is a scholarly discipline requiring knowledge of field techniques, competence in laboratory analysis of specimens, and the ability to prepare a detailed report of the investigations and their implications in archaeology. In times past, a number of leading archaeologists have acquired the necessary skills without formal training, but they, as well as archaeologists trained in scholarly techniques, have spent years in the study of archaeology as a science.

The Society for American Archaeology condemns uncontrolled excavation by persons who have not been trained in the basic techniques of field archaeology and scholarship. The Society for American Archaeology recommends the following formal training as a minimum qualification for persons planning to enter archaeology as a career. Individuals engaging in archaeology as a profession should acquire the B.A. or B.Sc. degree from an accredited college or university, followed by two years of graduate study with concentration in anthropology and specialization in archaeology during one of these programs. This formal training should be supplemented by at least two summer field schools or their equivalent under the supervision of archaeologists of recognized competence. A Master's thesis or equivalent in published reports is highly recommended. The Ph.D. in anthropology is recommended but not required.

Principles of Archaeological Ethics
Adopted 1996

Principle No. 1: Stewardship

The archaeological record, that is, *in situ* archaeological material and sites, archaeological collections, records and reports, is irreplaceable. It is the responsibility of all archaeologists to work for the long-term conservation and protection of the archaeological record by practicing and promoting stewardship of the archaeological record. Stewards are both caretakers of and advocates for the archaeological record for the benefit of all people; as they investigate and interpret the record, they should use the specialized knowledge they gain to promote public understanding and support for its long-term preservation.

Principle No. 2: Accountability

Responsible archaeological research, including all levels of professional activity, requires an acknowledgment of public accountability and a commitment to make every reasonable effort, in good faith, to consult actively with affected group(s), with the goal of establishing a working relationship that can be beneficial to all parties involved.

Principle No. 3: Commercialization

The Society for American Archaeology has long recognized that the buying and selling of objects out of archaeological context is contributing to the destruction of the archaeological record on the American continents and around the world. The commercialization of archaeological objects—their use as commodities to be exploited for personal enjoyment or profit—results in the destruction of archaeological sites and of contextual information that is essential to understanding the archaeological record. Archaeologists should therefore carefully weigh the benefits to scholarship of a project against the costs of potentially enhancing the commercial value of archaeological objects. Whenever possible they should discourage, and should themselves avoid, activities that enhance the commercial value of archaeological objects, especially objects that are not curated in public institutions, or readily available for scientific study, public interpretation, and display.

Principle No. 4: Public Education and Outreach

Archaeologists should reach out to, and participate in cooperative efforts with others interested in the archaeological record with the aim of improving the preservation, protection, and interpretation of the record. In particular, archaeologists should undertake to: 1) enlist public support for the stewardship of the archaeological record; 2) explain and promote the use of archaeological methods and techniques in understanding human behavior and culture; and 3) communicate archaeological interpretations of the past. Many publics exist for archaeology including students and teachers; Native Americans and other ethnic, religious, and cultural groups who find in the archaeological record important aspects of their cultural heritage; lawmakers and government officials; reporters, journalists, and others involved in the media; and the general public. Archaeologists who are unable to undertake public education and outreach directly should encourage and support the efforts of others in these activities.

Principle No. 5: Intellectual Property

Intellectual property, as contained in the knowledge and documents created through the study of archaeological resources, is part of the archaeological record. As such it should be treated in accord with the principles of stewardship rather than as a matter of personal possession. If there is a compelling reason, and no legal restrictions or strong countervailing interests, a researcher may have primary access to original materials and documents for a limited and reasonable time, after which these materials and documents must be made available to others.

Principle No. 6: Public Reporting and Publication

Within a reasonable time, the knowledge archaeologists gain from investigation of the archaeological record must be presented in accessible form (through publication or other means) to as wide a range of interested publics as possible. The documents and materials on which publication and other forms of public reporting are based should be deposited in a suitable place for permanent safekeeping. An interest in preserving and protecting *in situ* archaeological sites must be taken into account when publishing and distributing information about their nature and location.

Principle No. 7: Records and Preservation

Archaeologists should work actively for the preservation of, and long term access to, archaeological collections, records, and reports. To this end, they should encourage colleagues, students, and others to make responsible use of collections, records, and reports in their research as one means of preserving the *in situ* archaeological record, and of increasing the care and attention given to that portion of the archaeological record which has been removed and incorporated into archaeological collections, records, and reports.

Principle No. 8: Training and Resources

Given the destructive nature of most archaeological investigations, archaeologists must ensure that they have adequate training, experience, facilities, and other support necessary to conduct any program of research they initiate in a manner consistent with the foregoing principles and contemporary standards of professional practice.

Society for Historical Archaeology (SHA)
Reprinted by permission of The Society for Historical Archaeology
Ethical Principles
Adopted 21 June 2003

Historical archaeologists study, interpret and preserve archaeological sites, artifacts and documents from or related to literate societies over the past 600 years for the benefit of present and future peoples. In conducting archaeology, individuals incur certain obligations to the archaeological record, colleagues, employers and the public. These obligations are integral to professionalism. This document presents ethical principles for the practice of historical archaeology. All members of The Society for Historical Archaeology, and others who actively participate in society-sponsored activities, shall support and follow the ethical principles of the society. All historical archaeologists and those in allied fields are encouraged to adhere to these principles.

Principle 1
Members of the Society for Historical Archaeology have a duty to adhere to professional standards of ethics and practices in their research, teaching, reporting, and interactions with the public.

Principle 2
Members of the Society for Historical Archaeology have a duty to encourage and support the long-term preservation and effective management of archaeological sites and collections, from both terrestrial and underwater contexts, for the benefit of humanity.

Principle 3
Members of the Society for Historical Archaeology have a duty to disseminate research results to scholars in an accessible, honest and timely manner.

Principle 4
Members of the Society for Historical Archaeology have a duty to collect data accurately during investigations so that reliable data sets and site documentation are produced, and to see that these materials are appropriately curated for future generations.

Principle 5
Members of the Society for Historical Archaeology have a duty in their professional activities to respect the dignity and human rights of others.

Principle 6
Items from archaeological contexts shall not be traded, sold, bought or bartered as commercial goods, and it is unethical to take actions for the purpose of establishing the commercial value of objects from archaeological sites or property that may lead to their destruction, dispersal, or exploitation.

Principle 7
Members of the Society for Historical Archaeology encourage education about archaeology, strive to engage citizens in the research process and publicly disseminate the major findings of their research, to the extent compatible with resource protection and legal obligations.

World Archaeological Congress (WAC)

Reprinted by permission of the World Archaeological Congress
First Code of Ethics
Adopted 1990

Principles to Abide By:

Members agree that they have obligations to indigenous peoples and that they shall abide by the following principles:

1. To acknowledge the importance of indigenous cultural heritage, including sites, places, objects, artefacts, human remains, to the survival of indigenous cultures.

2. To acknowledge the importance of protecting indigenous cultural heritage to the well-being of indigenous peoples.

3. To acknowledge the special importance of indigenous ancestral human remains, and sites containing and/or associated with such remains, to indigenous peoples.

4. To acknowledge that the important relationship between indigenous peoples and their cultural heritage exists irrespective of legal ownership.

5. To acknowledge that the indigenous cultural heritage rightfully belongs to the indigenous descendants of that heritage.

6. To acknowledge and recognise indigenous methodologies for interpreting, curating, managing and protecting indigenous cultural heritage.

7. To establish equitable partnerships and relationships between Members and indigenous peoples whose cultural heritage is being investigated.

8. To seek, whenever possible, representation of indigenous peoples in agencies funding or authorising research to be certain their view is considered as critically important in setting research standards, questions, priorities and goals.

Rules to Adhere to:

Members agree that they will adhere to the following rules prior to, during and after their investigations:

1. Prior to conducting any investigation and/or examination, Members shall with rigorous endeavour seek to define the indigenous peoples whose cultural heritage is the subject of investigation.

2. Members shall negotiate with and obtain the informed consent of representatives authorised by the indigenous peoples whose cultural heritage is the subject of investigation.

3. Members shall ensure that the authorised representatives of the indigenous peoples whose culture is being investigated are kept informed during all stages of the investigation.

4. Members shall ensure that the results of their work are presented with deference and respect to the identified indigenous peoples.

5. Members shall not interfere with and/or remove human remains of indigenous peoples without the express consent of those concerned.

6. Members shall not interfere with and/or remove artefacts or objects of special cultural significance, as defined by associated indigenous peoples, without their express consent.

7. Members shall recognise their obligation to employ and/or train indigenous peoples in proper techniques as part of their projects, and utilise indigenous peoples to monitor the projects.

The new Code should not be taken in isolation; it was seen by Council as following on from WAC's adoption of the Vermillion Accord passed in 1989 at the South Dakota Inter-Congress.

The Vermillion Accord on Human Remains
Adopted 1989

1. Respect for the mortal remains of the dead shall be accorded to all, irrespective of origin, race, religion, nationality, custom and tradition.

2. Respect for the wishes of the dead concerning disposition shall be accorded whenever possible, reasonable and lawful, when they are known or can be reasonably inferred.

3. Respect for the wishes of the local community and of relatives or guardians of the dead shall be accorded whenever possible, reasonable and lawful.

4. Respect for the scientific research value of skeletal, mummified and other human remains (including fossil hominids) shall be accorded when such value is demonstrated to exist.

5. Agreement on the disposition of fossil, skeletal, mummified and other remains shall be reached by negotiation on the basis of mutual respect for the legitimate concerns of communities for the proper disposition of their ancestors, as well as the legitimate concerns of science and education.

6. The express recognition that the concerns of various ethnic groups, as well as those of science are legitimate and to be respected, will permit acceptable agreements to be reached and honoured.

The Tamaki Makau-rau Accord on the Display of Human Remains and Sacred Objects
Adopted 2006

In recognition of the principles adopted by the Vermillion Accord, the display of human remains and sacred objects is recognised as a sensitive issue. Human remains include any organic remains and associated material. Sacred objects are those that are of special significance to a community. Display means the presentation in any media or form of human remains and sacred objects, whether on a single occasion or on an ongoing basis, including conference presentations or publications. Community may include, but is not limited to, ethnic, racial, religious, traditional or Indigenous groups of people.

WAC reiterates its commitment to scientific principles governing the study of the human past. We agree that the display of human remains or sacred objects may serve to illuminate our common humanity. As archaeologists, we believe that good science is guided by ethical principles and that our work must involve consultation and collaboration with communities. The members of the WAC council agree to assist with making contacts within the affected communities.

Any person(s) or organisation considering displaying such material or already doing so should take account of the following principles:

1. Permission should be obtained from the affected community or communities.

2. Should permission be refused that decision is final and should be respected.

3. Should permission be granted, any conditions to which that permission is subject should be complied with in full.

4. All display should be culturally appropriate.

5. Permission can be withdrawn or amended at any stage and such decisions should be respected.

6. Regular consultation with the affected community should ensure that the display remains culturally appropriate.

Appendix 3
Suggested Readings

Below we have compiled eight bibliographies. As long as these lists are, there are many more books and articles we would have liked to include. Thus, the bibliographies aim to be comprehensive without necessarily being complete.

The edited volumes on archaeological ethics listed here typically crosscut all of the thematic sections used in this bibliography. To save space and to refrain from repetition, we rarely include the individual chapters from the edited volumes if the edited volume is listed. Hence, these edited volumes should be studied for most issues that concern the ethics of archaeological practice.

Introduction to Archaeological Ethics and Applied Ethics

Bracci, Sharon L., and Clifford G. Christians (editors)
  2002 *Moral Engagement in Public Life: Theorists for Contemporary Ethics.* Peter Lang, New York.
Brown, Michael F.
  2003 *Who Owns Native Culture?* Harvard University Press, Cambridge.
Callahan, Daniel, and Sissela Bok
  1980 *Ethics Teaching in Higher Education.* Hastings Center Series in Ethics. Springer, New York.
Caplan, Patricia.
  2003 *The Ethics of Anthropology: Debates and Dilemmas.* Routledge, London.
Cassell, Joan, and Sue-Ellen Jacobs
  1987 *Handbook on Ethical Issues in Anthropology.* American Anthropological Association, Washington, D.C.
Childs, S. Terry
  2004 *Our Collective Responsibility: The Ethics and Practice of Archaeological Collections Stewardship.* Society for American Archaeology, Washington, D.C.

Cooper, David E.
   2004 *Ethics for Professionals in a Multicultural World*. Pearson Prentice Hall, Upper Saddle River, NJ.
Drennan, Robert D., and Santiago Mora (editors)
   2002 *Archaeological Research and Heritage Preservation in the Americas*. Society for American Archaeology, Washington, D.C.
Edgeworth, Matt (editor)
   2006 *Ethnographies of Archaeological Practice: Cultural Encounters, Material Transformations*. AltaMira Press, Lanham, MD.
Elliott, Deni, and Judy E. Stern (editors)
   1997 *Research Ethics: A Reader*. University Press of New England, Hanover, NH.
Green, Ernestene L. (editor)
   1984 *Ethics and Values in Archaeology*. Free Press, New York.
Feder, Kenneth L.
   1999 *Frauds, Myths, and Mysteries: Science and Pseudoscience in Archaeology*. 3rd ed. Mayfield, Mountain View, KY.
Fluehr-Lobban, Carolyn (editor)
   2003 *Ethics and the Profession of Anthropology: Dialogue for Ethically Conscious Practice*. AltaMira Press, Walnut Creek, CA.
Harding, Sandra
   1998 *Is Science Multicultural? Postcolonialisms, Feminisms, and Epistemologies*. Indiana University Press, Bloomington.
Hodder, Ian (editor)
   2000 *Towards Reflexive Methods in Archaeology: The Example at Çatalhöyük*. McDonald Institute of Archaeological Research/British Institute of Archaeology at Ankara, Monograph 289. Oxbow Books, Oxford.
Holtorf, Cornelius
   2005 *From Stonehenge to Las Vegas: Archaeology as Popular Culture*. AltaMira Press, Lanham, MD.
Joukowsky, Martha S.
   1991 Ethics in Archaeology: An American Perspective. *Berytus* 39:11–20.
Karlsson, Håkan (editor)
   2004 *Swedish Archaeologists on Ethics*. Bricoleur Press, Lindome.
Laird, Sarah (editor)
   2002 *Biodiversity and Traditional Knowledge: Equitable Partnerships in Practice*. Earthscan, London.
Lampeter Archaeology Workshop
   1997 Relativism, Objectivity, and the Politics of the Past. *Archaeological Dialogues* 4(2):164–175.
Leone, Mark P., Parker B. Potter, Jr., and Paul A. Shackel
   1987 Towards a Critical Archaeology. *Current Anthropology* 28(3):251–302.
Little, Barbara J. (editor)
   2002 *Public Benefits of Archaeology*. University Press of Florida, Gainesville.
Lynott, Mark J.
   1997 Ethical Principles and Archaeological Practice: Development of an Ethics Policy. *American Antiquity* 62(4):589–599.

Lynott, Mark J., and Alison Wylie (editors)
  2000 *Ethics in American Archaeology: Challenges for the 1990's.* 2nd ed. Society for American Archaeology, Washington, D.C.
May, William F.
  1980 Doing Ethics: The Bearing of Ethical Theories on Fieldwork. *Social Problems* 27(3):358–370.
McBryde, Isabel (editor)
  1985 *Who Owns the Past?* Oxford University Press, Melbourne.
McGimsey, Charles R., III
  1972 *Public Archaeology.* Seminar Press, New York.
Meskell, Lynn, and Peter Pels (editors)
  2005 *Embedding Ethics: Shifting Boundaries of the Anthropological Profession.* Berg, Oxford.
Mihesuah, Devon A. (editor)
  2000 *Repatriation Reader: Who Owns American Indian Remains?* University of Nebraska Press, Lincoln.
Moody-Adams, Michele
  1997 *Fieldwork in Familiar Places: Morality, Culture, and Philosophy.* Harvard University Press, Cambridge.
Nicholas, George P., and Kelly P. Bannister
  2004 Copyrighting the Past? Emerging Intellectual Property Rights Issues in Archaeology. *Current Anthropology* 45(3):327–350.
O'Keefe, Patrick J.
  1998 Codes of Ethics: Form and Function in Cultural Heritage Management. *International Journal of Cultural Property* 7(1):32–51.
O'Rourke, Dennis H.
  2003 Anthropological Genetics in the Genomic Era: A Look Back and Behind. *American Anthropologist* 105(1):101–109.
Pels, Peter
  1999 Professions of Duplexity: A Prehistory of Ethical Codes in Anthropology. *Current Anthropology* 40(2):101–136.
Pluciennik, Mark (editor)
  2001 *The Responsibilities of Archaeologists: Archaeology and Ethics.* Lampeter Workshop in Archaeology 4, BAR S981. Archaeopress, Oxford
Rachels, James
  1998 *Ethical Theory.* Oxford University Press, Oxford.
  2002 *The Elements of Moral Philosophy.* 4th ed. McGraw-Hill, New York.
Rosenswig, Robert M.
  1997 Ethics in Canadian Archaeology: An International, Comparative Analysis. *Canadian Journal of Archaeology* 21(2):99–114.
Salmon, Merrilee H.
  1997 Ethical Considerations in Anthropology and Archaeology, or Relativism and Justice for All. *Journal of Anthropological Research* 53(1):47–63.
Scarre, Chris, and Geoffrey F. Scarre (editors)
  2006 *The Ethics of Archaeology: Philosophical Perspectives on Archaeological Practice.* Cambridge University Press, Cambridge.

Singer, Peter
   1993   *Practical Ethics*. 2nd ed. Cambridge University Press, Cambridge.
Turner, Trudy R. (editor)
   2005   *Biological Anthropology and Ethics: From Repatriation to Genetic Identity*. State
      University of New York Press, Albany.
Vitelli, Karen D., and Chip Colwell-Chanthaphonh (editors)
   2006   *Archaeological Ethics*. 2nd ed. AltaMira Press, Lanham, MD.
Wax, Murray L.
   1991   The Ethics of Research in American Indian Communities. *American Indian
      Quarterly* 15(4):431–56.
Wilk, Richard R., and K. Anne Pyburn
   1998   Archaeological Ethics. In *Encyclopedia of Applied Ethics*, vol. 1, edited by Ruth Chad-
      wick, Dan Callahan, and Peter Singer, pp. 197–207. Academic Press, New York.
Wood, John J., and Shirley Powell
   1993   An Ethos for Archaeological Practice. *Human Organization* 52(4):405–413.
Woodall, J. Ned (editor)
   1990   *Predicaments, Pragmatics, and Professionalism: Ethical Conduct in Archaeology*. Spe-
      cial Publication No. 1. Society of Professional Archaeologists, Washington, D.C.
Wylie, Alison
   1999   Science, Conservation, and Stewardship: Evolving Codes of Conduct in Archae-
      ology. *Science and Engineering Ethics* 5(3):319–336.
   2002   *Thinking from Things: Essays in the Philosophy of Archaeology*. University of Cali-
      fornia Press, Berkeley.
Zilinskas, Raymond A., and Peter J. Balint (editors)
   2001   *The Human Genome Project and Minority Communities: Ethical, Social, and Politi-
      cal Dilemmas*. Praeger, Westport, CT.
Zimmerman, Larry J., Karen D. Vitelli, and Julie Hollowell-Zimmer (editors)
   2003   *Ethical Issues in Archaeology*. AltaMira Press, Walnut Creek, CA.

Stakeholder Interests

Atalay, Sonya (editor)
   2006   Decolonizing Archaeology (Special Issue). *American Indian Quarterly* 30(3).
Barber, Ian
   2006   Is the Truth Down There? Cultural Heritage Conflict and the Politics of Archaeo-
      logical Authority. *Public History Review* 13:143–154.
Blakey, Michael L.
   1987   Skull Doctors: Intrinsic Social and Political Bias in the History of American
      Physical Anthropology, with Special Reference to the Work of Ales Hrlicka. *Cri-
      tique of Anthropology* 7:7–35.
   1999   The New York African Burial Ground Project: An Examination of Enslaved
      Lives, A Construction of Ancestral Ties. *Transforming Anthropology* 7(1):53–58.
Bray, Tamara L. (editor)
   2001   *The Future of the Past: Archaeologists, Native Americans, and Repatriation*. Garland,
      New York.

Bray, Tamara L., and Thomas W. Killion (editors)
1994 *Reckoning with the Dead: The Larsen Bay Repatriation and the Smithsonian Institute.* Smithsonian Institute Press, Washington, D.C.

Brown, Denise Fay
1999 Mayas and Tourists in the Maya World. *Human Organization* 58(3):295–304.

Brown, Michael F.
2005 Heritage Trouble: Recent Work on the Protection of Intangible Cultural Property. *International Journal of Cultural Property* 12(1):40–61.

Brown, Michael F., and Margaret M. Bruchac
2006 NAGPRA From the Middle Distance: Legal Puzzles and Unintended Consequences. In *Imperialism, Art and Restitution*, edited by John H. Merryman, pp. 193–217. Cambridge University Press, Cambridge.

Carmichael, David L., Jane Hubert, Brian Reeves, and Audhild Schanche (editors)
1994 *Sacred Sites, Sacred Places.* Routledge, London.

Carver, Martin
1996 On Archaeological Value. *Antiquity* 70(267):45–56.

Chippindale, Christopher
1986 Stoned Henge: Events and Issues at the Summer Solstice, 1985. *World Archaeology* 18(1):38–58.

Cleere, Henry
2001 Uneasy Bedfellows: Universality and Cultural Heritage. In *Destruction and Conservation of Cultural Property*, edited by Robert Layton, Peter Stone, and Julian Thomas, pp. 22–29. Routledge, London.

Colwell-Chanthaphonh, Chip, and T. J. Ferguson
2004 Virtue Ethics and the Practice of History: Native Americans and Archaeologists along the San Pedro Valley of Arizona. *Journal of Social Archaeology* 4(1):5–27.

Davidson, Iain, Christine Lovell-Jones, and Robyne Bancroft (editors)
1995 *Archaeologists and Aborigines Working Together.* University of New England Press, Armidale.

Deloria, Vine, Jr.
1969 *Custer Died for Your Sins: An Indian Manifesto.* MacMillan, London.
1992 Indians, Archaeologists, and the Future. *American Antiquity* 57(4):595–598.
1997 *Red Earth, White Lies.* Fulcrum Publishing, New York.

Derry, Linda, and Maureen Malloy (editors)
2003 *Archaeologists and Local Communities: Partners in Exploring the Past.* Society for American Archaeology, Washington, D.C.

Dongoske, Kurt E., Mark Aldenderfer, and Karen Doehner (editors)
2000 *Working Together: Native Americans and Archaeologists.* Society for American Archaeology, Washington, D.C.

Dongoske, Kurt E., Michael Yeatts, Roger Anyon, and T. J. Ferguson
1997 Archaeological Cultures and Cultural Affiliation: Hopi and Zuni Perspectives in the American Southwest. *American Antiquity* 62(4):600–608.

Dowdall, Katherine M., and Otis O. Parrish
2002 A Meaningful Disturbance of the Earth. *Journal of Social Archaeology* 3(1):99–133.

Dumont, Clayton W., Jr.
   2003 The Politics of Scientific Objections to Repatriation. *Wicazo Sa Review*
         18(1):109–128.
Echo-Hawk, Roger C.
   2000 Ancient History in the New World: Integrating Oral Traditions and the Archaeo-
         logical Record in Deep Time. *American Antiquity* 65(2):267–290.
Echo-Hawk, Roger C., and Walter R. Echo-Hawk
   1994 *Battlefields and Burial Grounds: The Indian Struggle to Protect Ancestral Graves in
         the United States.* Lerner Publications, Minneapolis.
Edgeworth, Matt (editor)
   2006 *Ethnographies of Archaeological Practice: Cultural Encounters, Material Transforma-
         tions.* AltaMira Press, Lanham, MD.
Ferguson, T. J.
   1996 Native Americans and the Practice of Archaeology. *Annual Review of Anthropology*
         25:63–79.
Fforde, Cressida, Jane Hubert, and Paul Turnbull (editors)
   2002 *The Dead and Their Possessions: Repatriation in Principle, Policy, and Practice.*
         Routledge, London.
Field, Judith, John Barker, Roy Barker, Essie Coffey, Loreen Coffey, Evelyn Crawford, Les
Darcy, Ted Field, Garry Lord, Brad Steadman, and Sarah Colley.
   2000 Coming Back: Aborigines and Archaeologists at Cuddie Springs. *Public Archaeol-
         ogy* 1(1):35–48.
Gathercole, Peter, and David Lowenthal (editors)
   1990 *The Politics of the Past.* Unwin Hyman, London.
Goldstein, Lynne, and Keith Kintigh
   1990 Ethics and the Reburial Controversy. *American Antiquity* 55(3):585–591.
Green, Lesley Fordred, David R. Green, and Eduardo Góes Neves
   2003 Indigenous Knowledge and Archaeological Science: The Challenges of Public
         Archaeology in the Reserva Uaçá. *Journal of Social Archaeology* 3(3):366–398.
Greer, Shelley, Rodney Harrison, and Susan McIntyre-Tamwoy
   2002 Community-Based Archaeology in Australia. *World Archaeology* 34(2):265–287.
Gulliford, Andrew
   1996 Bones of Contention: The Repatriation of Native American Human Remains.
         The Public Historian 18(4):119–143.
   2000 *Sacred Objects and Sacred Places: Preserving Tribal Traditions.* University Press of
         Colorado, Boulder.
Hamilakis, Yannis
   1999 La Trahison des Archeologues? Archaeological Practice as Intellectual Activity in
         Postmodernity. *Journal of Mediterranean Archaeology* 12(1):60–79.
Hemming, Steve, and Vivienne Wood
   2000 Researching the Past: Oral History and Archaeology at Swan Reach. In *The
         Archaeology of Difference: Negotiating Cross-Cultural Engagements in Oceania,*
         edited by Robin Torrence and Anne Clarke, pp, 331–359. Routledge, London.
Hill, Jonathan D.
   1992 Contested Pasts and the Practice of Anthropology. *American Anthropologist*
         94(4):809–815.

Hodder, Ian
  2002 Ethics and Archaeology: The Attempt at Çatalhöyük. *Near Eastern Archaeology* 65(3):174–181.
Johnson, Elden
  1973 Professional Responsibilities and the American Indian. *American Antiquity* 38(2):129–130.
Kerber, Jordan E. (editor)
  2006 *Cross-Cultural Collaboration: Native Peoples and Archaeology in the Northeastern United States.* University of Nebraska Press, Lincoln.
King, Thomas F.
  1983 Professional Responsibility in Public Archaeology. *Annual Review of Anthropology* 12:143–164.
Klesert, Anthony L., and Alan S. Downer (editors)
  1990 *Preservation on the Reservation: Native Americans, Native American Lands and Archaeology.* Navajo Nation Papers in Anthropology 26, Window Rock, AZ.
Klesert, Anthony L., and Shirley Powell
  1993 A Perspective on Ethics and the Reburial Controversy. *American Antiquity* 58(2): 348–354.
Lane, Kevin, and Alexander Herrera
  2005 Archaeology, Landscapes and Dreams: Science, Sacred Offerings, and the Practice of Archaeology. *Archaeological Review from Cambridge* 20(1):111–129.
Langford, Ros
  1983 Our Heritage—Your Playground. *Australian Archaeology* 16:1–6.
Layton, Robert (editor)
  1989a *Conflict in the Archaeology of Living Traditions.* Unwin Hyman, London.
  1989b *Who Needs the Past? Indigenous Values and Archaeology.* Unwin Hyman, London.
Lilley, Ian
  2006 Archaeology, Diaspora, and Decolonization. *Journal of Social Archaeology* 6(1):28–47.
Lea, Joanne, and Karolyn E. Smardz
  2000 Public Archaeology in Canada. *Antiquity* 74:141–147.
Lipe, William D.
  1984 Value and Meaning in Cultural Resources. In *Approaches to the Archaeological Heritage*, edited by Henry Cleere, pp. 1–11. Cambridge University Press, Cambridge.
Little, Barbara J., and Paul A. Shackel (editors)
  2007 *Archaeology as a Tool of Civic Engagement.* AltaMira, Lanham, MD.
Loring, Stephen, and Daniel Ashini
  2000 Past and Future Pathways: Innu Cultural Heritage in the Twenty-First Century. In *Indigenous Cultures in an Interconnected World*, edited by Claire Smith and Graeme Ward, pp. 167–189. Allen and Unwin, St. Leonards, New South Wales.
McDavid, Carol
  2002 Archaeologies That Hurt; Descendants That Matter: A Pragmatic Approach to Collaboration in the Public Interpretation of African-American archaeology. *World Archaeology* 23(2):303–314.

McGuire, Randall H.
  1992 Archaeology and the First Americans. *American Anthropologist* 94(4):816–836.
  1997 Why Have Archaeologists Thought the Real Indians Were Dead and What Can We Do about It? In *Indians and Anthropologists: Vine Deloria Jr. and the Critique of Anthropology*, edited by Thomas Biolsi and Larry J. Zimmerman, pp. 63–91. University of Arizona Press, Tucson.
  2004 Contested Pasts: Archaeology and Native Americans. In *A Companion to Social Archaeology*, edited by Lynn Meskell and Robert W. Preucel, pp. 374–395. Blackwell, Oxford.

McGuire, Randall, and Paul Reckner
  2003 Building a Working Class Archaeology: The Colorado Coal Field War Project. *Industrial Archaeology Review* 25(2):83–95.

McManamon, Francis P.
  1991 The Many Publics for Archaeology. *American Antiquity* 56(1):121–130.

McNiven, Ian J., and Lynette Russell
  2005 *Appropriated Pasts: Indigenous Peoples and the Colonial Culture of Archaeology*. AltaMira Press, Lanham.

Marshall, Yvonne
  2002 What Is Community Archaeology? *World Archaeology* 34(2):211–219.

Merrill, William L., Edmund J. Ladd, and T. J. Ferguson
  1993 The Return of the Ahayu:da: Lessons for Repatriation from Zuni Pueblo and the Smithsonian Institution. *Current Anthropology* 34(5):523–567.

Merriman, Nick (editor)
  2004 *Public Archaeology*. Routledge, New York.

Miller, Daniel
  1980 Archaeology and Development. *Current Anthropology* 21(6):709–726.

Moser, Stephanie, Darren Glazier, James E. Phillips, Lamya Nasser el Nemr, Mohammed Saleh Mousa, Rascha Nasr Aiesh, Susan Richardson, Andrew Conner, and Michael Seymour
  2002 Transforming Archaeology through Practice: Strategies for Collaborative Archaeology and the Community Archaeology Project at Quseir, Egypt. *World Archaeology* 23(2): 220–248.

Mulvaney, D. J.
  1991 Past Regained, Future Lost: The Kow Swamp Pleistocene Burials. *Antiquity* 65:12–21.

Murray, Tim
  1992 Aboriginal (Pre)History and Australian Archaeology: The Discourse of Australian Prehistoric Archaeology. In *Power, Knowledge, and Aborigines* edited by Bain Atwood and John Arnold, pp. 1–19. Journal of Australian Studies special edition 35 ed. LaTrobe University Press in association with National Centre for Australian Studies, Bundoora, Victoria.

Nicholas, George P.
  2007 Native Peoples and Archaeology. In *Encyclopedia of Archaeology*, Vol. 3, edited by Deborah M. Pearsall, pp. 1660–1669. Elsevier, Oxford.

Nicholas, George P., and Thomas D. Andrews (editors)
  1997 *At a Crossroads: Archaeology and First Peoples in Canada*. Archaeology Press, Burnaby.

Nicholas, George P., and Kelly P. Bannister
  2004 Intellectual Property Rights and Indigenous Cultural Heritage in Archaeology. In *Indigenous Intellectual Property Rights: Legal Obstacles and Innovative Solutions*, edited by Mary Riley, pp. 309–340. AltaMira Press, Walnut Creek, CA.
Nicholas, George, and Julie Hollowell
  2007 Ethical Challenges to a Postcolonial Archaeology: The Legacy of Scientific Colonialism. In *Archaeology and Capitalism: From Ethics to Politics*, edited by Yannis Hamilakas and Philip Duke, pp. 59–82. Left Coast Press, Walnut Creek, CA.
O'Regan, Gerard
  2006 Regaining Authority: Setting the Agenda in Maori Heritage through the Control and Shaping of Data. *Public History Review* 13:95–107.
Pagan-Jiménez, Jaime R.
  2004 Is All Archaeology at Present a Postcolonial One? Constructive Answers from an Eccentric Point of View. *Journal of Social Archaeology* 4(2):200–213.
Peck, Trevor, Evelyn Siegfried, and Gerald A. Oetelaar (editors)
  2004 *Indigenous People and Archaeology: Proceedings of the 32nd Annual Chacmool Conference.* Archaeological Association of the University of Calgary, Calgary.
Pokotylo, David
  2007 Archaeology and the "Educated Public": A Perspective from the University. *The SAA Archaeological Record* 7(3):14–18.
Pokotylo, David, and Neil Guppy
  1999 Public Opinion and Archaeological Heritage: Views From Outside the Profession. *American Antiquity* 64(3):400–416.
Pwiti, Gilbert
  1996 Let the Ancestors Rest in Peace? New Challenges for Cultural Heritage Management in Zimbabwe. *Conservation and Management of Archaeological Sites* 1(3):151–160.
Pyburn, K. Anne
  2003 We Have Never Been Post-modern: Maya Archaeology in the Ethnographic Present. In *Continuities and Changes in Maya Archaeology: Perspectives at the Millennium*, edited by Charles W. Golden and Greg Borgstede, pp. 287–294. Routledge, New York.
Ren, Avexnim Cojti
  2006 Maya Archaeology and the Political and Cultural Identity of Contemporary Maya in Guatemala. *Archaeologies* 2(1):8–19.
Riley, Mary (editor)
  2004 *Indigenous Intellectual Property Rights: Legal Obstacles and Innovative Solutions.* AltaMira Press, Walnut Creek, CA.
Rose, Jerome C., Thomas J. Green, and Victoria D. Green
  1996 NAGPRA is Forever: Osteology and the Repatriation of Skeletons. *Annual Review of Anthropology* 25:81–103.
Russell, Ian (editor)
  2006 *Images, Representations, and Heritage: Moving Beyond Modern Approaches to Archaeology.* Springer, New York.
Shackel, Paul A., and Erve J. Chambers (editors)
  2004 *Places in Mind: Public Archaeology as Applied Anthropology.* Routledge, New York.

Shankland, David
    1997 The Anthropology of an Archaeological Presence. In *On the Surface: The Re-
        opening of Çatalhöyük*, edited by Ian Hodder, pp. 186–202. McDonald Institute,
        Cambridge.
    1999 Integrating the Past: Folklore, Mounds and People at Çatalhöyük. In *Folklore and
        Archaeology*, edited by Cornelius Holtorf, pp. 139–157. Routledge, London.

Smith, Claire
    2007 The Indigenous Transformation of Archaeological Practice. *The SAA Archaeologi-
        cal Record* 7(2):35–39.

Smith, Claire, and H. Martin Wobst (editors)
    2005 *Indigenous Archaeologies: Decolonizing Theory and Practice*. London, Routledge.

Smith, Linda T.
    1999 *Decolonizing Methodologies: Research and Indigenous Peoples*. Zed Books, London.

Sorovi-Vunidilo, Tarisi
    2003 Developing Better Relationships between Researchers and Local Pacific Commu-
        nities: The Way Forward. In *Pacific Archaeology Assessments and Prospects: Proceed-
        ings of the International Conference for the 50th Anniversary of the First Lapita
        Excavation, Koné-Nouméa 2002*, edited by Christophe Sand, pp. 371–374. Les
        Cahiers de l'Archéologie en Nouvelle-Calédonie 15. Service des Musees et du
        Patrimonie de Nouvelle-Caledonie, Noumea.

Stephenson, Janet
    2006 Conflict in the Landscape: A Case Study of the Cultural Values Model. *Public
        History Review* 13:35–52.

Stipe, Robert E.
    1987 Historic Preservation: The Process and the Actors. In *The American Mosaic: Pre-
        serving a Nation's Heritage*, edited by Robert E. Stipe and Antoinette J. Lee. U.S.
        Committee, International Council on Monuments and Sites and Preservation
        Press, Washington, D.C.

Stroulia, Anna
    2001 On the Other Side of Kiladha Bay: Local Perspectives on Archaeological Sites and
        Archaeologists. *Aegean Archaeology* 4:101–113.

Swidler, Nina, Kurt E. Dongoske, Roger Anyon, and Alan S. Downer (editors)
    1997 *Native Americans and Archaeologists: Stepping Stones to Common Ground*. AltaMira
        Press, Walnut Creek.

Thomas, David Hurst
    2000 *Skull Wars: Kennewick Man, Archaeology, and the Battle for Native American Iden-
        tity*. Basic Books, New York.

Trigger, Bruce G.
    1980 Archaeology and the Image of the American Indian. *American Antiquity*
        45(4):662–676.

Ucko, Peter J.
    1987 *Academic Freedom and Apartheid: The Story of the World Archaeological Congress*.
        Duckworth, London.

Watkins, Joe E.
    2000 *Indigenous Archaeology: American Indian Values and Scientific Practice*. AltaMira
        Press, Walnut Creek, CA.

2002 Marginal Native, Marginal Archaeologist: Ethnic Disparity in American Archaeology. *The SAA Archaeological Record* 2(4):36–37.

2003 Beyond the Margin: American Indians, First Nations, and Archaeology in North America. *American Antiquity* 68(2):273–285.

2005 Through Wary Eyes: Indigenous Perspectives on Archaeology. *Annual Review of Anthropology* 34:429–449.

2006 Communicating Archaeology: Words to the Wise. *Journal of Social Archaeology* 6(1):100–118.

Watkins, Joe E., and T. J. Ferguson

2005 Working with and Working for Indigenous Communities. In *Handbook of Archaeological Methods, Vol. II*, edited by Herbert D. G. Maschner and Christopher Chippindale, pp. 1372–1406. AltaMira Press, Lanham, MD.

Whitley, David S.

2007 Indigenous Knowledge and 21st Century Archaeological Practice: An Introduction. *The SAA Archaeological Record* 7(2):6–8.

Woodbury, Nathalie F. S.

1992 When My Grandmother Is Your Database: Reactions to Repatriation. *Anthropology Newsletter* 33(3):6.

Wylie, Alison

1995 Alternative Histories: Epistemic Disunity and Political Integrity. In *Making Alternative Histories: The Practice of Archaeology and History in Non-Western Settings*, edited by Peter Schmidt and Thomas Patterson, pp. 255–272. School of American Research, Santa Fe.

Yellowhorn, Eldon C.

2002 Awakening Internalist Archaeology in the Aboriginal World. Ph.D. Dissertation, Department of Anthropology, McGill University, Montreal.

Zimmerman, Larry J.

1998 When Data Become People: Archaeological Ethics, Reburial, and the Past as Public Heritage. *International Journal of Cultural Property* 7(1):69–86.

2005 Public Heritage, a Desire for a "White" History of America, and Some Impacts of the Kennewick Man/Ancient One Decision. *International Journal of Cultural Property* 12(2):261–270.

2005 Consulting Stakeholders. In *Archaeology in Practice: A Student Guide to Archaeological Analyses*, edited by Jane Balme and Alistair Paterson, pp. 39–58. Blackwell, London.

Ethics in Cultural Resource Management

Allison, John
  1999   Self-determination in Cultural Resource Management: Indigenous People's Inter-
         pretation of History and of Places and Landscape. In *The Archaeology and Anthro-
         pology of Landscapes*, edited by Peter J. Ucko and Robert Layton, pp. 264–283.
         Routledge, London.
Anyon, Roger, and T. J. Ferguson
  1995   Cultural Resources Management at the Pueblo of Zuni, New Mexico, USA.
         Antiquity 69:913–30.
Budhwa, Rick
  2005   An Alternative Model for First Nations Involvement in Resource Management
         Archaeology. *Canadian Journal of Archaeology* 29(1):20–45.
Byrne, Denis
  1991   Western Hegemony in Archaeological Heritage Management. *History and
         Anthropology* 5(2):269–276.
Cleere, Henry (editor)
  1984   *Approaches to the Archaeological Heritage: Comparative Study of World Resource
         Management Systems*. Cambridge University Press, Cambridge.
  1989   *Archaeological Heritage Management in the Modern World*. Unwin Hyman, London.
Craib, Donald Forsyth
  2000   *Topics in Cultural Resource Law*. Society for American Archaeology, Washington,
         D.C.
Creamer, Howard
  1990   Aboriginal Perceptions of the Past: The Implications for Cultural Resource Man-
         agement in Australia. In *The Politics of the Past*, edited by Peter Gathercole and
         David Lowenthal, pp. 130–140. Routledge, London.
Downum, Christian E., and Laurie J. Price
  1999   Applied Archaeology. *Human Organization* 58(3):226–239.
Egloff, Brian
  1998   Practicing Archaeology and the Conservation of Tam Ting, Lao People's Democra-
         tic Republic. *Conservation and Management of Archaeological Sites* 2(3):163–175.
Epp, Henri, and Brian F. Spurling
  1984   The Other Face of Janus: Research in the Service of Archaeological Resource
         Management. *Canadian Journal of Archaeology* 8(2):95–113.
Ferguson, T. J.
  2003   Anthropological Archaeology Conducted by Tribes: Traditional Cultural Proper-
         ties and Cultural Affiliation. In *Archaeology is Anthropology*, edited by Susan D.
         Gillespie and Deborah L. Nichols, pp. 137–144. Archaeological Papers of the
         American Anthropological Association No. 13. American Anthropological Asso-
         ciation, Washington, D.C.
Ferguson, T. J., and Roger Anyon
  2001   Hopi and Zuni Cultural Landscapes: Implications of Social Identity and Cultural
         Affiliation Research for Cultural Resources Management. In *Native Peoples of the
         Southwest: Negotiating Land, Water, and Ethnicities*, edited by Laurie Weinstein,
         pp. 99–122. Bergin and Garvey, Westport, CT.

Ferris, Neal
1998 'I Don't Think We're in Kansas Anymore ...' The Rise of the Archaeological Consulting Industry in Ontario. In *Bringing Back the Past Historical Perspectives on Canadian Archaeology*, edited by Pamela Smith and Donald Mitchell, pp. 225–247. Museum of Civilization, Archaeological Survey of Canada, Mercury Series, Paper 158. Canadian Museum of Civilization/Musée Canadien des Civilisations, Gatineau QC.

Fitting, James, and Albert Goodyear
1979 Client-Oriented Archaeology. *Journal of Field Archaeology* 6:352–360.

Green, William, and John Doershuk
1998 Cultural Resource Management and American Archaeology. *Journal of Archaeological Research* 6(2):121–167.

Greene, Joseph A.
1999 Preserving Which Past for Whose Future? The Dilemma of Cultural Resource Management in Case Studies from Tunisia, Cyprus and Jordan. *Conservation and Management of Archaeological Sites* 3(1&2):43–60.

Gutiirrez, Marma de la Luz, Enrique Hambleton, Justin Hyland, and Nicholas Stanley Price
1996 The Management of World Heritage Sites in Remote Areas: The Sierra de San Francisco, Baja California, Mexico. *Conservation and Management of Archaeological Sites* 1(4):209–225.

Holt, H. Barry
1983 A Cultural Resource Management Dilemma: Anasazi Ruins and the Navajos. *American Antiquity* 48(3):594–599.

Holtorf, Cornelius
2001 Is the Past a Nonrenewable Resource? In *Destruction and Conservation of Cultural Property*, edited by Robert Layton, Peter Stone, and Julian Thomas, pp. 286–297. Routledge, London.

Kerber, Jordan
1994 *Cultural Resource Management: Archaeological Research, Preservation Planning, and Public Education in the Northeastern United States*. Bergin and Garvey, Connecticut.

Killebrew, Ann E.
1999 From Canaanites to Crusaders: The Presentation of Archaeological Sites in Israel. *Conservation and Management of Archaeological Sites* 3:17–32.

King, Thomas F.
1983 Professional Responsibility in Public Archaeology. *Annual Review of Anthropology* 12:143–164.
1998 *Cultural Resource Laws and Practice: An Introductory Guide*. AltaMira Press, Walnut Creek, CA.
2002 *Thinking About Cultural Resource Management: Essays from the Edge*. AltaMira Press, Walnut Creek, CA.
2003 *Places That Count: Traditional Cultural Properties in Cultural Resource Management*. AltaMira Press, Walnut Creek, CA.

Kristiansen, Kristian
1998 Between Rationalism and Romanticism: Archaeological Heritage Management in the 1990s. *Current Swedish Archaeology* 6:115–122.

Lertrit, Sawang
  2000   Cultural Resource Management and Archaeology at Chiang Saen, Northern
    Thailand. *Journal of Southeast Asian Studies* 31(1):137–161.
Lipe, William D.
  1974   A Conservation Model for American Archaeology. *The Kiva* 39(3–4): 213–245.
McIntosh, Susan Keech
  1993   Archaeological Heritage Management and Site Inventory Systems in Africa. *Journal of Field Archaeology* 20(4):500–504.
McKercher, Bob, and Hilary Du Cros
  2002   *Cultural Tourism: The Partnership Between Tourism and Cultural Heritage Management.* Haworth Press, New York.
McManamon, Francis P., and Alf Hatton (editors)
  2000   *Cultural Resource Management in Contemporary Society: Perspectives on Managing and Presenting the Past.* Routledge, London.
Midgley, Emma, Dirk H. R. Spennemann, and Harvey Johnston
  1998   The Impact of Visitors on Aboriginal Sites in Mungo National Park. *Archaeology in Oceania* 33(3):221–231.
Palumbo, Gaetano, Abdul Sami' Abu Dayyeh, Khawla Qussous, and Mohammad Waheeb
  1995   Cultural Resource Management and National Inventory of Archaeological and Historic Sites: The Jordanian Experience. *Studies in the History and Archaeology of Jordan* 5:83–90.
Ravesloot, John C.
  1990   On the Treatment and Reburial of Human Remains: The San Xavier Bridge Project, Tucson, Arizona. *American Indian Quarterly* 14(1):35–50.
Smith, Laurajane
  2004   *Archaeological Theory and the Politics of Cultural Heritage.* Routledge, London.
  2006   *The Uses of Heritage.* Routledge, London.
Spain, James N.
  1982   Navajo Culture and Anasazi Archaeology: A Case Study in Cultural Resource Management. *The Kiva* 47(4):273–278.
Stoffle, Richard W., and Michael J. Evans
  1990   Holistic Conservation and Cultural Triage: American Indian Perspectives on Cultural Resources. *Human Organization* 49(2):91–99.
Swidler, Nina, David C. Eck, T. J. Ferguson, Leigh J. Kuwanwisiwma, Roger Anyon, Loren Panteah, Klara Kelley, and Harris Francis
  2000   Multiple Views of the Past: Integrating Archeology and Ethnography in the Jeddito Valley. *CRM* 23(9):49–53.
Vitelli, Karen D., and K. Anne Pyburn
  1997   Past Imperfect, Future Tense: Archaeology and Development. *Nonrenewable Resources* 6(2):71–84.
Willems, Willem J. H.
  1998   Archaeology and Heritage Management in Europe: Trends and Developments. *European Journal of Archaeology* 1(3):293–311.

Collectors and Commercialization

Atwood, Roger
  2004 *Stealing History: Tomb Raiders, Smugglers, and the Looting of the Ancient World.* St. Martin's Press, New York.
Barkan, Elazar, and Ronald Bush (editors)
  2002 *Claiming the Stones/Naming the Bones: Cultural Property and the Negotiation of National and Ethnic Identity.* Getty Research Institute, Los Angeles.
Bator, Paul M.
  1983 *The International Trade in Art.* University of Chicago Press, Chicago.
Belk, Russell W.
  1995 *Collecting in a Consumer Society.* Routledge, London.
Berlo, Catherine (editor)
  1992 *The Early Years of Native American Art History: The Politics of Scholarship and Collecting.* University of Washington Press, Seattle.
Bieder, Robert E.
  1992 The Collecting of Bones for Anthropological Narrative. *American Indian Culture and Research Journal* 16(2):21–36.
Blum, Orly
  2002 The Illicit Antiquities Trade: An Analysis of Current Antiquities Looting in Israel. *Culture without Context* 11(Autumn). Available: www.mcdonald.cam.ac.uk/iarc/culturewithoutcontext/issue11/blum.htm. Accessed: 20 March 2007.
Breckenridge, Carol A.
  1989 The Aesthetics and Politics of Colonial Collecting: India at World Fairs. *Comparative Studies in Society and History* 31(2):195–216.
Brodie, Neil, and Kathryn Walker Tubb
  2002 *Illicit Antiquities: The Theft of Culture and the Extinction of Archaeology.* Routledge, London.
Brodie, Neil, and Colin Renfrew
  2005 Looting and the World's Archaeological Heritage: The Inadequate Response. *Annual Review of Anthropology* 34:343–361.
Brodie, Neil, Jennifer Doole, and Colin Renfrew (editors)
  2001 *Trade in Illicit Antiquities: The Destruction of the World's Archaeological Heritage.* McDonald Institute for Archaeological Research, Cambridge.
Brodie, Neil J., Jennifer Doole, and Peter Watson
  2000 *Stealing History.* McDonald Institute for Archaeological Research, Cambridge.
Brodie, Neil, Morag M. Kersel, Christina Luke, and Kathryn Walker Tubb (editors)
  2006 *Archaeology, Cultural Heritage, and the Antiquities Trade.* University Press of Florida, Gainesville.
Cameron, Catherine (editor)
  1997 Special Issue on The Loss of Cultural Heritage: An International Perspective. *Nonrenewable Resources* 6(2).
Bruhns, Karen Olsen
  2000 www.plunderedpast.com. *Society for American Archaeology Bulletin* 18(2):14–15, 17.

Chamberlin, Russell
  1983   *Loot! The Heritage of Plunder.* Facts on File, New York.
Chase, Arlen F., Diane Z. Chase, and Harriot W. Topsey
  1988   Archaeology and the Ethics of Collecting. *Archaeology* 41(1):56–60, 87.
Chippindale, Christopher, and David W. J. Gill
  2000   Material Consequences of Contemporary Classical Collecting. *American Journal of Archaeology* 104:463–511.
Coe, Michael C.
  1993   From *Huaquero* to Connoisseur: The Early Market in Pre-Columbian Art. In *Collecting the Pre-Columbian Past*, edited by Elizabeth H. Boone, pp. 271–290. Dumbarton Oaks, Washington, D.C.
Coggins, Clemency
  1969   Illicit Traffic of Pre-Columbian Antiquities. *Art Journal* 29(1):94–98, 114.
Cole, Douglas
  1985   *Captured Heritage: The Scramble for Northwest Coast Artifacts.* University of Washington Press, Seattle.
Colwell-Chanthaphonh, Chip
  2004   Those Obscure Objects of Desire: Collecting Cultures and the Archaeological Landscape in the San Pedro Valley of Arizona. *Journal of Contemporary Ethnography* 33(5):571–601.
Constable, Giles
  1983   The Looting of Ancient Sites and the Illicit Trade in Works of Art. *Journal of Field Archaeology* 10:482–485.
Cook, Brian F.
  1991   The Archaeologist and the Art Market: Policies and Practice. *Antiquity* 65:533–537.
Dorfman, John
  1998   Getting Their Hands Dirty? Archaeologists and the Looting Trade. *Lingua Franca* May/June:28–36.
Ede, James
  1998   Ethics, the Antiquities Trade, and Archaeology. *International Journal of Cultural Property* 7(1):128–131.
Elia, Ricardo J.
  1992   The Ethics of Collaboration: Archaeologists and the *Whydah* Project. *Historical Archaeology* 26(4):105–117.
  1993   A Seductive and Troubling Work. *Archaeology* 46(1):64, 66–69.
  1997   Looting, Collecting, and the Destruction of Archaeological Resources. *Nonrenewable Resources* 6(2):85–98.
  2001   Analysis of the Looting, Selling, and Collecting of Apulian Red-Figure Vases: A Quantitative Approach. In *Trade in Illicit Antiquities: The Destruction of the World's Archaeological Heritage,* edited by Neil Brodie, Jennifer Doole, and Colin Renfrew, pp. 145–153. McDonald Institute Monographs, Cambridge.
Gill, David W. J.
  1997   Sotheby's, Sleaze and Subterfuge: Inside the Antiquities Trade. *Antiquity* 71:468–471.

Gill, David W. J., and Christopher Chippindale
   1993 Material and Intellectual Consequences of Esteem for Cycladic Figures. *American Journal of Archaeology* 97:601–659.
Greenfield, Jeanette
   1995 *The Return of Cultural Treasures.* 2nd ed. Cambridge University Press, Cambridge.
Griffin, Gillett G.
   1986 In Defense of the Collector. *National Geographic* 169(4):462–465.
   1999 Collecting Pre-Columbian Art. In *The Ethics of Collecting Cultural Property: Whose Culture? Whose Property?* edited by Phyllis Mauch Messenger, pp. 103–116. University of New Mexico Press, Albuquerque.
Hamilakis, Yannis
   1999 Stories from Exile: Fragments from the Cultural Biography of the Parthenon (or 'Elgin') Marbles. *World Archaeology* 31(2):303–320.
Heath, Dwight B.
   1973 Economic Aspects of Commercial Archeology in Costa Rica. *American Antiquity* 38(3):259–65.
Herscher, Ellen
   2001 Scourge of the Forgery Culture. *Archaeology* 54(1):61–66.
Hinsley, Curtis M.
   1992 Collecting Cultures and Cultures of Collecting: The Lure of the American Southwest, 1880–1915. *Museum Anthropology* 16(1):12–20.
   1996 Digging for Identity: Reflections on the Cultural Background of Collecting. *American Indian Quarterly* 20(2):180–196.
Hitchens, Christopher, and Graham Binns
   1998 *The Elgin Marbles: Should They be Returned to Greece?* Verso, London.
Hollowell, Julie
   2006 Moral Arguments on Subsistence Digging. In *The Ethics of Archaeology: Philosophical Perspectives on the Practice of Archaeology*, edited by Chris Scarre and Geoffrey F. Scarre, pp. 69–93. Cambridge University Press, Cambridge.
Hollowell-Zimmer, Julie
   2003 Digging in the Dirt - Ethics and "Low-End Looting". In *Ethical Issues in Archaeology*, edited by Larry J. Zimmerman, Karen D. Vitelli and Julie Hollowell-Zimmer, pp. 45–56. AltaMira Press, Walnut Creek, CA.
Holtorf, Cornelius
   1995 Object-Orientated and Problem-Orientated Approaches of Archaeological Research - Reconsidered. *Hephaistos* 13: 7–18.
Howell, Carol L.
   1996 Daring to Deal with Huaqueros. In *Archaeological Ethics*, edited by Karen D. Vitelli, pp. 47–53. AltaMira Press, Walnut Creek, CA.
Jones, Schuyler
   1975 Afghan Cultural Heritage Threatened by Art and Antiquities Traffic. *Cultural Anthropology* 16(3):443.
Judd, Neil M.
   1924 Report on Illegal Excavations in Southwestern Ruins. *American Anthropologist* 26(3):428–432.

Kirkpatrick, Sidney D.
  1992   *Lord of Sipan: A Tale of Pre-Inca Tombs, Archaeology, and Crime.* William Morrow and Company, New York.
Kleiner, Fred S.
  1990   On the Publication of Recent Acquisitions of Antiquities. *American Journal of Archaeology* 94:525–527.
Krech, Shepard, III, and Barbara A. Hail (editors)
  1999   *Collecting Native America, 1870–1960.* Smithsonian Institution Press, Washington, D.C.
Layton, Robert, and Julian Thomas
  2003   The Destruction and Conservation of Cultural Property. *World Archaeological Bulletin* 18:29–72.
Lazrus, Paula
  1995   Is Field Survey Always Non-Destructive? Thoughts on Survey, Looting and the International Traffic in Antiquities. *Journal of Field Archaeology* 22(1):131–135.
McIntosh, Susan K., Colin Renfrew, and Steven Vincent
  2000   The Good Collector: Fabulous Beast or Endangered Species? *Public Archaeology* 1:73–81.
McLaughlin, Robert H.
  1998   The American Archaeological Record: Authority to Dig, Power to Interpret. *International Journal of Cultural Property* 7(2):342–375.
Mallouf, Robert J.
  2000   An Unraveling Rope: The Looting of America's Past. In *Repatriation Reader: Who Owns American Indian Remains?* edited by Devon A. Mihesuah, pp. 59–73. University of Nebraska Press, Lincoln.
Marks, Peter
  1998   The Ethics of Art Dealing. *International Journal of Cultural Property* 7(1):116–127.
Matsuda, David
  1998   The Ethics of Archaeology, Subsistence Digging, and Artifact Looting in Latin America: Point, Muted Counterpoint. *International Journal of Cultural Property* 7(1):87–97.
Mazariegos, Oswaldo C.
  1998   Archaeology and Nationalism in Guatemala at the Time of Independence. *Antiquity* 72:376–386.
Merryman, John Henry
  1998   Cultural Property Ethics. *International Journal of Cultural Property* 7(1):21–31.
  2000   A Licit International Trade in Cultural Objects. In *Thinking about the Elgin Marbles: Critical Essays on Cultural Property, Art and Law,* edited by John Henry Merryman, pp. 176–226. Kluwer Law International, Cambridge.
Messenger, Phyllis M. (editor)
  1999   *The Ethics of Collecting Cultural Property: Whose Culture? Whose Property?* Originally published 1989. University of New Mexico Press, Albuquerque.
Meyer, Karl E.
  1973   *The Plundered Past: The Story of the Illegal International Traffic in Works of Art.* Atheneum, New York.

Migliore, Sam
1991 Treasure Hunting and Pillaging in Sicily: Acquiring a Deviant Identity. *Anthropologica* 33:161–75.
Miller, Samuel C.
1998 A Syrian Odyssey: The Return of Syrian Mosaics by the Newark Museum. *International Journal of Cultural Property* 7(1):166–169.
Monreal, Luis
1979 Problems and Possibilities in Recovering Dispersed Cultural Heritages. *Museum* 31(1):49–57.
Muscarella, Oscar White
1984 On Publishing Unexcavated Artifacts. *Journal of Field Archaeology* 11:61–65.
2000 *The Lie Became Great: The Forgery of Ancient Near Eastern Cultures*, vol. I. Studies in the Art and Archaeology of Antiquity. STYX Publications, Groningen.
Nicholas, George P., and Alison Wylie
in press Archaeological Finds: Legacies of Appropriation, Modes of Response. In *Stolen Goods? The Ethics of Cultural Appropriation,* edited by Conrad Brunk and James Young. Blackwell, New York.
Nicholas, Lynn H.
1994 *The Rape of Europa: The Fate of Europe's Treasures in the Third Reich and the Second World War.* Vintage Books, New York.
O'Keefe, Patrick J.
1997 *Trade in Antiquities: Reducing Theft and Destruction.* Archetype Publications and UNESCO, London and Paris.
Paredes Maury, Sofia
1998 Surviving the Rainforest: The Realities of Looting in the Rural Villages of El Peten, Guatemala. Foundation for the Advancement of Mesoamerican Studies, Crystal River. http://www.famsi.org/reports/95096/index.html (Last accessed 13 January 2008)
Parezo, Nancy J.
1985 Cushing as Part of the Team: The Collecting Activities of the Smithsonian Institution. *American Ethnologist* 12(4):763–774.
2006 Collecting Diné Culture in the 1880s: Two Army Physicians and Their Ethnographic Approaches. *Museum Anthropology* 29(2):95–117.
Pearce, Susan M.
1995 *On Collecting*. Routledge, London.
1998 *Collecting in Contemporary Society*. AltaMira Press, Walnut Creek, CA.
Pringle, P. M.
1939 Getting Down to Business, From a Collector's Point of View. *American Antiquity* 4(3):273–276.
Renfrew, Colin
2000 *Loot, Legitimacy, and Ownership*. Duckworth, London.
Rose, Mark, and Ozgen Acar
1996 Turkey's War on the Illicit Antiquities Trade. In *Archaeological Ethics*, edited by Karen D. Vitelli, pp. 71–89. AltaMira Press, Walnut Creek, CA.

Rowan, Yorke, and Uzi Baram (editors)
  2004 *Marketing Heritage: Archaeology and the Consumption of the Past.* AltaMira Press, Walnut Creek, CA.
Sackler, Elizabeth A.
  1998 The Ethic(s) of Collecting. *International Journal of Cultural Property* 7(1):132–140.
Schmidt, Peter, and Roderick McIntosh (editors)
  1996 *Plundering Africa's Past.* Indiana University Press, Bloomington.
Sheets, Payson D.
  1973 The Pillage of Prehistory. *American Antiquity* 38(3):317–320.
Smith, Kimbra L.
  2005 Looting and the Politics of Archaeological Knowledge in Northern Peru. *Ethnos* 70(2):149–170.
St. Clair, William
  1999 The Elgin Marbles: Questions of Stewardship and Accountability. *International Journal of Cultural Property* 8(2):391–521.
Tubb, Kathryn W. (editor)
  1995 *Antiquities Trade or Betrayed: Legal, Ethical and Conservation Issues.* Archetype Publications, London.
Udvardy, Monica, Linda L. Giles, and John B. Mitsanze
  2003 The Transatlantic Trade in African Ancestors: Mijikenda Memorial Statues (Vigango) and the Ethics of Collecting and Curating Non-Western Cultural Property. *American Anthropologist* 105(3):566–580.
Vitelli, Karen D.
  2000 E-commerce in Antiquities. *Society for American Archaeology Bulletin* 18(4):4–5.
White, Shelby
  1998 A Collector's Odyssey. *International Journal of Cultural Property* 7(1):170–176.
Whittaker, John C., and Michael Stafford
  1999 Replicas, Fakes, and Art: The Twentieth Century Stone Age and its Effects on Archaeology. *American Antiquity* 64(2):203–214.
Wylie, Alison
  1996 Ethical Dilemmas in Archaeological Practice: Looting, Repatriation, Stewardship, and the (Trans)formation of Disciplinary Identity. *Perspectives on Science* 4(2):154–194.

Ethics and Museums

Ames, Michael
  2003 How to Decorate a House: The Renegotiation of Cultural Representation at the UBC Museum of Anthropology. In *Museums and Source Communities*, edited by Laura Peers and Alison K. Brown, pp. 171–180. Routledge, London.
Andrei, Mary Anne, and Hugh H. Genoways
  1997 Museum Ethics. *Curator* 40(1):6–12.
Archambault, JoAllyn
  1993 American Indians and American Museums. *Zeitschrift Für Ethnologie* 118:7–22.

Barringer, Tim, and Tom Flynn (editors)
  1998 *Colonialism and the Object: Empire, Material Culture and the Museum.* Routledge, London.
Bogdanos, Matthew, and William Patrick
  2005 *Thieves of Baghdad.* Bloomsbury, New York.
Castañeda, Quetzil E.
  1996 *In the Museum of Maya Culture: Touring Chichén Itzá.* University of Minnesota Press, Minneapolis.
Coggins, Clemency
  1998 A Proposal for Museum Acquisition Policies in the Future. *International Journal of Cultural Property* 7:434–437.
Conn, Steven
  1998 *Museums and American Intellectual Life, 1876–1926.* University of Chicago Press, Chicago.
Crane, Susan A.
  1997 Memory, Distortion, and History in the Museum. *History and Theory* 36(4):44–63.
Curtis, Neil G. W.
  2003 Human Remains: The Sacred, Museums, and Archaeology. *Public Archaeology* 3(1):21–32.
des Portes, Elisabeth
  1998 Museums and Ethics: Long History, New Developments. *International Journal of Cultural Property* 7(1):141–148.
Dubin, Steven C.
  1999 *Displays of Power: Memory and Amnesia in the American Museum.* New York University Press, New York.
Fine-Dare, Kathleen S.
  2002 *Grave Injustice: The American Indian Repatriation Movement and NAGPRA.* University of Nebraska Press, Lincoln.
Gable, Eric, and Richard Handler
  2006 Persons of Stature and the Passing Parade: Egalitarian Dilemmas at Monticello and Colonial Williamsburg. *Museum Anthropology* 29(1):5–19.
Handler, Richard, and Eric Gable
  1996 After Authenticity at an American Heritage Site. *American Anthropologist* 98(3):568–578.
  1997 *The New History in an Old Museum: Creating the Past at Colonial Williamsburg.* Duke University Press, Durham.
Hollowell, Julie
  2005 Ancient Art from Where We Live Surfaces in the Art World. *American Anthropologist* 107(3):489–497.
Herle, Anita
  1994 Museums and First Peoples in Canada. *Journal of Museum Ethnography* 6:39–66.
Hervik, Peter
  1998 The Mysterious Maya of National Geographic. *Journal of Latin American Anthropology* 4(1):166–197.

Isaac, Gwyniera, Wendy Fontenelle, and Tom Kennedy
  1997 A:shiwi A:wan: 'Belonging to the Zuni People' Interviews from the A:shiwi A:wan Museum and Heritage Center in Zuni, NM. *Cultural Survival Quarterly* 21(1):41–46.

Karp, Ivan, Christine M. Kreamer, and Steven D. Lavine (editors)
  1992 *Museums and Communities: The Politics of Public Culture.* Smithsonian Institution Press, Washington, D.C.

Kelly, John D.
  2000 Nature, Natives, and Nations: Glorification and Asymmetries in Museum Representation, Fiji and Hawaii. *Ethnos* 65(2):195–216.

King, Mary Elizabeth
  1980 Curators: Ethics and Obligations. *Curator* 23(1):10–18.

Kreps, Christina F.
  2003 *Liberating Culture: Cross-Cultural Perspectives on Museums, Curation, and Heritage Preservation.* Taylor & Francis, London.

Lavine, Steven D., and Ivan Karp
  1991 *Exhibiting Cultures: The Poetics and Politics of Museum Display.* Smithsonian Institution Press, Washington, D.C.

Levy, Janet
  2006 Prehistory, Identity, and Archaeological Representation in Nordic Museums. *American Anthropologist* 108(1):135–147.

Lowry, Glenn D.
  1998 Cultural Property: A Museum Director's Perspective. *International Journal of Cultural Property* 7(2):438–445.

Mauzé, Marie
  2003 Two Kwakwaka'wakw Museums: Heritage and Politics. *Ethnohistory* 50(3):503–522.

McEwan, Colin, Chris Hudson, and Maria-Isabel Silva
  1994 Archaeology and Community: A Village Cultural Center and Museum in Ecuador. *Practicing Anthropology* 16(1):3–7.

McManus, Paulette M. (editor)
  2000 *Archaeological Displays and the Public: Museology and Interpretations.* Archetype, London.

Monreal, Luis
  1979 Problems and Possibilities in Recovering Dispersed Cultural Heritages. *Museum* 31(1):49–57.

Moser, Stephanie
  2003 Representing Archaeological Knowledge in Museums: Exhibiting Human Origins and Strategies for Change. *Public Archaeology* 3(1):3–20.

Peers, Laura, and Alison K. Brown (editors)
  2003 *Museums and Source Communities: A Routledge Reader.* Routledge, London.

Price, Richard, and Sally Price
  1995 Executing Culture: Musee, Museo, Museum. *American Anthropologist* 97(1):97–109.

Rosenblum, Amalia
  1996 Prisoners of Conscience: Public Policy and Contemporary Repatriation Discourse. *Museum Anthropology* 20(3):58–71.

Sabloff, Jeremy A.
  1999   Scientific Research, Museum Collections, and the Rights of Ownership. *Science and Engineering Ethics* 5(3):347–354.
Sandell, Richard
  1998   Museums as Agents of Social Inclusion. *Museum Management and Curatorship* 17(4):401–418.
  2006   *Museums, Prejudice, and the Reframing of Difference.* Routledge, London.
Sandler, Lauren
  2004   The Thieves of Baghdad. *Atlantic Monthly* 294(4):175–182.
Scheper-Hughes, Nancy
  2001   Ishi's Brain, Ishi's Ashes. *Anthropology Today* 17(1):12–18.
Silverman, Helaine (editor)
  2006   *Archaeological Site Museums in Latin America.* University Press of Florida, Gainesville.
Simpson, Moira G.
  1996   *Making Representations: Museums in the Post-Colonial Era.* Routledge, London.
Stocking, George W., Jr. (editor)
  1985   *Objects and Others: Essays on Museums and Material Culture.* University of Wisconsin Press, Madison.
Yelvington, Kevin A., Neill G. Goslin, and Wendy Arriaga
  2002   Whose History? Museum Making and Struggles over Ethnicity and Representation in the Sunbelt. *Critique of Anthropology* 22(3):343–379.

Training Students and Public Education

Bender, Susan J., and George S. Smith (editors)
  2000   *Teaching Archaeology in the Twenty-First Century.* Society for American Archaeology, Washington, D.C.
Burke, Heather, and Claire Smith
  2007   *Archaeology to Delight and Instruct: Active Learning in the University Classroom.* Berg, Oxford.
Davis, Elaine M.
  2005   *How Students Understand the Past: From Theory to Practice.* AltaMira Press, Walnut Creek.
Frink, Douglas S.
  1997   Managing the Public's Cultural Resources: from Presentation to Participation. *Journal of Middle Atlantic Archaeology* 13:161–165.
Jameson, John H., Jr. (editor)
  1997   *Presenting Archaeology to the Public.* AltaMira Press, Lanham, MD.
Ludlow Collective
  2001   Archaeology of the Colorado Coal Field War, 1913–1914. In *Archaeologies of the Contemporary Past,* edited by Victor Buchli and Gavin Lucas, pp. 94–107. Routledge, London.
Malone, Caroline, Peter Stone, and Mary Baxter
  2000   Education in Archaeology. *Antiquity* 74:122–126.

Merriman, Nick, and Tim Schdla-Hall (editors)
2004 *Public Archaeology.* Routledge, London.
Potter, Parker B., Jr.
1994 *Public Archaeology in Annapolis: A Critical Approach to History in Maryland's "Ancient City."* Smithsonian Institution Press, Washington, D.C.
Potter, Parker B., Jr., and Mark P. Leone
1987 Archaeology in Public in Annapolis: Four Seasons, Six Sites, Seven Tours, and 32,000 Visitors. *American Antiquity* 6(1):51–61.
Pryor, Francis
1989 Look What We've Found—A Case Study in Public Archaeology. *Antiquity* 63:51–61.
Ramos, Maria, and Davis Duganne
2000 *Exploring Public Perceptions and Attitudes About Archaeology.* Harris Interactive for the Society for American Archaeology, Washington D.C.
Smardz, Karolyn, and Shelley J. Smith (editors)
2000 *The Archaeology Education Handbook: Sharing the Past with Kids.* AltaMira Press, Walnut Creek.
Society for American Archeology (SAA)
1990 *Save the Past for the Future: Actions for the '90s.* Final Report, Taos Working Conference on Preventing Archeological Looting and Vandalism (May 7–12, 1989). On file, SAA Office of Government Relations, Washington, D.C.
Stone, Peter, and Robert MacKenzie (editors)
1994 *The Excluded Past: Archaeology in Education.* Routledge, London.
Stone, Peter G., and Brian L. Molyneaux (editors)
1994 *The Presented Past: Heritage, Museums, and Education.* Routledge, London.
Stone, Peter G., and Philippe Planel (editors)
1999 *The Constructed Past: Experimental Archaeology, Education, and the Public.* Routledge, London.
Stacy, V. K. Pheriba
1998 Training O'Odham as Desert Archaeologists: A Historical Remembrance. *Kiva* 64(2):201–209.

Gender Equity

Arnold, Bettina
2005 Teaching with Intent: The Archaeology of Gender. *Archaeologies* 1(2):83–93.
Bacus, Elisabeth A., Alex W. Barker, Jeffrey D. Bonevich, Sandra L. Dunavan, J. Benjamin Fitzhugh, Debra L. Gold, Nurit S. Goldman-Finn, William Griffin, and Karen M. Mudar
1993 *A Gendered Past: A Critical Bibliography of Gender in Archaeology.* Technical Report 25. University of Michigan Museum of Anthropology, Ann Arbor.
Bart, Jody (editor)
2000 *Women Succeeding in the Sciences: Theories and Practices Across Disciplines.* Purdue University Press, West Lafayette, IN.
Burkholder, Jo Ellen
2006 Doing It for Ourselves: Women and Participation in the SAA Annual Meetings. *SAA Archaeological Record* 6(2):27–31.

Claassen, Cheryl (editor)
1994 *Women in Archaeology*. University of Pennsylvania Press, Philadelphia.

Conkey, Margaret W.
2005 Dwelling at the Margins, Action at the Intersection? Feminist and Indigenous Archaeologies, 2005. *Archaeologies* 1(1):9–59.

Conkey, Meg W., and Joan M. Gero
1997 Programme to Practice: Gender and Feminism in Archaeology. *Annual Review of Anthropology* 26:411–437.

Diaz-Andreu, Margarita, and Marie L.S. Sørensen
1998 *Excavating Women: A History of Women in European Archaeology*. Routledge, London.

Du Cros, Hilary, and Laurajane Smith
1993 Women in Archaeology: A Feminist Critique. In *Occasional Papers in Archaeology*, vol. 23. Canberra Department of Prehistory, Research School of Pacific Studies, Australian National University, Canberra.

Gero, Joan M., and Margaret W. Conkey (editors)
1991 *Engendering Archaeology: Women and Prehistory*. Basil Blackwell, Oxford.

Hutson, Scott R.
1998 Institutional and Gender Effects on Academic Hiring Practices. *Society for American Archaeology Bulletin* 16(4):19–21, 26.
2002 Gendered Citation Practices in American Antiquity and Other Archaeological Journals. *American Antiquity* 67(2):331–342.

Irwin-Williams, Cynthia
1990 Women in the Field: The Role of Women in Archaeology before 1960. In *Women in Science: Righting the Record*, edited by G. Kass-Simon and Patricia Farnes, pp. 1–41. Indiana University Press, Bloomington.

Nakane, Chie
1982 Becoming an Anthropologist. In *Women Scientists: The Road to Liberation*, edited by Derrek Richter, pp. 45–60. MacMillan Press, London.

Nelson, Margaret C., Sarah M. Nelson, and Alison Wylie (editors)
1994 *Equity Issues for Women in Archaeology*. Archaeological Papers of the American Anthropological Association, Washington, D.C.

Nelson, Sarah M.
1999 Indiana Jones and the Female Archaeologist. *Discovering Archaeology* 4:1–3.

Parezo, Nancy J. (editor)
1993 *Hidden Scholars: Women Anthropologists and the Native American Southwest*. University of New Mexico Press, Albuquerque.

Stark, Barbara L., Katherine A. Spielmann, Brenda Shears, and Michael Ohnersorgen
1997 The Gender Effect on Editorial Boards and in Academia. *Society for American Archaeology Bulletin* 15(4):1–8.

Two Bears, Davina
2000 A Navajo Student's Perception: Anthropology and the Navajo Nation Archaeology Department Student Training Program. In *Working Together: Native Americans and Archaeologists*, edited by Kurt E. Dongoske, Mark Aldenderfer, and Karen Doehner, pp. 15–22. Society for American Archaeology, Washington D.C.

Wennerás, Christine, and Agnes Wold
  2001 Nepotism and Sexism in Peer-Review. In *Women, Science, and Technology: A Reader in Feminist Science Studies,*, edited by Mary Wyer, Mary Barbercheck, Donna Geisman, Hatice Örün Öztürk, and Marta Wayne, pp. 46–52. Routledge, New York.

Wright, Rita P.
  2003 Gender Matters—A Question of Ethics. In *Ethical Issues in Archaeology*, edited by Larry J. Zimmerman, Karen D. Vitelli and Julie Hollowell-Zimmer, pp. 225–238. AltaMira Press, Walnut Creek, CA.

Wylie, Alison
  1992 The Interplay of Evidential Constraints and Political Interests: Recent Archaeological Research on Gender. *American Antiquity* 57(1):15–35.

The Nation and the Law

Abu el-Haj, Nadia
  1998 Translating Truths: Nationalism, the Practice of Archaeology, and the Remaking of Past and Present in Contemporary Jerusalem. *American Ethnologist* 25(2):166–188.

Appadurai, Arjun
  2002 The Globalization of Archaeology and Heritage. *Journal of Social Archaeology* 1(1):35–49.

Appiah, Kwame A.
  2006 Whose Culture Is It? *The New York Review of Books* 53(2):38–41.

Arnold, Bettina
  1992 The Past as Propaganda: Totalitarian Archaeology in Nazi Germany. *Antiquity* 64:464–478.

  1999 The Contested Past. *Anthropology Today* 15(4):1–4.

  2002 Justifying Genocide: Archaeology and the Construction of Difference. In *Annihilating Difference: The Anthropology of Genocide*, edited by Alex Hinton, pp. 95–116. University of California Press, Berkeley.

Ashton, Paul, and Jennifer Cornwall
  2006 Corralling Conflict: The Politics of Australian Federal Heritage Legislation Since the 1970s. *Public History Review* 13:53–65.

Atkinson, John A., Iain Banks, and Jerry O'Sullivan (editors)
  1996 *Nationalism and Archaeology*. Cruithne Press, Glasgow.

Bernbeck, Reinhard, and Susan Pollock
  1996 Ayodhya, Archaeology, and Identity. *Current Anthropology* 37(supp):138–142.

Boylan, Patrick J.
  2002 The Concept of Cultural Protection in Times of Armed Conflict: From the Crusades to the New Millennium. In *Illicit Antiquities: The Theft of Culture and the Extinction of Archaeology*, edited by Kathryn W. Tubb and Neil Brodie, pp. 43–108. Routledge, London.

Brodie, Neil
  2003 Spoils of War. *Archaeology* 56(4):16–19.

Bruner, Edward M.

1996 Tourism in Ghana: The Representation of Slavery and the Return of the Black Diaspora. *American Anthropologist* 98(2):290–304.

Bruning, Susan B.

2006 Complex Legal Legacies: The Native American Graves Protection and Repatriation Act, Scientific Study, and Kennewick Man. *American Antiquity* 71(3):501–521.

Butler, Beverley

2001 Return to Alexandria: Conflict and Contradiction in Discourses of Origins and Heritage Revivalism. In *Destruction and Conservation of Cultural Property*, edited by Robert Layton, Peter Stone, and Julian Thomas, pp. 55–74. Routledge, London.

Carman, John

1996 *Valuing Ancient Things: Archaeology and Law.* Leicester University, London.

Chapman, John

1994 Destruction of a Common Heritage: The Archaeology of War in Croatia, Bosnia and Hercegovina. *Antiquity* 68:120–126.

Cheek, Annetta L.

1991 Protection of Archaeological Resources on Public Lands: History of the Archaeological Resources Protection Act. In *Protecting the Past*, edited by George Smith and John E. Ehrenhard, pp. 33–39. CRC Press, Boca Raton, FL.

Clark, Geoffrey A.

1999 NAGPRA, Science, and the Demon-Haunted World. *Skeptical Inquirer* 23(3):44–48.

Coggins, Clemency

1998 United States Cultural Property Legislation: Observations of a Combatant. *International Journal of Cultural Property* 7(1):52–68.

Coningham, Robin, and Nick Lewer

1999 Paradise Lost: The Bombing of the Temple of the Tooth—A UNESCO World Heritage Site in Sri Lanka. *Antiquity* 73:857–866.

Cunningham, Richard B.

2006 *Archaeology, Relics, and the Law.* 2nd ed. Carolina Academic Press, Durham.

Daher, Rami F.

1999 Gentrification and the Politics of Power: Capital and Culture Emerging in Jordanian Heritage Industry. *Traditional Dwellings and Settlement Review* 10(2):33–45.

Diaz-Andreu, Margarita

1993 Theory and Ideology in Archaeology: Spanish Archaeology Under the Franco Regime. *Antiquity* 67:74–82.

Diaz-Andreu, Margarita, and Timothy Champion (editors)

1996 *Nationalism and Archaeology in Europe.* University College London Press, London.

Dietler, Michael

1994 'Our Ancestors the Gauls': Archaeology, Ethnic Nationalism, and the Manipulation of Celtic Identity in Modern Europe. *American Anthropologist* 96(3):584–605.

Downum, Christian E., and Laurie J. Price
  1999 Applied Archaeology. *Human Organization* 58(3):226–239.
Ehrentraut, Adolf W.
  1996 Maya Ruins, Cultural Tourism and the Contested Symbolism of Collective Identities. *Culture* 16(1):15–32.
Erickson, Clark
  1998 Applied Archaeology and Rural Development: Archaeology's Potential Contribution to the Future. In *Crossing Currents: Continuity and Change in Latin America* edited by Michael B. Whiteford and Scott Whiteford, pp. 34–45. Prentice-Hall, Upper Saddle, NJ.
Farrer, Claire R.
  1994 Who Owns the Words? An Anthropological Perspective on Public Law 101–601. *Journal of Arts Management, Law and Society* 23(4):317–326.
Fawcett, Clare
  1986 Politics of Assimilation in Japanese Archaeology. *Archaeological Review of Cambridge* 5(1):43–57.
Ferris, Neal
  2003 Between Colonial and Indigenous Archaeologies: Legal and Extra-legal Ownership of the Archaeological Past in North America. *Canadian Journal of Archaeology* 27(2):154–190.
Fine-Dare, Kathleen
  2005 Anthropological Suspicion, Public Interest and NAGPRA. *Journal of Social Archaeology* 5(2):171–192.
Fitschen, Thomas
  1996 Licit International Art Trade in Times of Armed Conflict? *International Journal of Cultural Property* 5(1):127–132.
FitzGibbon, Kate (editor)
  2005 *Who Owns the Past? Cultural Policy, Cultural Property, and the Law.* Rutgers University Press and Council for Cultural Policy, New Brunswick, NJ.
Fowler, Don D.
  1987 Uses of the Past: Archaeology in the Service of the State. *American Antiquity* 52(2):230–247.
Funari, Pedro
  2001a Destruction and Conservation of Cultural Property in Brazil: Academic and Practical Challenges. In *Destruction and Conservation of Cultural Property*, edited by Robert Layton, Peter Stone, and Julian Thomas, pp. 93–101. Routledge, London.
  2001b Public Archaeology from a Latin American Perspective. *Public Archaeology* 1(4):239–243.
Ganado, Albert
  1999 The Protection of Cultural Heritage in Maltese Law. *Journal of Mediterranean Studies* 9(1):122–134.
Garlake, Peter S.
  1982 Prehistory and Ideology in Zimbabwe. *Africa* 52(3):1–19.
Gatewood, John B., and Catherine M. Cameron
  2004 Battlefield Pilgrims at Gettysburg National Park. *Ethnology* 43(3):193–216.

Gerstenblith, Patty
  1995 Identity and Cultural Property: The Protection of Cultural Property in the United States. *Boston University Law Review* 75:559–688.
  2004 *Art, Cultural Heritage, and the Law: Cases and Materials.* Carolina Academic Press, Durham.
Gerstenblith, Patty (editor)
  1998 Ethical Considerations and Cultural Property (Special Issue). *International Journal of Cultural Property* 7(1).
Glover, Ian C.
  1999 Letting the Past Serve the Present—Some Contemporary Uses of Archaeology in Viet Nam. *Antiquity* 73:594–602.
Gosden, Chris
  2001 Postcolonial Archaeology: Issues of Culture, Identity, and Knowledge. In *Archaeological Theory Today*, edited by Ian Hodder, pp. 241–261. Polity Press, Cambridge.
Green, William
  1998 Cultural Resource Management and American Archaeology. *Journal of Archaeological Research* 6(2):121–167.
Gugolz, Alessandro
  1996 The Protection of Cultural Heritage in the Sultanate of Oman. *International Journal of Cultural Property* 5(2):291–309.
Hall, Martin
  2001 Cape Town's District Six and the Archaeology of Memory. In *Destruction and Conservation of Cultural Property*, edited by Robert Layton, Peter Stone, and Julian Thomas, pp. 298–311. Routledge, London.
Haglund, William D., Melissa Connor, and Douglas D. Scott
  2001 The Archaeology of Contemporary Mass Graves. *Historical Archaeology* 35(1):57–69.
Hamilakis, Yannis
  2003 Iraq, Stewardship and the "Record": An Ethical Crisis for Archaeology. *Public Archaeology* 3:104–111.
  2005 Whose World and Whose Archaeology? The Colonial Present and the Return of the Political. *Archaeologies* 1(2):94–101.
Hamilakis, Yannis, and Phillip Duke (editors)
  2007 *Archaeology and Capitalism: From Ethics to Politics.* Left Coast Press, Walnut Creek.
Harmon, David, Francis P. McManamon, and Dwight T. Pitcaithley (editors)
  2006 *The Antiquities Act: A Century of American Archaeology, Historic Preservation, and Nature Conservation.* University of Arizona Press, Tucson.
Harris, Charles H., and Louis R. Sadler
  2003 *The Archaeologist Was a Spy: Sylvanus G. Morley and the Office of Naval Intelligence.* University of New Mexico Press, Albuquerque.
Heffernan, Thomas F.
  1988 *Wood Quay: The Clash Over Dublin's Viking Past.* University of Texas Press, Austin.

Henderson, Joan
   2003 Ethnic Heritage as a Tourist Attraction: The Peranakans of Singapore. *International Journal of Heritage Studies* 9(1):27–44.
Hingley, Richard
   1996 Ancestors and Identity in the Later Prehistory of Atlantic Scotland: The Reuse and Reinvention of Neolithic Monuments and Material Culture. *World Archaeology* 28(2):231–243.
Hutt, Sherry, Elwood W. Jones, and Martin McAllister
   1992 *Archaeological Resource Protection*. Preservation Press, Washington, D.C.
Hutt, Sherry, and C. Timothy McKeown
   1999 Control of Cultural Property as Human Rights Law. *Arizona State Law Journal* 31(2):363–389.
Ikawa-Smith, Fumiko
   1999 Construction of National Identity and Origins in East Asia: A Comparative Perspective. *Antiquity* 73:626–629.
Jansen, Stef
   2002 The Violence of Memories: Local Narratives of the Past After Ethnic Cleansing in Croatia. *Rethinking History* 6(1):77–94.
Jones, Sian
   1994 Nationalism, Archeology, and the Interpretation of Ethnicity: Israel and Beyond. *Anthropology Today* 10(5):19–21.
Kaarsholm, P.
   1989 The Past as Battlefield in Rhodesia and Zimbabwe: The Struggle of Competing Nationalisms over History from Colonization to Independence. *Culture and History* 6:85–106.
Kane, Stephanie
   2003 *The Politics of Archaeology and Identity in a Global Context*. Archaeological Institute of America, Boston.
Kohl, Philip L., and J. A. Perez Gollan
   2002 Religion, Politics, and Prehistory. *Current Anthropology* 43(4):561–575.
Kohl, Phillip L., and Clare Fawcett (editors)
   1995 *Nationalism, Politics and the Practice of Archaeology*. Cambridge University Press, Cambridge.
Lertrit, Sawang
   1997 Who Owns the Past? A Perspective from Chiang Saen, Thailand. *Conservation and Management of Archaeological Sites* 2(2):81–92.
Lilley, Ian (editor)
   2000 Native Title and the Transformation of Archaeology in the Postcolonial World. *Oceania Monographs* 50. University of Sydney.
Linenthal, Edward T., and Tom Engelhardt
   1996 *History Wars: The Enola Gay and Other Battles for the American Past*. Henry Holt, New York.
Lowenthal, David
   1985 *The Past is a Foreign Country*. Cambridge University Press, Cambridge.
   1998a *The Heritage Crusade and the Spoils of War*. Cambridge University Press, Cambridge.

1998b Fabricating Heritage. *History and Memory* 10(1):5–25.

Lundstrvm, Inga, and Marja-Leena Pilvesmaa
  1998 Reflections on an Unreflected Sphere: Archaeological Exhibitions and Nationalism. *Current Swedish Archaeology* 6:143–151.

McIntosh, Roderick J., Boubacar Hama Diaby, and Tereba Togola
  1997 Mali's Many Shields of Its Past. *Nonrenewable Resources* 6(2):111–129.

Mahadin, Kamel A., and Taleb Rifai
  1995 Preservation of an Archaeological Heritage: 'Ayn Ghazal. *Studies in the History and Archaeology of Jordan* 5:111–117.

Martin, Joann
  1993 Contesting Authenticity: Battles Over the Representation of History in Morelos, Mexico. *Ethnohistory* 40(3):438–465.

Masson, Vadim Mihailovich
  1987 Modern Soviet Archaeology: Organization, Methodology and Politics of the Past. *Acta Archaeologica* 58:201–206.

Mazariegos, Oswaldo C.
  1998 Archaeology and Nationalism in Guatemala at the Time of Independence. *Antiquity* 72:376–386.

McAlister, Melani
  1996 "The Common Heritage of Mankind": Race, Nation, and Masculinity in the King Tut Exhibit. *Representations* 54:80–103.

Merryman, John H.
  1986 Two Ways of Thinking about Cultural Property. *American Journal of International Law* 80:831–853.
  1998 Cultural Property Ethics. *International Journal of Cultural Property* 7(1):21–31.
  2005 Cultural Property Internationalism. *International Journal of Cultural Property* 12(1):11–39.

Meskell, Lynn
  2002 Negative Heritage and Past Mastering in Archaeology. *Anthropological Quarterly* 75(3):557–574.
  2005 Archaeological Ethnography: Conversations around Kruger National Park. *Archaeologies* 1(1):81–100.

Meskell, Lynn (editor)
  1998 *Archaeology Under Fire: Nationalism, Politics, and Heritage in the Eastern Mediterranean and Middle East.* Routledge, London.

Miller, Daniel
  1980 Archaeology and Development. *Current Anthropology* 21(6):709–726.

Morphy, Howard, and Frances Morphy
  1984 The "Myths" of Ngalakan History: Ideology and Images of the Past in Northern Australia. *Man* 19(3):459–478.

Mortensen, Lena
  2001 The Local Dynamics of Global Heritage: Archaeotourism at Copán, Honduras. *Mesoamerica* 42:104–134.

Munson, Cheryl A., Marjorie Jones, and Robert Fry
  1995 The GE Mound: An ARPA Case Study. *American Antiquity* 60(1):131–149.

Musitelli, Jean
  2003 World Heritage, Between Universalism and Globalization. *International Journal of Cultural Property* 11(2):323–336.
Nas, Peter J. M.
  2002 Masterpieces of Oral and Intangible Culture: Reflections on the UNESCO World Heritage List. *Current Anthropology* 43(1):139–148.
Nash, Steve
  2004 Battles Over Battlefields. *Archaeology* 57(5):24–29.
Ndoro, Webber
  1997 Marketing the Past: The 'Shona Village' at Great Zimbabwe. *Conservation and Management of Archaeological Sites* 2(1):3–8.
Olsen, Bjvrnar
  1986 Norwegian Archaeology and the People without (Pre-)History or How to Create a Myth of a Uniform Past. *Archaeological Review of Cambridge* 5(1):25–42.
Owens, Bruce McCoy
  2002 Monumentality, Identity, and the State: Local Practice, World Heritage, and Heterotopia at Swayambhu, Nepal. *Anthropological Quarterly* 75(2):269–316.
Pai, Hyung Il
  1999 Nationalism and Preserving Korea's Buried Past: The Office of Cultural Properties and Archaeological Heritage Management in South Korea. *Antiquity* 73:619–625.
Pak, Yangjin
  1999 Contested Ethnicities and Ancient Homelands in Northeast Chinese Archaeology: The Case of Koguryo and Puyo Archaeology. *Antiquity* 73:613–618.
Pearson, Richard J.
  1976 The Social Aims of Chinese Archaeology. *Antiquity* 50:8–10.
Pinsky, Valerie, and Alison Wylie (editors)
  1989 *Essays in the Philosophy, History, and Sociopolitics of Archaeology.* Cambridge University Press, New York.
Ploss, S. I.
  1960 The Bolshevik Past as the First Secretary Likes It. *World Politics* 13(1):77–98.
Pollock, Susan, and Catherine Lutz
  1994 Archaeology Deployed for the Gulf War. *Critique of Anthropology* 14(3):263–284.
Pringle, Heather
  2006 *The Master Plan: Himmler's Scholars and the Holocaust.* Hyperion, New York.
Prott, Lyndel V., and Patrick J. O'Keefe
  1984 *Law and the Cultural Heritage.* 3 vols. Professional Books, Abingdon, Oxon.
Randsborg, Klavs
  2000 National History, Non-National Archaeology: The Case of Denmark. *Oxford Journal of Archaeology* 19(2):211–222.
Richman, Jennifer R., and Marion P. Forsyth
  2004 *Legal Perspectives on Cultural Resources.* AltaMira Press, Walnut Creek.
Ritter, David
  2006 Many Bottles for Many Flies: Managing Conflict over Indigenous Peoples' Cultural Heritage in Western Australia. *Public History Review* 13:125–142.

Robson, Eleanor, Luke Treadwell, and Chris Gosden (editors)
  2006 *Who Owns Objects? The Ethics and Politics of Collecting Cultural Artefacts.* Oxbow Books, London.
Rosen, Lawrence
  1980 The Excavation of American Indian Reburial Sites: A Problem in Law and Professional Responsibility. *American Anthropologist* 82(1):4–27.
Rountree, Kathryn
  2002 Re-Inventing Malta's Neolithic Temples: Contemporary Interpretations and Agendas. *History and Anthropology* 13(1):31–51.
Scham, Sandra A.
  1998 Mediating Nationalism and Archaeology: A Matter of Trust? *American Anthropologist* 100(2):301–308.
Scham, Sandra A., and Adel Yahya
  2003 Heritage and Reconciliation. *Journal of Social Archaeology* 3(3):399–416.
Schmidt, Peter R., and Thomas C. Patterson (editors)
  1995 *Making Alternative Histories: The Practice of Archaeology and History in Non-Western Settings,* School of American Research, Santa Fe.
Scott, Barbara G.
  1996 Archaeology and National Identity: The Norwegian Example. *Scandinavian Studies* 68(3):321–342.
Silberman, Neil A.
  1982 *Digging for God and Country.* Knopf, New York.
Silverman, Helaine
  1999 Archaeology and the 1997 Peruvian Hostage Crisis. *Anthropology Today* 15(1):9–13.
  2002 Touring Ancient Times: The Present and Presented Past in Contemporary Peru. *American Anthropologist* 104(3):881–902.
Simpson, Elizabeth (editor)
  1997 *The Spoils of War: World War II and Its Aftermath.* Harry N. Abrams, New York.
Smith, George, and John E. Ehrenhard (editors)
  1991 *Protecting the Past.* CRC Press, Boca Raton, FL.
Stanley, Nick, and Siu King Chung
  1995 Representing the Past as the Future: The Shenzhen Chinese Folk Culture Villages and the Marketing of Chinese Identity. *Journal of Museum Ethnography* 7:25–40.
Trigger, Bruce G.
  1984 Alternative Archaeologies: Nationalist, Colonialist, Imperialist. *Man (N.S.)* 19:355–370.
Tunbridge, John
  2006 Empire, War and Nation: Heritage Management Perspectives from Canada And Malta. *Public History Review* 13:4–22.
Van der Veer, Peter
  1992 Ayodhya and Somnath: Eternal Shrines, Contested Histories. *Social Research* 59(1):85–109.
Vossler, Greg
  2006 Sense or Nonsense? New Zealand Heritage Legislation in Perspective. *Public History Review* 13:66–85.

Watkins, Joe
  2005 Cultural Nationalists, Internationalists, and "Intra-Nationalists": Who's Right and Whose Right? *International Journal of Cultural Property* 12(1):78–94.
Weiner, James
  1999 Culture in a Sealed Envelope: The Concealment of Australian Aboriginal Heritage and Tradition in the Hindmarsh Island Bridge Affair. *Journal of the Royal Anthropological Institute* 5(2):193–105.
Weingrod, Alex
  1995 Dry Bones: Nationalism and Symbolism in Contemporary Israel. *Anthropology Today* 11(6):7–12.
Whittaker, Elvi
  1994 Public Discourse on Sacredness: The Transfer of Ayers Rock to Aboriginal Ownership. *American Ethnologist* 21(2):310–334.
Woost, Michael D.
  1993 Nationalizing the Local Past in Sri Lanka: Histories of Nation and Development in a Sinhalese Village. *American Ethnologist* 20(3):502–521.
Wylie, Alison
  1997 Contextualizing Ethics: Comments on Ethics in Canadian Archaeology by Robert Rosenswig. *Canadian Journal of Archaeology* 21(2):115–120.
Zerubavel, Yael
  1995 *Recovered Roots: Collective Memory and the Making of Israeli National Tradition.* University of Chicago Press, Chicago.